SAS THE GREAT TRAIN RAID

Damien Lewis

SAS

THE GREAT TRAIN RAID

THE MOST DARING
SAS MISSION OF WWII

QUERCUS

First published in Great Britain in 2025 by Quercus
Part of John Murray Group

1

Copyright © 2025 Omega Ventures Limited

Map by Bill Donohoe

A CIP catalogue record for this book is available
from the British Library

HB ISBN 978 1 52944 116 1
TPB ISBN 978 1 52944 117 8
EBOOK ISBN 978 1 52944 119 2

Typeset in Minion by CC Book Production

Printed and bound in Great Britain by Clays Ltd, Elcograf S.p.A.

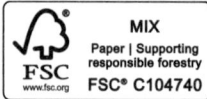

Quercus
Carmelite House
50 Victoria Embankment
London EC4Y 0DZ

John Murray Group
Part of Hodder & Stoughton Limited
An Hachette UK company

The authorised representative in the EEA is Hachette Ireland,
8 Castlecourt Centre, Dublin 15, D15 XTP3, Ireland (email: info@hbgi.ie)

For those who liberated Pisticci,
Italy's first concentration camp.

And for Bob Lancaster.
Once a pilgrim.

Honi soit qui mal y pense.
Evil be to him who thinks evil.

Malo Mori Quam Foedari.
I Prefer Death to Dishonour.

Contents

Picture Credits

Picture credits (in order of appearance):

1, 3, 9, 10, 25, 27, 28, 29, 32 – Imperial War Museum; 2 – nsf/ Alamy Stock Photo; 4, 5 – Courtesy of the family of Charlie Hackney; 6, 8, 34, 35 – Courtesy of the Cary-Elwes family; 7, 20, 21 – Author's collection; 11, 19 – Alamy; 12 – Fossoli Foundation; 13 – Bundesarchiv; 14 – Sueddeutsche Zeitung Photo/Alamy; 15 – Courtesy of Debbie Hussey; 16, 17 – Courtesy of David Bruce; 18 – Archivo GBB; 22 – Pictorial Press Ltd/Alamy; 23, 24 – Courtesy of the Simonds family; 26 – Courtesy of the National Army Museum, London; 29, 30, 31 – Courtesy of the US Army; 33 – HarperField/BNPS; 36, 37, 38, 39 – Courtesy of Bob Lancaster.

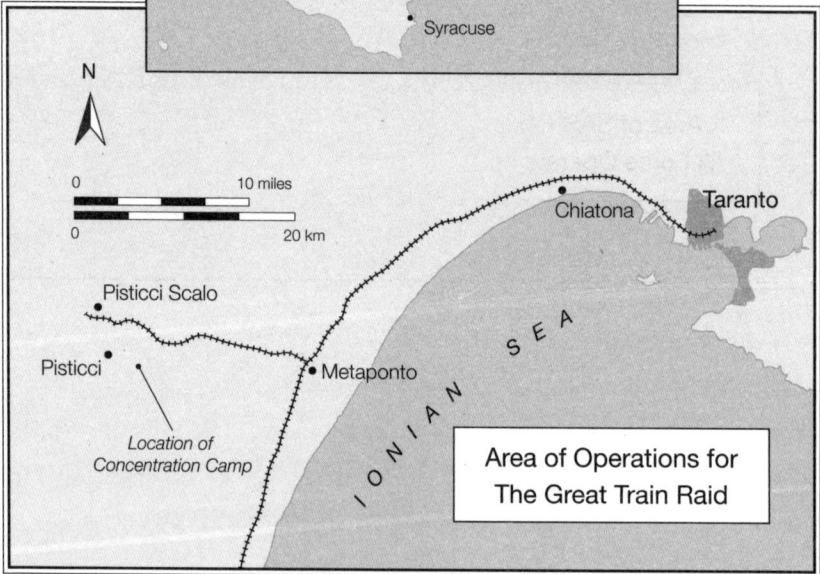

Area of Operations for
The Great Train Raid

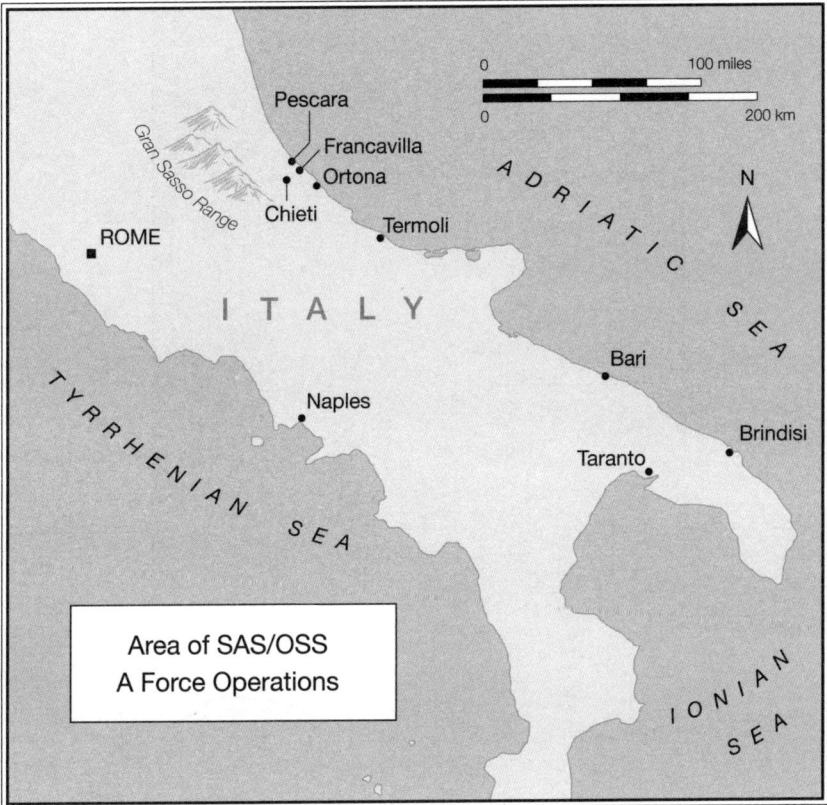

Area of SAS/OSS
A Force Operations

Author's Note

There are sadly very few survivors from the Second World War operations told in these pages. I have been in contact with as many as possible, and crucially with the surviving family members of those who have passed away. For all these contributions and input I am immensely grateful. If there are further witnesses to the stories told here who are inclined to come forward, please do get in contact with me, as I will endeavour to include further recollections of the operations portrayed in future editions.

The time spent by Allied servicemen and women as Special Service volunteers was often traumatic and wreathed in layers of secrecy; many chose to take their stories to their graves. Memories tend to differ and apparently none more so than those concerning operations deep behind enemy lines. The written accounts that do exist tend to differ in their detail and timescale, and locations and chronologies are sometimes contradictory. Nevertheless, I have endeavoured to provide an accurate sense of place, timescale and narrative to the story depicted in these pages.

Where various accounts of a mission appear to be particularly contradictory, the methodology I have used to reconstruct where, when and how events took place is the 'most likely' scenario. If two or more testimonies or sources point to a particular time or place or sequence of events, I have opted to use that account as most likely, while also taking into account the relative verisimilitude of each of those accounts.

The above notwithstanding, any mistakes herein are entirely of my own making, and I would be happy to correct any in future editions. Likewise, while I have attempted to locate the copyright holders of the photos and other images, and of the written material used in this book, this has not always been straightforward or easy. Again, I would be happy to correct any mistakes in future editions.

As it was originally conceived as an airborne outfit – using parachutes to drop behind enemy lines – the unit was named the Special *Air* Service (my emphasis). In due course many other forms of insertion into target were adopted – on foot, by vehicle, by submarine and landing craft, or, as in this case, by train.

This is a true story. Any sections of speech are taken from contemporary accounts of reported dialogue, diary entries, letters, or memoirs written by those involved. Any number of the source documents I have relied upon– war diaries, scribbled notes, signals logs, letters home – were written under the most difficult circumstances and often in some haste and/or under duress. Doubtless, they were never intended for publication. Accordingly, I have standardised spelling, corrected grammar and simplified acronym use, to make the book easier to read (e.g. 'Amm' is rendered as ammunition; 'Ack' becomes acknowledge). References to the source documents can be found in the detailed notes provided at the end of this book.

Likewise, I have faithfully reproduced the language and tenor of the accounts written at the time, complete with what we might now consider as their archaisms and anachronisms.

Chapter 1

NAKED LUNCH

The training camp was a desperately barren and inhospitable place at the best of times. But right now, in the dying days of the summer of 1943, it felt blisteringly hot and suffocatingly humid, as the fierce African sun beat down and the dust mingled with the clouds of whining mosquitoes. But that wasn't what most bothered the small body of elite warriors who had gathered to hear their mission orders. It was how the briefing had ended and just what that might signify for their chances of survival.

Captain Eric 'Bill' Barkworth, the highly regarded intelligence officer of the Special Air Service, had laid out the specifics of the coming operation, at the end of which, the red-haired Lieutenant Anthony Greville-Bell, one of the few officers present, had pointed out the obvious: Barkworth had made no mention of how they were to get home again, once they'd parachuted deep behind enemy lines to cause untold havoc and mayhem.

'What about getting back?' Greville-Bell asked, pointedly.

To those gathered it seemed an entirely reasonable question. While several of their previous missions had been nigh-on suicidal, at least they'd had fast motor torpedo boats (MTBs) or stealthy submarines standing by, ready to pull them out of enemy territory and spirit them back to Allied lines. So what was the plan for the coming mission? What was the exit strategy? How were they supposed to make it home?

'That's up to you,' Barkworth answered, baldly.

On one level, the casual-seeming response didn't exactly surprise those present. In Lieutenant Colonel William 'Bill' Stirling's 2 SAS – the 2nd Special Air Service Regiment, modelled upon the original SAS founded by his brother, David Stirling – nothing was viewed as being impossible. Nothing was deemed as being too much to ask of the men, nor beyond the boundaries of the human spirit or the capabilities of such finely honed and seasoned operators.

That was especially so right then, for Bill Stirling's intention was to deploy scores of such raiding parties far behind the lines, as Allied forces endeavoured to crowbar open fascist and Nazi Europe's fearsome defences. These thirteen men were the forerunners, their mission to be proof of concept. If they could pull it off, Bill Stirling would have shown that his notion of mass small-scale raids designed to paralyse the enemy's supply lines had real promise and might even turn the tide of the war. In short, this mission might earn Stirling the blessing to ensure that the SAS would be used as he intended – something that was far from being a given, as the Allies prepared to make their first landings on European shores.

Still, as one of those present would remark, regarding the lack of any getaway plan: 'In other words, after completing the mission we would be on our own.'

That man, Sergeant Horace Stokes, was no shrinking violet. Having volunteered for the army at the outbreak of war, at age eighteen, Stokes had missed out on the battle for France and the miraculous rescue of so many from the Dunkirk beaches. Losing several close friends in the fighting, he'd hungered to hit back. He'd volunteered for Special Service – for hazardous duties of a top-secret nature – and despite the fact that barracks rumour had it that these were to be 'suicide squads'. He'd gone on to train with No. 12 Commando, taking part in a string of raids, including the daring attack on the oil tanks of the Lofoten Islands, in northern Norway, codenamed Operation Claymore.

Stokes had found his natural home in the commandos, where there was 'as little bullshit as possible' in the ranks. A city boy by upbringing, he'd learned to stalk a deer with a knife – 'bloody hard' – and to operate at night until 'darkness was our daylight'. As an added blessing, his commanding officer, Captain Philip Hugh Pinckney, turned out to be 'one of the finest officers of the war'. Pinckney had taken the all-for-one, egalitarian nature of 12 Commando to new heights, allowing the men to dress as they liked, to suit the conditions they were facing, flagrantly disobeying orders to the contrary. Such matters, he argued, were 'a man's personal concern'. His patrol thus 'queerly garbed . . . attracted the disapproval of every passing general'. But Pinckney basked in the sheer delight of 'disobeying an order which he considered unreasonable'.

During the Lofoten raid, Pinckney had taken a very dim view of a propaganda film being shot of the Norwegian villagers welcoming the British raiders. If it was broadcast in Britain, they would surely pay the price of Nazi reprisals, he reasoned. His answer was to grab the reels of film and throw them into the sea during the voyage home. For this Pinckney had faced a court martial. Utterly unrepentant, he'd argued his case forcefully and been let off with a fine of £75. Even that he had contested vociferously.

During another operation, a July 1941 raid on German positions on the Calais coastline, Pinckney had been obliged to storm a machine-gun post, to stop it from sinking the landing craft that had dropped his men ashore. Encouraged afterwards to put the key individuals forward for medals, Pinckney had proceeded to recommend every man for a decoration, arguing that all had shared the same level of risk. Such an egalitarian attitude hadn't always won him friends in high places, but Pinckney was a fierce champion of those under his command and utterly single-minded in his convictions.

A recent episode at their SAS training camp illustrated this attitude perfectly – his 'hatred of all the bad, petty side of soldiering'. Pinckney, Stokes and their troop had just returned from a tough sojourn in the desert, looking like 'a rag tag lot', only to discover that so-called discipline was to be tightened. A recent influx of officer trainees hailing from 'pukka' Guards regiments had infused the place with their characteristic sense of how things ought to be done, including a distinct smartening of dress. Previously, it had been accepted that seasoned SAS veterans returning from punishing missions needed to relax as they saw fit, dressing in shorts and little else.

Abhorring the pointlessness of 'spit and polish soldiering', Pinckney didn't dress particularly differently from his men, reflecting the ethos of the SAS, which was founded on the basis of merit above rank. But the incoming recruits seemed to find the SAS captain's 'eccentric' appearance most irregular. Orders were duly posted that all those dining in the Officer's Mess were to dress formally. For most, the idea of having to 'sweat your way into proper dress to sit stickily at dinner' was no idea of fun. Pinckney was singled out for a private word, and asked whether he wouldn't mind wearing a tie to dinner. By way of response, he'd told his men to 'tactically conceal' themselves outside the Officer's Mess, to provide him with a little useful cover.

Stokes and his fellows had duly obliged, eyeing the officers as they'd arrived in 'all their finery'. Shortly, the tables were filling up, and still there was no sign of Captain Pinckney. Eventually, when everyone seemed to be seated, a figure emerged from the night 'stark bollock naked' apart from a tie. In that manner Pinckney had strolled into the Officer's Mess and proceeded to take one of the few empty seats. There was a long moment of stunned silence, before the place had erupted into laughter. Pinckney had proceeded to dine just as he was. The next day fresh orders were issued, excusing Captain Pinckney from having to dress for dinner. A point had been made, and in a manner that typified the man.

Pinckney believed passionately that he was fighting to defeat the forces of fascism and Nazism, but in his defence of Britain and the civilised world he had a certain dark conviction that he 'owed it to his country to be killed'. As Sergeant Stokes was painfully aware, even prior to their present mission all was not well with their commander, for Pinckney had fractured his spine during a previous jump. He had confided only in Stokes, who was sworn to secrecy, and especially since Bill Stirling would have grounded the SAS captain had he found out about the injury.

By fair means or foul Stokes had managed to procure some painkillers and ointment for Pinckney, but even so he was in agony. Remaining stoically silent, he'd insisted on leading their present mission. The SAS medic had got wind of Pinckney's injury and tried to stop him from deploying, but he was having none of it. Instead, he'd persuaded the doctor to apply a spray-on 'freezing mixture' to kill the pain. But worryingly, Operation Speedwell, as their mission was codenamed, seemed to have even the indomitable Pinckney rattled. He had a certain premonition of his own death, which proved deeply unsettling to anyone who sensed it. It tended to rub off. As Stokes would remark, 'I knew in my heart that the next operation was likely to be my last.'

With departure looming, the lack of any escape plan was dealt with in typical fashion – devil-may-care humour. Take-off was to be from Kairouan airbase, in northern Tunisia, a few hours' drive from the SAS camp. The thirteen men gathered, decked out in their US Army overalls – a makeshift parachuting jumpsuit – plus their fighting knives, and American M1 carbines, the lightweight semi-automatic rifle then favoured by the SAS. Breaking down into their two sticks, there was time to kill before mounting up the aircraft, which would fly them almost a thousand kilometres to the drop zone.

Bill Stirling joined Pinckney's party, as they spread out one of their parachutes to form a DIY card table. Gambling proved high-spirited and fierce, as condemned men jousted at baccarat, the popular casino card game, and hundreds of pounds changed hands. The second Speedwell stick was commanded by Captain Pat Dudgeon, another longstanding veteran of the unit. He and his men passed around a bottle of whisky, as they traded stories about the 'respective merits of Italian wine and women', amid much laughter and wisecracks.

Take-off was scheduled for 6.30 p.m., and the evening was fine and clear – perfect flying conditions. The parachutists boarded the two waiting Armstrong Whitworth Albermarles – light, twin-engine transport aircraft – and took to the skies. The lead aeroplane was carrying Pinckney's stick, and it struck a course north across the Mediterranean for the five-hour flight to their designated drop zone, which lay deep in Italy's rugged Apennine mountains some 400 kilometres due north of Rome.

The twin-engine Albermarle – already obsolete – was not a popular aircraft. As one SAS veteran would remark, for parachutists it was a death trap. With a narrow hold and a low ceiling, the last jumper sat crammed up next to the aircraft's rear gunner, risking his parachutist's kit getting tangled with the belts of ammunition. The jump itself took place through an aperture set in the floor – 'a trapdoor . . . what a hole!' Getting free of an Albermarle was a blessing for any parachutist, for it was an 'awful aircraft to jump from', as Stokes himself fully appreciated.

The roar of the twin Bristol Hercules engines was deafening, and all they could do was yell the odd word to one another, through cupped hands. Most dozed, but Stokes was beset by worry, and mostly for their commanding officer. Even as they'd gone to board the Albermarle, Pinckney had made a half-joking reference about how unsettled he was. 'I don't feel too good about this one. But then, I always get that feeling at the start, you know, the feeling that every operation might be the last.' It was so unlike Pinckney to be unnerved, and especially in view of his previous track record.

Over a year earlier, in June 1942, the then commando captain had dreamt up an utterly audacious raid, codenamed Operation Airthief. The plan was to land from a motor torpedo boat (MTB) by canoe in northern France, to put ashore with Jeffrey Quill, an RAF test pilot, and aim to infiltrate a Luftwaffe airbase to steal a Focke-Wulf Fw 190, the advanced German fighter aircraft that was wreaking havoc with the RAF. They'd sneak in at first light, while the Fw 190's engine was being warmed up, and kill the ground staff, enabling Quill to steal the warplane and fly it back to Britain, after which Pinckney would execute an escape and evasion on foot, heading for neutral Spain.

As matters transpired, Airthief was overtaken by events, a disoriented German pilot mistakenly landing an Fw 190 on British soil. It was captured and flown by Quill to RAF Farnborough for in-depth study. Typically, Pinckney was 'outraged' that Airthief had been so unexpectedly foiled. As Quill observed, 'One might have encountered him accompanying Drake's raid on Spanish treasure trains ... or steering a fireship amongst the Armada anchored off Calais, or with Shackleton on his epic open-boat journey from Antarctica to South Georgia ... his exploits became a sort of legend wherever he went.'

Then, in the spring of 1943, Bill Stirling had founded 2 SAS, after his brother, David Stirling, had been captured on operations in North Africa. On learning of this, Pinckney had hand-picked several of his commandos, and all had stepped forward to volunteer for the SAS, Sergeant Stokes being top of the list. In one of their earliest actions, they'd taken a jeep to probe enemy lines, riding at the vanguard of the American forces that had landed in North Africa under Operation Torch. Their overall commander was General Dwight D. Eisenhower, and a large part of the SAS's mission was to demonstrate to the US high-ups how Special Forces should be used in war.

Frustratingly, Eisenhower's headquarters staff had proved 'almost as suspicious of the SAS' as their British counterparts, regular military commanders finding it so hard to grasp the concept of these kinds of missions. In an effort to show them, Pinckney and his men had advanced across the terrain to recce a seemingly deserted village, the jeep's rapid-firing twin Vickers K machine guns at the ready. Aware of their drills and with 'senses on full alert', they'd skirted the settlement, even as someone cried out a warning that they'd spotted a vehicle on the far side. Racing towards a patch of desert scrub, they'd spotted a German armoured car, the gunner of which was traversing his cannon to open fire. That weapon could make short work of their open-topped jeep, which meant that speed and untold aggression were their chief allies right then.

Both forces let rip at the same instant. Just as the SAS intended, the enemy gunner missed their speeding jeep, while the combined firepower of half a dozen Vickers K guns tore into the armoured car, a storm of armour-piercing and incendiary rounds sparking all along its metal flanks. With the Vickers K – originally a weapon designed for aircraft, due to its rapid rate of fire – mounted on a pivot, it was possible to shoot from a moving vehicle with some degree of accuracy. With its impressive rate of fire, the jeep's combined weaponry was punching out some 6,000 rounds per minute at the enemy.

But even as battle was joined, so the buildings in the village seemed to erupt with flame, as muzzle flashes blazed away from every window, roof and doorway. The entire place proved to be 'crawling with Germans'. While that lone SAS jeep was more than capable of holding its own against one armoured car, this was a whole different ball game. The role of the SAS was not to stand and fight, but to hit and run; to gather intelligence or to wreak sabotage, and to melt away swiftly thereafter. By now those riding in that jeep had discovered all they needed to know – this was a heavily defended enemy position.

With the 'adrenalin pumping', and making a decision in the split second that separates life from death, they reacted with 'razor sharp senses', executing an abrupt about-turn. As they raced back towards friendly lines they got hit several times by enemy fire, but thankfully suffered no casualties. Their quick thinking and carefully honed drills had saved the day, and they'd brought back vital intelligence for the American commanders about that enemy stronghold.

On another occasion, Pinckney had emerged from a long stint behind the lines looking like 'an enormous man with a long beard, most indecently exposed in the ragged remains of his uniform and carrying a Tommy gun', but also bearing crucial intelligence. For what followed he would be recommended for a 'very high American decoration'. With the Allied advance stalled, Pinckney had set out in a jeep to lead US forces across enemy lines. When the track he was following petered out, he went ahead alone on foot, returning three days later with detailed sketches of the German frontline positions.

He then volunteered to lead the Americans through those defences, so as to hit the enemy from the rear. An entire US regiment 'was ordered to follow him'. At one stage during his solo reconnaissance he'd been lying in the undergrowth some twenty metres from an enemy machine-gun position, when the German troops started to burn the vegetation 'to improve their field of fire'. Pinckney had been forced to remain 'absolutely motionless' as the flames crackled and roared all around him, grasping a rock in either hand to beat out the fire whenever it drew too close.

Stokes and Pinckney had bonded on countless such missions, but in a sense theirs was an odd partnership, one that could very likely only have been forged in such a unit as this at war. Pinckney was descended from one of William the Conqueror's knights, and the family boasted a long line of foremost warriors, lawyers and the likes in its ranks. Educated at St. Neot's preparatory school and Eton, one of his great-great-great uncles had been Eton's headmaster. Moving on to Trinity College, Cambridge, Pinckney had lasted barely a year before wanderlust got the better of him, and he'd gone off to join his father's tea business in India. Impetuous, an intense individualist, Pinckney 'was such a strong character nobody who knew him could ever forget him', as one of his friends would remark. Crucially, he was blessed with a 'deep interest in people', regardless of their class, race or economic background, 'so long as they were the kind of people Phil liked'.

Stokes was clearly one such person, despite the gulf between their backgrounds. The SAS sergeant had been brought up in abject poverty and with precious little education. One of ten children raised in a two-bedroom terraced house, he'd grown up in the shadow of Birmingham FC (now Birmingham City) football ground. He'd been sent to school sans underwear, for the family couldn't afford any, and with cardboard stuffed into the holes in his shoes. His bed was a mattress filled with straw, and his clothes were flea-ridden, heavily patched hand-me-downs. His father, a factory worker, owned only the one suit – his 'Sunday best'. Often, Stokes's mother would have to pawn it, to tide the family over until payday.

A bright child often coming top of his class, Stokes was offered a place at the local grammar school, but instead was sent to work as a greengrocer's barrow boy, at age fourteen. One of the perks of the job was to take the sacks of discarded cabbage leaves to 'people in posh houses', to feed to their pets. The 'few coppers' he earned bolstered his meagre pay, and his family were in dire need of the money. It was hard, physical labour alongside some 'bloody tough folk', as Stokes would describe them, but likewise it had toughened him for life, teaching him how to 'stick up' for himself come what may.

Known as 'Stokey' to his comrades, he'd proved an SAS stalwart. But as with all aboard that Albermarle, he sensed that what lay before them would eclipse their previous missions. Operation Speedwell was to be their testing. Southern Italy was to be the point at which the Allies would make their first landings on Europe's shores. As all appreciated, the country was shaped like a long, thin boot. Allied invasion forces were poised to hit the toe and heel of the country, which is around a thousand kilometres from end to end. From there, the intention was to advance up the peninsula, pushing north towards Austria and Germany itself.

But Hitler had other ideas. He'd vowed that Italy would not fall. Once Allied troops hit the beaches, German soldiers and armour would pour south to bolster the enemy's frontlines. This was where the Operation Speedwell raiders came in. Key to rushing in those German reinforcements were the railway lines that traversed Italy and extended into the nations beyond. Pinckney and his men were to parachute into the mountains around the northern Italian city of Bologna, charged to sabotage those key supply routes. More specifically, they were to blow up German troops and armour as the heavily laden trains passed through tunnels, with the aim of blocking those routes for as long as possible.

If they could start to paralyse the nation's rail networks, that would play a pivotal role in the coming battle for Italy. If scores more such SAS raiding parties could be parachuted in on similar missions, the effects would snowball and might well change the course of the war. Italy was Winston Churchill's much-vaunted 'soft underbelly of Europe'. Success there was absolutely vital at this stage of the conflict. Bill Stirling's mass sabotage raids held real promise to deliver it, that was if the Speedwell raiders hit home.

It was just before midnight when the lead Albermarle climbed above the mountains that marked out the drop zone (DZ). Despite his 'hatred of discipline', Pinckney was a born leader, and all 'would have followed him anywhere'. Several of those riding in that aircraft had been with him since first volunteering for special duties, and he enjoyed an undying loyalty from those he commanded. Typically, and despite his hidden injuries, he insisted on being the first to make the jump, leading his men into whatever might await. Below, the terrain was bathed in fine moonlight, an icy mountain air rushing in through the open jump hatch. The DZ was marked out by the small village of Castiglione, which lay beside a distinctive-looking lake.

As he waited for the jump light to switch to 'green for go', Stokes mentally congratulated the pilot for putting them 'bang on our DZ right on time'. It was an impressive feat both of navigation and of flying. Having made one pass over the DZ, the pilot sent back a warning: there was mist at ground level, and winds were gusting to 25 mph. These were borderline conditions in which to attempt a parachute drop, but no one doubted that they were going anyway. Moments later Pinckney gave his signature bellowing war cry as the light switched to green and he dropped through the hole. Unless one knew otherwise, he gave all the appearances of being in the very finest fettle.

Instantly Stokes leapt after him, plummeting into thin air. As the parachute silk snapped open and his oscillations lessened, he found that he had time to study the view. They'd been released at around 7,000 feet, but as the mountains thereabouts reared up to considerable heights, dropping from such an altitude was an absolute necessity. Above him blossomed five further 'chutes, as the rest of the stick made a seemingly perfect exit. Stokes could make out everyone, Pinckney included, in the clear moonlight. It looked as if they'd all made a fine drop.

As he drifted lower, he studied the expanse of the lake, which stretched out like a silvery-blue finger reaching far to the north. Preparing for touchdown, he felt himself being grabbed by a sudden gust of wind. As it tore at his 'chute, making it crack and snap like a ship's sail, Stokes sensed that he was being swept out of line. A familiar voice drifted up to him, yelling out a warning.

'Watch your drift, Stokes! Watch your drift!'

'Yes, sir,' he cried.

Pinckney half waved one arm to acknowledge, and Stokes reciprocated.

Even with the fierce wind, Stokes figured they should land with little distance separating the two of them, which meant that linking up should be child's play. Maybe Speedwell was going to turn out like so many previous missions when they'd feared the worst, but somehow had made it out unscathed. Right now, things were looking up. They'd been dropped bang on the DZ, not an enemy soldier was in sight, and the terrain appeared deserted of human habitation. Just the one, isolated farmhouse protruded from the thin cloak of ground mist, and even that betrayed not a chink of light nor sign of life.

But as Stokes dropped lower, the wind strengthened. Inexorably, it propelled him towards that isolated farmstead. Moments later, Murphy's Law – if it can go wrong, it will – came into full effect.

A gust drove Stokes sideways, slamming him into the farmstead's chimney. The moment he made impact he sensed he'd done some real damage. The pain was horrendous, and to Stokes it felt like he'd ruptured his groin. Worse still, he came to a crashing, juddering halt hung up in his parachute, suspended from the roof of the building. Below, he could hear the occupants waking up, and for a moment he feared it would all end like this, 'dangling here, shot in my harness'.

Blanking his mind to the pain, Stokes grabbed his knife and cut himself free. He tumbled to the ground, cursing his injuries, before he bolted into the darkness, leaving the billowing expanse of his 'chute dangling from the farmhouse chimney. This was totally against all training, of course, for the first thing to do when landing in enemy territory was to bundle up your 'chute and bury it, along with your jump helmet, to hide all signs of your presence. But needs must.

Each man knew the drill upon touching down. As quickly as possible they were to 'roll up the stick'. Each jumper was to remain exactly where he'd landed, so that the first man, in this case, Pinckney, could follow the line of the drop, locating number two, after which they'd repeat the process until all were reunited. But as Stokes scanned the moonlit landscape, there seemed to be no sign of the SAS captain anywhere. By rights, he should be hurrying back to Stokes's position, yet the familiar figure of Pinckney was nowhere to be seen.

Eventually Stokes was forced to abandon the wait and search for jumper number three – fellow sergeant Tim 'Robby' Robinson. Stokes and Robinson went way back, for they'd joined No. 12 Commando together. Over the months that followed the two had become inseparable. They shared an added bond in that they both revered their commander. 'No man I ever met in the Army ever talked ill of him,' Robinson would remark of Pinckney. 'He was a man, a gentleman and an officer, a very rare combination. The only man I ever met to come near his standard was Major Appleyard.'

Major Geoffrey Appleyard had been another prime recruit into Bill Stirling's 2 SAS; by this stage of the war he'd already been awarded a Distinguished Service Order (DSO), Military Cross (MC) and bar. Pinckney and Appleyard had served together on many a previous raid. Sadly, Appleyard was to be killed five days after Pinckney and his men dropped into the far north of Italy, as he ushered in another SAS raiding party in support of the Allied landings. The death of such a highly regarded and long-experienced officer would constitute a devastating loss for 2 SAS. And right now, here in northern Italy, the unit was about to be struck another body blow.

While Robinson had landed flat on his face, executing desperate evasive action to avoid hitting a tree, a few cuts and bruises were the most he had suffered. In turn the two sergeants located Greville-Bell, but his condition appeared to be almost as bad as that of Stokes. As the wind had driven him towards the lake, Greville-Bell had been forced to initiate the drill for landing on water. He'd struggled out of his parachute harness, until he was left hanging by his hands. That way, when he hit the lake he would be able to swim free of the mass of tangled lines and silk. Otherwise, he might end up trapped beneath it and drown.

Drifting towards the water, another gust had caught him and driven him back towards land. Moments later Greville-Bell's 'chute had snagged in some branches, and the forward momentum had swung him around violently, smashing him into the trunk of a tree. In the process he'd broken several ribs and was in a great deal of pain. One by one the men rolled up the remainder of the stick, all except for Pinckney. Still there was no sign of their mission commander.

One man, Corporal Pete Tomasso, had news of him. Tomasso had seen Pinckney descend some 300 metres away, but on the far side of a small hill. As he'd slipped from view, Tomasso had heard Pinckney cry out his name. He'd found that somewhat odd, for he was the fourth jumper in the stick, and Stokes and Robinson were far closer. They began to search for their missing commander, making the cry of the curlew, a large wading bird that inhabits this kind of lakeland terrain. It was the agreed call to attract each other's attention. The distinctive, eerie sound, like a rising, piercing *tuuh-weet*, echoed around the landscape, but there was not the sniff of any response.

What did it signify? Had Pinckney made a bad landing? Was he stumbling around injured and disoriented in the semi-darkness? In the back of Stokes's mind was the knowledge, to which only he was privy, of Pinckney's pre-existing injury. His greatest fear was that the SAS captain's back had given way when he landed. Though it went against their orders – they were supposed to get away from the DZ as quickly as possible, for obvious reasons – they spent an hour scouring the landscape, but eventually were forced to give up.

With Pinckney missing, Greville-Bell was now the senior officer. His injuries were acute, and the hour spent searching for Pinckney had proved totally exhausting. To keep him warm the others wrapped Greville-Bell in one of their silk parachutes, and using that as a makeshift stretcher they dragged him away from the DZ. Their patrol had been dropped so far behind enemy lines that they were well out of radio range of 2 SAS headquarters in North Africa. There was no way of making contact, to report what had happened. Friendly forces 'felt like a long way away', as Stokes remarked.

In so many ways they were on their own.

Chapter 2

BANDIT COUNTRY

While Greville-Bell was in a 'really bad way', so too was Stokes, but he decided to keep his problems to himself. Having shared out the injured SAS lieutenant's kit, and having emptied the drop-containers of their rucksacks, weapons and explosives, the two sergeants, Stokes and Robinson, led the way. It proved tough, challenging going, for the hillside above was a mass of dense, dark trees. Finally, they found a spot to lie up and await day-break. Perhaps come first light there might be good news. Maybe they would locate Pinckney and be reunited with their mission commander.

Sunrise brought no such respite. Instead, the six men were forced to watch as the village below was searched end-to-end by a mass of enemy troops. Clearly, their presence here had been reported, which was hardly surprising, considering Stokes's unfortunate arrival atop that farmhouse chimney, and the distinctive calling card that he had left behind. They had to presume they would now be hunted all the way, as they endeavoured to execute their mission.

With no other option, Greville-Bell reorganised the patrol into two groups of three. One consisted of Stokes and Robinson, plus Private Len Curtis, a man of real character and a talented footballer. The other was made up of Greville-Bell, Sergeant George 'Bebe' Daniels, plus Corporal Tomasso, the latter being an invaluable asset to their team. Tomasso was a Scotsman of Italian extraction, whose family owned one of Glasgow's top ice-cream parlours. With his dark good looks and fashionable Ronald Colman-style Hollywood moustache, he could easily pass as a local.

Greville-Bell had taken two doses of morphine to deaden the pain, but he was in little doubt as to his limited capabilities. He explained to the men what he had in mind. While each party was to strike out for their respective targets, Sergeant Daniels was to command his own force. A fresh recruit into 2 SAS, Daniels had served three years in a regular infantry regiment, before finding his way into the unit in which he would finally feel at home. Daniels had never much fancied getting killed for 'some obscure reason', and about which he'd had very little say. By contrast, in the SAS you were obliged to use your initiative, and knew exactly what your target was and why it mattered.

Teams set, it was time to divide their kit. Most importantly, there were the 16 pounds of plastic explosives, plus a variety of detonators and fuses. All was split evenly between the patrols. After that, they turned to their meagre rations, the greatest proportion of which consisted of 4½ pounds of cheese. As Greville-Bell would later report, 'I consider the food we took to be most inappropriate and to be a bad choice on our part, consisting as it did of cheese, sardines, biscuits, sugar and compo tea.' In truth, it was the sheer paucity of supplies that would prove most debilitating.

Before setting off, Greville-Bell voiced his opinion on what he feared must have happened to Pinckney. Disorientated in the high winds, he must have set out on the wrong bearing to roll up the stick, and in doing so had got himself lost in the hills. That was one theory, but privately Stokes feared that Pinckney had suffered a very different fate. Together, the six heavily laden men began their climb into the mountains. By mid-afternoon they'd reached a point that marked the parting of the ways. They paused to shake hands and to joke about how they would meet in Rome for a boozy evening, doing their best to disguise how low their fortunes had sunk.

In truth things were pretty dire. Their highly respected mission commander was missing, his second in command all-but incapacitated. The enemy knew the SAS were here and they would be on the scent. The six raiders were bound to be pursued all the way to their targets, if they even got there. After which there was only one way to escape and evade: somehow, they'd have to cross the 800 kilometres of enemy territory that separated them from the Allied landings, and all under their own steam.

To many soldiers this would have proven a daunting, perhaps crushing, proposition. As it was, they were off – Sergeant Daniels leading his party west towards their target, situated around the town of Porretta Terme, amid some of the highest peaks of the Apennines, while Stokes, Robinson and Curtis headed southeast, towards the stretch of rail track that linked the cities of Prato and Bologna. Though they didn't like to admit it, the two SAS sergeants were relieved to be shot of the wounded Greville-Bell. Despite his own injuries, Stokes figured they should now be able to move at a 'cracking pace'.

He and Robinson laid out a plan. They'd 'travel at night until they reached the objective', and continue to do so for the escape and evasion phase thereafter. That decided, they found a patch of dense forest in which to lie up for the remaining hours of daylight. After enjoying a handful of raisins, two hard biscuits and a swig of water each, they settled down to sleep. It was late afternoon on 8 September 1943, and they reckoned that four nights of hard marching should bring them to their target.

Come nightfall they got moving again. As they'd feared, 'humping full kit over really harsh terrain' made for incredibly tough going, especially since they were forced to survive on a few handfuls of food per day. But still they endured. In fact, lack of water was becoming their chief problem. They'd parachuted in with two full bottles per man, and they were forced to ration themselves piteously. While pushing themselves relentlessly they could do without food, but proper hydration was essential.

Forty-eight hours into their journey they stopped in the darkness before dawn, choosing a lie-up point with clear escape routes. They awoke in the late morning of 10 September to the faint sound of running water. A stream lay near by. It allowed the three men to slake their thirst, after which they indulged in the luxury of a wash and a shave. As Stokes would note, it was amazing how such a 'small act can lift your spirits (even when done in cold water)'. He topped it off with the even greater luxury of a cigarette, smoked in the shelter of his sleeping bag – 'absolutely fantastic!' In truth the SAS sergeant was in great pain, but he reckoned he would just have to 'get on with it' for as long as he could.

Pulses quickened when they heard a train in the distance. A few hours later they actually saw one – the locomotive threading a plume of thick smoke through the landscape. Observing the railway from their vantage point, they decided upon the best time to attack, plus their route to target. The settlement of Verino lay between them and it, so they would have to be 'extremely cautious'. It was the early hours of 13 September, five days after dropping in, when they flitted through Verino's dark outskirts. Here and there they paused, grabbing tomatoes and bunches of grapes from back gardens. As Stokes admitted, 'we stuffed our faces as we were bloody starving and dehydrated. Bliss.'

A dog barked a warning. No one seemed to pay any attention. A faint humming echoed from up ahead, where a powerhouse provided electricity to the railway line. Moments later they were at the tracks – the steel rails polished with use, stretching into the silvery distance under the starlight. Moving along them in well-practised silence, they peered into the generator house itself. The lone guard seemed utterly uninterested in whatever might be going on outside. Beyond lay the target – the gaping mouth of a tunnel burrowing deep into the mountains.

Using a dry riverbed as cover, they stole towards that dark horseshoe of shadow. As Stokes noted, it was 'a good feeling being exactly bang on target, and we stopped short and listened, ready to deal with any sentry'. Luckily, this stretch of track appeared to be unguarded. The three men paused for a while longer, pressing their ears to the silky-smooth, cold surface of the rails. Not the slightest vibration from any in-bound train could they detect.

With Robinson and Curtis covering him, Stokes, their demolition man, crept into the tunnel entrance itself. Using the feel of the rails underfoot, he let them guide him deeper into the darkness. It felt cold, and the air was dank and stale. Loosening his pack, Stokes lowered it to one side and unwrapped one of the parcels of plastic explosives, the unmistakable odour of almonds filling the air. The SAS used a type of explosive known as 'Nobel 808', which had the appearance of green plasticine, plus that distinctive smell. He taped the first charge to the rails. They needed around 3 pounds to blow one length of track, so with the eight pounds that Stokes carried he could afford to lay two such charges.

Once all was set, he connected the explosives to a 'fog signal' detonator, an ingenious invention of the Special Operations Executive (SOE), otherwise known as Churchill's Ministry for Ungentlemanly Warfare. Convinced that this war would be a total war waged on all possible fronts, Churchill had established the SOE to do all the things that are strictly forbidden in law: assassinations, bribery, corruption, blackmail, smuggling, money laundering and more. A standard fog signal was a piece of equipment used on the railways. As the name suggested, it would be fitted to a rail to alert a train driver if a stop signal up ahead was obscured by fog. As the locomotive ran over the device, it would detonate, the sharp bang warning the driver to slow down. But SOE had adapted the standard device so as to trigger an explosive charge lying *ahead* of a speeding locomotive, thus causing the train to derail.

In the pitch darkness of a tunnel like this, the driver would have little chance of spying the charge. Amid such narrow confines, the derailment should cause the carriages to concertina, blocking the tunnel from floor to ceiling with a mass of twisted debris. That at least was the plan.

No sooner had he set the explosives, than Stokes made a move to leave. He had no desire to linger any longer, for obvious reasons. Rejoining his comrades, he whispered the good news: *charges set*. Beside the tunnel entrance lay a disused quarry, with typically sheer sides. At the top there was a thick clump of trees. Perfect cover from which to observe the effects of their handiwork.

The three men had only just reached the woodland when they detected the 'very faint sound of a train in the distance', echoing down the tunnel. There was a locomotive approaching.

Sound seemed to travel further in the stillness of the night. The train was some distance away, which gave Stokes ample time to worry about the charges he had set, but there was 'absolutely nothing more I could do', he noted. Either his handiwork would do the business, or he would be forced to return to the tunnel to check the explosives. Stokes kept 'everything crossed' as he prayed he'd done the job just right.

'We waited with bated breath,' observed Robinson. The sound grew in intensity, until the rhythmic, whooshing, hissing onrush of the locomotive seemed to fill the three watchers' ears. Even as the noise of the engine reached a crescendo, there was a blinding flash which lit up the entire night sky, followed by the earth-shattering roar of the explosion, the force of which tore along the valley, echoing deafeningly from peak to peak.

That intense cataclysm of sound and light was followed by a most eerie, 'unearthly silence', which seemed to last for an age. It was broken only by the hiss of escaping steam, occasional cries, plus the groans of tortured metal. Finally, the spell seemed to break. A barked cry of alarm split the silence, followed by a sharp burst of gunfire. Moments later 'all hell broke loose', as a firefight erupted on the tracks below the trio of watching saboteurs. No one had the slightest clue as to who the enemy might be shooting at, for it certainly wasn't at any of them.

Either way, they seized the opportunity to vanish, knowing their job had been done and done well. Against all odds, they had struck the very blow that they had intended. As the three men slipped into the darkness and began to climb, battle raged below.

Not for the first time, Stokes reflected upon how people who had been attacked tended to 'fire at anything, everything, even if they didn't know what they were firing at'. He decided that this was really 'quite funny', the noise of gunfire and explosions only fading away as they drew further and further into the heights.

Disregarding his injuries, Stokes and his two companions 'broke nearly every speed marching record', as they strove to put distance between themselves and that tunnel. Other than the moment of their landing, this was the most dangerous time. For hours they traversed intensely challenging ground, seeking out the most inhospitable terrain. Over time, Stokes began to feel his injuries, coupled with the exhaustion, catching up with him. Sustaining this kind of pace over this kind of landscape was aggravating his ruptured groin, though he was yet to confess that he was carrying such an injury.

It was on 17 September, three days after the attack, that the last of their rations ran out. Driven to desperation, the three fugitives began moving by daylight, and they risked using some of the cash they carried to buy food. It was difficult for any of them to pose convincingly as locals, and especially for Stokes with his shock of blonde hair. They just had to hope that the local rural folk would take them for German troops. At one stage they managed to purchase an entire loaf of bread, plus eggs and cheese – 'like a feast fit for a king'. At another they managed to enjoy a full 'bath' in a stream, sheltered by thick woodland, followed by a cup of tea. Sheer bliss.

A week after their tunnel demolition work, the trio bumped into their first enemy troops. On a track deep in some woodland they encountered a knot of Italian soldiers. By now the fugitives had all the appearances of being wild mountain men, but they were still dressed in full uniform and were heavily armed. The Italians seemed disinclined to put up any sort of fight. In short order, they offered an explanation as to why. According to them, British and Italian troops were now supposedly the best of friends. Apparently, while the raiders had been wreaking devastation in the mountains, the Italians had surrendered to the Allies. In theory at least, they were now all on the same side.

More Italian soldiers emerged from hiding. From one the trio heard an account of the very sabotage operation that they had executed – 'a devastating attack on a German armoured train deep in the mountains at Verino'. The three raiders exchanged knowing glances, but they were not letting on. As far as the Italians knew, they were escaped prisoners of war. That was their cover story. At every turn the trio kept their ears open for any word of their missing commander, Captain Pinckney. But no one seemed to have the slightest news. It was as if the SAS captain had disappeared into thin air.

Two of the Italian soldiers turned out to be fellow paratroopers. One was travelling south towards his home city of Naples. He offered to take the three SAS men with him by train. This struck Stokes as being somewhat ironic, especially since they had just blown up one of the main Apennine rail routes. Even so, he summed up their collective sentiments thus: 'Bollocks – it had to be better than walking.'

Ditching their main weapons, packs and uniform, the three fugitives used some of their cash to purchase civilian clothes and suitcases, into which they loaded their pistols and grenades, plus some food. It was a distinctly unsettling experience heading for the nearest railway station thus attired, especially since the place was thronged with German troops. Still, they held their nerve.

It was 24 September when they boarded a train heading south, but their luck ran out while they were well north of Rome. At all points further south the Germans were checking 'travel documents, identity cards and papers'.

This was the end of the line.

With the help of their Italian paratrooper friend they avoided the nearest checkpoint, made it to a safe house, but were forced to flee when the Germans launched house-to-house searches. A series of stop-start journeys ensued, first by farmer's cart, then on foot, dodging enemy convoys. But with the air turning distinctly autumnal the weather began to worsen. They were soaked to the skin and freezing cold in their thin civilian clothing. Though they often found shelter with incredibly brave locals – anyone caught harbouring Allied troops faced the worst – Stokes's condition deteriorated fast.

Eventually, he was forced to reveal to the others the extent of his injuries. Though he tried to struggle on, by 7 October Stokes accepted the inevitable, telling Robinson that he couldn't continue. More to the point, he was slowing down his comrades. With immense reluctance, Robinson was forced to agree. They'd found shelter with a farmer at Fabriano, a town some 200 kilometres north of Rome. Amazingly, Stokes had covered a far greater distance than that already, but this was the end.

'I'll never forget the parting,' Stokes would write of the moment of farewell. 'As Robby turned to wave from the top of the valley I think both of us thought we would never meet again. That was a hard day.' As for Robinson, each time he glanced back the sight of the ailing Stokes 'down in a small valley watching' was stamped ever more indelibly on his mind.

Stokes, alone now apart from his farmer host, was fading

fast. Without proper medical attention he would surely die. His groin had turned septic, he was erupting in pustulous boils, and his body was giving up on him. He was also in immense pain. Staying put would spell the end. He knew that Rome was the right direction of travel, and that the Vatican lay in Rome. It was neutral and there was a chance that it might harbour and succour a fugitive such as him. He also knew that Rome boasted a long-established POW support network. Getting there was the problem. No way could he walk.

A week after parting from Robinson and Curtis, Stokes decided to steal a bicycle and he set out on his seemingly impossible journey, aiming to cycle 220 kilometres into the heart of Italy's capital city. As he would write of what followed: 'That journey took every ounce of my physical and mental strength.' By the time he had reached Rome, found his way into the Vatican and tried to convince those who received him that he was an escaped Allied POW, he was at death's door. Though they doubted his bona fides, they could tell that Stokes was in dire peril.

Via Vatican escape line mastermind Monsignor Hugh O'Flaherty, an Irish clergyman and longstanding Vatican priest, Stokes was spirited into a Rome safe house. There, a young Yugoslav medical student – himself a dissident – was asked to operate on the ailing British soldier, in an effort to save his life. That man, Dr Milko Škofič, consented. As Stokes would later write, 'I have no doubt he saved my life.' Brought back from death's door, Stokes was safe, for now. But of course, in Nazi-occupied Rome he was still a very long way from home.

By now, the men of Operation Speedwell had been listed as 'missing in action' by SAS headquarters, though it was hoped that they were making their way back to Allied lines. In a sense their fate did little to alter the overall assessment of Speedwell's outcomes, for their chances of making it home had never been overly high. Regardless, Speedwell was judged as being an out-and-out success. Not only had Stokes's party struck home, but in a carbon copy attack so too had Greville-Bell's. In fact, they had blown up three trains in three separate attacks. The second Speedwell stick, that commanded by Captain Dudgeon, had also hit the bullseye, derailing two trains in the depths of a tunnel.

While their numbers were too small to keep those crucial railway lines out of action for ever, 'if the whole regiment had been used, the railway system could have been halted . . .' As it was, Speedwell had 'proved Bill Stirling's thesis that small parties inserted by parachute could inflict vast amounts of damage upon the enemy at comparatively little cost'. The results spoke for themselves: 'Trains were buried deep in the mountains, taking days of clearance and the supply of German armour heading south was held up, disrupting their reinforcement plans.' But despite such upbeat assessments, the reward for such an epic undertaking was not to be as Stirling had hoped.

The commander of 2 SAS argued that his entire regiment be used on similar missions, for they were 'prepared to accept rough, unreconnoitred landings which can be easily undertaken . . . with advantages too obvious to mention'. A 'force of 300 men could work over hundreds of miles in up to 140 parties, with shattering effect . . . mountainous areas could be infested with small parties, which, if sufficiently numerous will completely saturate local defences and paralyse communications.' Flooding Northern Italy with two- or three-man SAS teams engaged on Speedwell-like missions held enormous promise, Stirling averred.

'A lot of people think war is just about killing people; it isn't. It's occupying ground and if the enemy feel so nervous that they retreat you've won the battle and with minimum casualties.'

Bill Stirling was without doubt a visionary. But the commander of 2 SAS was to be thwarted. In a bitter disappointment his request to launch multiple such missions was stymied. Instead, senior commanders at 15th Army Group, Stirling's overall chain of command – which combined the forces of the British Eighth Army and the Seventh United States Army – had a very different kind of mission in mind. It was not a typical SAS task and was eminently unsuited to their independent, audacious, maverick-spirited means of waging war. In many ways, Stirling and his men were about to have their wings savagely clipped. Not for the first time, the famed *esprit de corps* and the core strengths of the SAS were to be largely ignored, its potential squandered.

But either way, the die was cast.

Chapter 3

SLAPSTICK

The knife-cut prow of the USS *Boise* cut through the Mediterranean calm, her passage throwing up barely a plume of spray as she cleaved the waters. With her twin raked funnels and multiple, six-inch gun turrets, normally the light cruiser would strike a decidedly graceful, if warlike, note. But right now her classic lines were all rather cluttered and befuddled, for items of kit – entire vehicles, even – were strapped to every available inch of deck space, including some of the most unlikely of places.

Some 150 of Bill Stirling's SAS were crammed aboard a warship that was hardly designed as a troop carrier, not to mention as much of their kit as she could handle. Their jeeps had been 'slung in odd places all over the ship, and were even lashed to the tops of the gun-turrets'. It meant that the *Boise* would be seriously hampered if she were called upon to fight, for with her crowded decks her guns could hardly be brought to bear. In a calculated risk taken by Allied commanders, she was but one of several warships similarly encumbered, forming an invasion fleet that was steaming north from the Tunisian port city of Bizerte, aiming to hit southern Italian shores.

Typically, their deployment had been a horrendously hurried, last-minute affair. Fully five SAS squadrons had been ordered to move, and they'd spent all night packing kit and weaponry. While everyone understood they were heading for Italy, no one knew the exact reason or the nature of their mission. It had all been chaotic and very hush-hush. So much so that some of the official records from the time would even get the key names wrong: 'Posted with 2 SAS Regiment Bizerta in USS *Boygey*,' read one.

Somewhat fittingly, this cobbled-together deployment had been codenamed Operation Slapstick. The one major bonus about riding aboard the USS *Boise* proved to be the food. Compared to what the SAS were used to, the American rations were the best. Many had not tasted fresh baked bread for weeks. Most stopped wondering about their destination or the nature of their mission as soon as the call went out over the ship's Tannoy system: 'Come on, you Limeys! Come 'n' get your ice cream and cookies!' 'Limey' was common American slang for Brits, the name originating in the practice of Royal Navy ship's crews being given a daily lime juice ration, to prevent scurvy, a disease caused by lack of vitamin C.

The SAS shared the wider convoy with the men of the 1st Airborne Division, a British unit that had seen little previous action. Officially some 12,000 strong, the division was markedly understrength, having suffered casualties in recent days during the invasion of Sicily.

Deploying at such short notice, no aircraft were available to fly them in, hence their present means of conveyance. So cramped were the ships that only half of the division was present in this first wave, and there was room for 'very few guns and practically no transport'. Typically, the men had only a day's rations plus 'the ammunition they could carry on their person'. They would have to rely upon improvisation, requisitioning local vehicles and capturing enemy equipment and weaponry.

In truth, their mission was in direct response to a momentous development in the course of the war. Few of those present knew anything about this, or had any idea how such warships could possibly land troops such as theirs on hostile shores. Nothing made a great deal of sense, at least not until they heard the 'startling news over the loudspeakers that Italy had surrendered'. After a few seconds' stunned silence, a tremendous cheer swept the decks of the ship. To all present, it felt as if their efforts to gain victory in North Africa had paid off, and that 'part of the debt of Dunkirk had been wiped out'. As the ship's bar was declared open, all went to celebrate, and to drink to comrades 'who could not be with us and to those who would never drink again', as one of the SAS men observed.

Coming some forty-eight hours into their journey, the announcement filled all with 'tremendous excitement', and triggered 'a great wave of speculative rumour'. Further news followed: the Italian naval fleet had supposedly come over to the Allied side, and the port of Taranto was being cleared for the Allies. Shortly, there was concrete evidence of this, as a flotilla of Italian warships steamed past the invasion fleet, bound for Malta where their formal surrender would be taken. Still, the American vessels – and the one British ship in their number, the minesweeper, HMS *Abdiel* – did their best to keep their guns trained on their erstwhile enemies, at least until they were well out of range.

That done, the USS *Boise* steamed onwards towards Italian shores. No one knew if the Taranto landings would be opposed, or whether German troops still occupied the port city. Only time would tell. Further announcements made clear just what was expected of the invasion forces. Situated on the heel of the Italian boot, Taranto was one of the foremost naval bases in Italy. Many of the Italian warships that had steamed past hailed from there. In their wake, the US-British invasion fleet was to steal into Taranto itself, to seize the port and its naval installations, which were to be held at all costs.

That was the prize which supposedly justified all the rush and confusion of the present deployment. The men of 2 SAS – doubtless, the most battle-experienced of those present – had landed a role which though it might provoke resentment and frustration, was bound to put them in the thick of the action. Of course, in theory there should be little Italian resistance. But the forces of the German 1st Parachute Division – long-experienced and battle-hardened – were known to be on the ground. Word was that they'd strung a cordon of steel around the port city itself. The prize of Taranto would lure the Allied forces in, and then the trap would be sprung.

Once the invasion troops got ashore, they would be the only Allied forces holding the entire 'heel' of Italy and very thinly spread. Bearing in mind the stakes involved and the odds, it would have been churlish for the men of the SAS not to get into the swing of things. Charged to act as the eyes and ears of the division, their role was to race far ahead, rooting out and fixing the enemy. There was one major problem with such a mission, apart from its unsuitability. As with their airborne brethren, the SAS were woefully short of vehicles. Of the five squadrons, only one had a full complement of jeeps. Of the remainder, they either had few or none, so would have to seize whatever transport they might find.

*

It was a beautiful day as the USS *Boise* approached landfall. To either side, 'tiny red-roofed villages' clustered along the azure shoreline, making Taranto look 'more European and more like home that anything we had seen in North Africa', one of the SAS commanders observed. Deeply suspicious of the Italians' intentions – their supposed surrender, and the handing over of such a prize – the escort destroyers steamed ahead of the main fleet, guns at the ready as they hustled towards the harbour. Ashore, there was movement. The SAS studied it through their binoculars. 'We saw German tanks and trucks moving along the promenade,' observed one; 'we feared the worst.'

The leading warship, a destroyer, raced ahead and opened fire. Those crowded aboard the *Boise* threw themselves down on the decks, expecting the cruiser to follow suit with her six-inch guns.

'Clear the decks for action,' came the cry over the ship's speakers, not that there was exactly anywhere for the SAS to go.

Crawling behind the nearest cover, they saw the *Boise*'s five triple-gun turrets swing around to menace the shore. But instead of hearing the deafening blast of shells tearing overhead, there echoed across the water a series of explosions. To the experienced ears of the men of the SAS, it sounded as if the enemy might be 'blowing up ammo dumps in preparation for leaving'. That they took as a positive sign. Shortly, the USS *Boise* moved cautiously along the line of buoys that marked the route to the docks, passing a fleet of Italian tugs, the crews of which eyed the men aboard the American warship 'with the same curiosity with which we regarded them'.

By now, the waterfront seemed to be utterly deserted of civilians, Taranto itself like a ghost town. The inhabitants, fully expecting a massive naval bombardment, had fled into the hills. A few Italian sailors lined the docks, studying the newcomers uncertainly. One indicated where the USS *Boise* should tie up. The ship's captain, not fancying the look of that berth, opted to choose an adjacent one. It was to prove a fateful decision.

Shortly, HMS *Abdiel*, the British minelayer, slipped into the space that the *Boise* had rejected. Launched in April 1940, the *Abdiel* had scored a string of successes, at one stage laying a minefield that had sunk the Italian destroyer *Carlo Mirabello*, the gunboat *Pellegrino Matteucci*, plus the German transports *Kybfels* and *Marburg*, which were carrying a large contingent of the 2nd Panzer Division to Taranto. Unbeknown to her captain, the *Abdiel* was about to face a similar fate.

Mines had been planted in that very berth by a departing German naval crew. Two exploded beneath the heavily laden minelayer, which sank within three minutes, claiming scores of lives, and with 150 or more injured. Apart from the ship's crew, most of the dead were the airborne troops that she was carrying. In one fell swoop, the ranks of the 6th (Royal Welch) Parachute Battalion had been devastated. So much for the so-called surrender and ceasefire, for the Italians looked to have been complicit in the attack. It was first blood to the enemy, and a very lucky escape for the USS *Boise* and the men she carried.

To many of the SAS, the *Abdiel*'s grim fate underlined the duplicity and treachery that all would now have to guard against. As one of them, Corporal Albert 'Charlie' Hackney, a long-standing SAS veteran, would note, as they watched the unfolding disaster from the deck of the *Boise,* they were convinced that an Italian torpedo bomber had pounced on the *Abdiel*, the aircrew of which either 'did not know of the Italian surrender, or chose to ignore it!' Who knew where the truth lay? Where they were heading, who would be able to tell friend from foe?

Hackney just hoped that the firepower and versatility of their US-made Willys jeeps would lend them an edge. 'The combination of twin Vickers machine guns, Browning .50 machine guns, Bren guns, personal weapons (the Tommy gun was the most favoured sub-machine gun), grenades and explosives offered colossal firepower to the armed jeeps.' But as they prepared to unload the first of those 4x4s from the *Boise*, it was glaringly obvious how few they were in number. One sweep of the docks also revealed a dearth of usable vehicles. With the city's inhabitants having fled, Termoli had been emptied of its transport.

With the *Boise* having docked, scramble nets were tossed over the side and figures began to swarm ashore. Foremost among them was SAS Lieutenant Alistair McGregor and his five men, his stick of six having been given a vital objective. They were to execute a dash to 'secure the dock gates'. As the *Boise* had cruised north across the Mediterranean, McGregor and his men had studied their maps and memorised the route that lay ahead. Now, as they swung down the ship's side, each man had an M1 Carbine or a Tommy gun slung over his shoulder, six grenades and a fighting knife and pistol stuffed in his belt, plus a bulging rucksack strapped on his back.

'If the scramble had been down the side of a four master,' remarked one, 'and we were carrying knives in our mouths, we could have been transported to Hollywood as Captain Kidd and his boys,' – in other words, the notorious Scottish pirate and his crew. Ever since volunteering for the SAS together, McGregor's patrol had worked as one. They'd 'learned each other's good points, our faults and we learned to trust each other'. This was one of the standout facets of Bill Stirling's 2 SAS: he encouraged commanders to pick and choose their own teams, valuing the close bonds that would be forged.

The Captain Kidd comparison had been made by Trooper George Arnold, who was especially close to the man that they all knew simply as 'The Boss' – Lieutenant McGregor. Before volunteering for the SAS, Arnold and McGregor had been serving in North Africa and had executed a night assault against a dug-in German machine gun. The site of a feared 'Spandau' – a rapid-firing MG 42 machine gun, also known as 'Hitler's Buzzsaw' due to its fearsome noise – it had cut down several of McGregor's men. Under cover of darkness, he and Arnold had belly-crawled up to it, grenades gripped in either hand with the pins removed. Striking by complete surprise, they'd lobbed the grenades, before finishing off the MG 42 crew at close quarters.

Lieutenant McGregor had just turned 25 as they'd sailed for Italy. He'd been educated at Epsom College, a top private school on the outskirts of London. There he'd excelled at the kind of gentleman's pursuits that suited his combative, adventurous spirit – boxing, fencing, shooting and rugby. Signing up to the military at the outbreak of war, he'd fought with the British Expeditionary Force (BEF) in the defence of France, before weathering 'a hazardous evacuation from Dunkirk'. He'd gone on to see service in North Africa, but after an 'altercation with the authorities at Battalion Headquarters' he had been ordered back to Britain. McGregor, it seemed, had other ideas; he was damned if he was going to miss out on the Italian landings.

Instead, he'd jumped off a train en route to the port, made contact with Bill Stirling's 2 SAS and was promptly invited to join them. Married in 1942 to Magda, a Hungarian, the stocky, gruff and impetuous-seeming SAS lieutenant was actually blessed with a fine battle instinct and considerable charm. He'd brought most of his regulars into the SAS with him, urging Arnold and several others to volunteer. 'Devilishly handsome', as he would be described, McGregor was known for being a charismatic and determined leader, one who had the confidence to allow his men to have their say. That side of his nature – his inclusive spirit – had made of men like Arnold utterly loyal and dedicated recruits.

Arnold, two years McGregor's senior, was likewise married – to Nellie, and they had one infant son, John. But in contrast to the SAS lieutenant, Arnold hailed from a very different background. He'd left school, Heigham Elementary, in Norwich, at age fourteen, to work as a shoemaker, for the family needed the money. In fact, Arnold had precious little family to speak of. His father, Edward, a soldier, had been brought up in an orphan's home, but he had been killed in the First World War. Arnold had never got to know him. Worse still, his mother, Eleanor, had abandoned him, after which Arnold had been cared for by his grandmother, Mrs E. Webster.

Two years after leaving school he'd enlisted as a boy soldier, going on to join a cavalry regiment, and deploying to North Africa as part of an armoured unit. It was there that he'd come under the command of McGregor, and experienced at first hand the horrors of war, as their armoured vehicles had got shot up by the Germans' fearsome 88mm anti-tank guns, seeing his comrades reduced to 'corpses, their bloated bodies full of hungry flies in the burning sun'.

When war broke out, Arnold had been in India, patrolling the rugged North-West Frontier Province on horseback. Assessed as being 'a good rider but too hasty to be a good horseman', his military record was littered with infractions: 'absent without leave', 'neglecting to obey orders', 'rank insubordination', 'breaking out of camp' and more. Repeatedly, he'd had pay docked, been confined to barracks, reprimanded or otherwise disciplined. That was until July 1943, when he'd joined the SAS. There, he'd found his true home. This was a unit whose only disciplinary measure was to be returned to unit (RTU'd) – in other words, expelled from the exalted fraternity; the brotherhood. In Arnold's case, as with so many, that was all the discipline that he seemed to need – self-discipline.

At five foot five inches tall and weighing just 119 pounds, the diminutive Arnold was known as 'Blondie' to all, due to his shock of wild, sandy hair. There was one problem with the scramble nets flung down the USS *Boise*'s side: they stopped ten feet short of the harbour wall. Not great, when, like Arnold, you were one of the shortest men in the unit. But having spent weeks during training flinging themselves off scaffolding towers, or even moving vehicles, in an effort to prepare themselves for executing a parachute jump for real, disembarking from the *Boise* should be child's play.

Dropping the last ten feet, McGregor and his men picked themselves up and glanced around; 'it looked as if the whole place was deserted'. Moving silently on their rubber-soled boots, they began to head along the route they'd memorised: 'take the first turn left, then the first turn left again, pass three buildings, then turn right and the gates will be about fifty yards in front . . .' Evening was settling over the city, the shadows lengthening, as they traced their path, weapons at the ready. They rounded the final bend, but 'my God, in front of us was a machine gun pointing at us'. Before the dock gates a gun crew were gathered around their weapon. The central figure had it gripped 'by the handles and it looked as if his fingers were on the trigger'.

Just a few months back Arnold and McGregor had stalked that MG 42 post, but at least then they'd been cloaked in darkness. Now, it was light enough to see and to aim; to shoot to kill. Diving into the cover of the nearest building, McGregor and his men levelled their weapons. But they were under strict orders not to shoot unless fired upon. Those figures manning that machine gun could well be Italians, who in theory were their new-found allies. McGregor and his men lay stock still, studying their adversaries. The machine-gun crew did exactly the same – 'just there, staring at us', as Arnold observed. Stalemate.

Each side was wondering what to do. Finally, McGregor turned to Arnold. 'Okay, Blondie, Swill – follow me! Let's see how close we can get. The rest of you – cover us. If there is any sign of movement, open fire.'

Trooper 'Swill' Sutton had volunteered for the SAS alongside McGregor and Arnold. Rising to their feet, the trio set off, moving closer to the machine gun, the gaping barrel of which was pointed directly at them. 'It was like walking the gallows,' as Arnold noted, 'all tensed up, fingers itching on triggers.' They got to within twenty metres, when the man directly behind the weapon rose to his feet. He just stood there, stock still, staring at the three SAS men, not speaking or seeming to move a muscle. They half expected him to raise his hands in surrender. But not a bit of it. Another of the gun-crew got to his feet and did likewise.

McGregor, Arnold and Sutton crept closer, until they were within spitting distance of the machine gun. Still no one had said a damn word. Suddenly, the figure nearest McGregor made a move. He must have recognised their uniforms, for he flung his arms around the SAS lieutenant, crying out in Italian, '*Buongiorno! Viva gli Inglesi! Viva gli Inglesi!*' Before any of the SAS trio could think how to react, the other two Italians had embraced Arnold and Swill, and were likewise crying out their greetings. 'We did not know what to do except return the gesture,' observed a somewhat nonplussed Arnold.

Once they'd disentangled themselves from the Italians' embraces, McGregor gestured for the soldiers to unload their gun, at which point they dissolved into laughter. They indicated that McGregor should inspect it. It turned out not to be loaded, and neither did the Italians have any ammunition. It had all been an absurd piece of theatre, just in case McGregor and his men were Germans. McGregor indicated that the Italians should head for the Allied ships lying at berth, where they could get fed and processed. Meanwhile he and his men stepped towards the dock gates, which were locked and bolted.

An old man emerged from a nearby hut, jabbering away and brandishing some keys. He was obviously the gatekeeper. He proceeded to unlock the gates and to swing them wide. McGregor led his men through. Inside, there was a crowd of silent, terrified-looking civilians. They eyed the newcomers 'as if we were lepers', shrinking back from their presence. Then, from out of the crowd emerged a figure 'who looked as if he had just stepped out of a comic opera'. Dressed in gleaming riding boots, breeches, and a blue tunic that was 'adorned with more gold than the Bank of England', his get-up was topped off by an enormous tricorne hat.

Recognising McGregor and his men as British troops, the Carabinieri officer – a commander of the Italian paramilitary police – began to explain in English how the people of Taranto welcomed the Allies and how they would do 'all in their power to get rid of the hated Tedeschi', for 'no Italians wanted this terrible war'. '*Tedeschi*' was Italian for Germans. In response, McGregor told the carabiniere to order the townsfolk to go home and to stay there. There could be fighting on the streets. They had to remain inside.

With the docks secured, McGregor led his men across a bridge that connected the port area to the main city. Next objective was the railway station. They reached Taranto's main square. Utterly deserted, not a light showed anywhere. 'The silence could almost be felt,' Arnold observed. A shot rang out. The bullet ploughed into the wall not so far from him. Search as they might, they could not locate the gunman. They moved on to the railway yard. The gates were locked, so they vaulted over the perimeter wall. The entire place seemed eerily devoid of life. Ghostly. A train was lying in the station, abandoned. Its carriages proved to be chock-full of foodstuffs, mortar shells, plus a Mercedes vehicle.

Moving up the railway tracks, McGregor and his men spied 'some blazing truck headlights'. Coming down the road was a convoy. Dashing for cover, they took up firing positions, forming a snap ambush. Arnold had dived into a ditch from where he readied his Bren light machine gun. A favourite of British troops, though it had less than half the rate of fire of the MG 42, the equivalent German weapon, the Bren was far more accurate and could even be used as a sniping weapon. As he lay in that ditch preparing to open fire, a sickening smell filled Arnold's nostrils. It seemed to be coming from right beneath him. He had no time to worry about it right then.

The seconds ticked down, before McGregor gave a yell: 'Hold your fire!'

Arnold could not believe his eyes. McGregor stepped into the road. He began to move towards the leading truck with one hand raised in the stop position, and with his pistol levelled at the windscreen. The convoy was racing towards him, and it looked as if he was going to get run over or gunned down. Instead, he cried out: 'Halt! *Inglesi!*' It worked. The convoy ground to a sudden stop. The lead driver jumped from his cab, and moments later he was giving McGregor the same kind of treatment as his comrades had at the dock gates. This was an Italian military convoy, and the soldiers were seeking to surrender. They had deserted from the Germans, and the trucks were full of food and ammunition.

Getting to his feet, Arnold was struck by that sickening smell again. He glanced down. A human hand was sticking out of the earth. He bent and scraped some soil away, 'and there was the face of a dead woman. I must have had the legs of the Bren on her chest.' He spoke to some of the Italians and showed them what he'd found. They offered to exhume the body, put it in one of the trucks and drive it into Taranto for a proper burial.

That sorted, McGregor urged his men on. They reached a vantage point, which overlooked the railway. McGregor told his men to each choose an olive tree that offered good cover, and in pairs to take a break for a brew. While one made tea, the other would be on watch. They'd just started doing so, when Trooper 'Della' Dellow gave a low hiss of alarm. Dellow, a Jew hailing from London's Soho district, was blessed with an unbelievably wicked sense of humour, but he wasn't joking now. With a famous weakness for nuts – he'd eat 'anything that came out of a shell' – he'd been about to tuck in to his own private stash when he'd spied movement.

'Look towards the railway line,' he whispered.

Figures were darting through the half-light, 'flitting over the railway embankment through the trees'. Arnold alerted McGregor, who'd taken cover perched in the branches of a nearby tree. From his vantage point the SAS lieutenant could see that they were German troops. He opened fire with his Tommy gun, the blazing muzzle flash lighting up the branches all around him in dramatic silhouette. That was the signal for all to do likewise. Arnold let rip with his Bren, the accurate fire from which cut down two of the distant figures.

More enemy soldiers rose from the cover of the embankment and Arnold fired again. It was at the limit of the accurate range of the Tommy guns, but not the Bren. Two more fell, but 'whether they were just ducking for cover', Arnold didn't know. While their fire was delaying the enemy, McGregor expected them to launch an attack 'at any moment'. Opting to stay where they were in good cover, they resolved to fight it out. Movement would only risk drawing the enemy's fire, for they'd have to cross open ground in either direction. McGregor and his men hunkered down.

The enemy were closing in. Trap set.

Chapter 4

AMBUSH ALLEY

Back at the USS *Boise* the last of the SAS vehicles had been unloaded and readied for battle, as they sought to secure Termoli from the enemy. First to nose cautiously into the darkening city with their jeeps were the men of D Squadron, SAS, commanded by the redoubtable Major Roy Farran. As with the missing Pinckney and Appleyard, Farran was another of Bill Stirling's earliest and most prized recruits. The city felt hot and oppressive, the dusk streets thick with silence, the air's sticky humidity stirred here and there only by a faint sea breeze.

Farran, a long-term veteran of the war in North Africa, was no stranger to such conditions. As Corporal Hackney would remark, the SAS commander's track record spoke volumes. 'Major Farran, originally a Cavalry Officer, had been wounded and captured in the battle for Crete, but had escaped from a POW camp ... Wounded again in the retreat to the Alamein line, he later fetched up in Algeria ... One day he bumped into an old friend ... who organised an interview for Farran with the CO, Bill Stirling.' Brought into the SAS to lead D Squadron, Farran was to prove an outstanding commander. But in truth, he had only made it into the SAS by the skin of his teeth.

In his second episode of being wounded in battle, Farran had been hit in a Luftwaffe dive-bombing attack, during the 1942 retreat to El Alamein. Shot in the arm, he'd lost the use of two of his middle fingers and was slated to be invalided out of the military. Evacuated to a South African hospital, he'd managed to bribe a nurse with 'a bottle of gin and a bunch of flowers', and absconded from the ward to spend his time lounging by a pool and chasing after the ladies. 'Many of us only avoided marriage by a narrow margin in these happy days,' he would remark of his South African interlude, 'while others fell by the wayside.'

Having refused surgery, 'since there was nothing I could not do except play the piano (which I had never learned anyway)', Farran was dispatched to Britain, to go before the Medical Board to assess his injuries. Somehow, he managed to convince them to upgrade him to 'Category A' – fighting fit. Pulling strings with one or two generals, Farran got himself back into the war. Posted to a regular unit, he'd been branded as an 'untrusted upstart', what with his medals – he'd been awarded an MC for his heroism on Crete, plus a bar for his epic escape – and his unconventional military mindset.

After his North African experiences, Farran was a diehard believer in the need to 'threaten the security of the enemy's lines of communication, those vital life lines without which an army cannot exist', plus the need for 'long-range harassing attacks made by small raiding parties, possibly independent of the main theatre of operations'. Ostracised within the unit to which he had been posted, he'd been welcomed with open arms into Bill Stirling's 2 SAS. From the very first, Farran recognised the battle-winning potential of their jeeps, 'the ideal vehicle for this type of warfare. They had a tremendous load-carrying capacity, an enormous range . . . a fine cross-country performance and great firepower . . .'

Farran's D Squadron was lucky enough to have a full complement of the vehicles, the only one to do so. That put him and his men at the very tip of the spear. 'There was an uncanny air about our silent advance up that deserted highway,' Farran would write, as the column of jeeps nosed north through the darkening city. Apart from having a vague smattering of intelligence that the German 1st Parachute Division was somewhere up ahead, Farran and his men knew nothing. With no friendly forces to either side, he felt 'half proud to be the advance guard of a new army on foreign soil, half afraid of the unknown'.

The route north into Taranto took the form of a wide, tree-lined boulevard. Farran's jeep was second in the line of march, his deputy, twenty-two-year-old Lieutenant James 'Big Jim' Mackie, taking point. The column-like moon-shadows of the trees punctuated the highway, each marking their onwards passage, only the faint growl of the jeep's engines disturbing the deathly silence. The SAS maxim was: 'Good reconnaissance is done by the eyes in the daylight and by the ears at night.' Frequently, Mackie brought the entire convoy to a standstill, as he stopped to execute a 'listening watch' – straining his ears for the slightest sound, and with senses on high alert. Still, there seemed to be not a sniff of any hostile presence.

Mackie, a tall, sandy-haired fellow hailing from Edinburgh, would be first to hit any trouble. For a man who never 'harboured an evil thought in his life', as Farran would describe him, Big Jim was eager to be first into the fight. With a father who was a Professor of Bacteriology and the Dean of Medicine at Edinburgh University, Mackie had been keen to follow in his footsteps, but he'd been obliged to put aside his medical studies to go to war. Loyal to a fault, when Mackie stopped and beckoned Farran silently forward, the SAS major did as he was bid.

Mackie indicated a number of armed figures just visible in the gloom, clustered around a key bridge. As Farran and Mackie studied them, trying to identify who they might be, a voice cried out a challenge in Italian. It looked as if these were Italian troops, so the SAS's supposed Allies.

'*Inglesi*,' Farran yelled back. British troops. Coming through.

Alone, he started the long walk. As he did, he remarked to Sergeant Major Bill Mitchell, one of the gunners on his jeep, to cover him with his Bren light machine gun. Farran approached the bridge, which was occupied by a group of shadowy figures in indistinct green uniforms. Suddenly, one rushed towards him, rifle raised, and fired a round at almost point blank range. Miraculously, it failed to hit home, instead passing clean between Farran's legs. The instant the shot was fired, Mitchell opened up and peppered the gunman 'with a whole magazine of Bren bullets'.

The standoff ended when each side managed to identify the other. The gallant defenders on the bridge were indeed Italians. Their officer produced a bottle of wine, and after 'profound apologies on both sides' the case of mistaken identity was cleared up. Drinking a somewhat forced toast to their 'new alliance' – British with Italians – the dead sentry lay ignored and unmourned, 'crumpled in the dust – an innocent victim of an accident of war'.

Having garnered what little intelligence he could, Farran got the convoy under way again, pushing north out of the city. A little way further along the night-dark highway, Mackie became unsure of the route. He pulled to a stop, and in his halting Italian asked a figure at the roadside for directions.

The response he got was an unintelligible snort, and with a punch to his chest the one word answer: 'Tedesco'.

None the wiser, Mackie turned to Corporal Clarke, the most well-educated fellow on his vehicle. 'Corporal Clarke, what does "Tedesco" mean?'

Clarke stared mouth agape for an instant, before swivelling his weapon around and yelling out: 'Germans!'

The soldier was indeed German, and seeming resigned to his fate he muttered a subdued 'Ach-so,' as he was made to climb into the back of the jeep, to be taken prisoner. Four more German soldiers were captured in this way, before the quiet of the night was torn apart by a sustained burst of fire, tracer rounds streaking through the darkness and ricocheting all around the leading jeeps. The gunfire had the signature tattoo of the 'Schmeisser', the German Maschinenpistole 40 (MP 40) sub-machine gun that was favoured by many of the SAS – Farran included – whenever they could get their hands on one. In the chaos and confusion, the Vickers K guns – 'perhaps the best machine gun in the world for quick retaliation' – more than proved their worth, as Farran and his men pumped 'magazine after magazine of tracer into the darkness'.

They managed to break off the contact without taking any casualties. In the process, one of their prisoners had bolted, but by then Farran had discovered exactly what he needed to know. The position up ahead, Massafra, a town lying some 25 kilometres north of Taranto harbour, was well and truly occupied by the Tedeschi. Farran's response was simple: he steered the convoy of jeeps left down a side road, in an effort to box around the enemy. At first light they reached the tiny village of Pogiano. After a night spent on the move and under intense stress and strain, they grabbed a few hours' precious kip in the shadows of the cactus hedges that lined the streets.

By mid-morning, orders had come through to push further north, so as to infiltrate well to the rear of the German positions. The jeeps inched ahead for a dozen kilometres, before they reached a crossroads. Bizarrely, an Italian policeman was there standing traffic duty. Seeming to be one of the 'good Italians' – those whose sympathies lay with the Allies – he informed Farran that the roads thereabouts were crammed with German vehicles, most of which were heading to their base at Ginosa, to the northwest of Taranto. As feared, the enemy were pouring troops into the area to stem the Allied offensive, which meant that this was as good a place as any to try to stop them.

Farran directed his men into hidden ambush positions. The last jeep was busy backing into some trees, when the SAS commander spied a large convoy approaching the crossroads. Throwing himself into the cover of a roadside ditch, he readied his Tommy gun. All knew to open up if and when Farran pulled the trigger. Suspecting the convoy to be Italian, the lead truck was almost upon them before Farran recognised the symbol on the driver's cap. They were German troops all right. The moment he opened fire the combined force of some forty Vickers K guns – augmented by the heavier-calibre Brownings – let rip, cutting into the German column 'at practically "nil" range'.

The report in the SAS War Diary from the time described a 'Successful ambush, capturing two trucks and 42 men, and destroying 10 vehicles . . .' The reality on the ground was far more visceral, as Farran and his raiders hammered in the fire all along the length of that enemy convoy. Rounds tore through thin steel and canvas, shattering glass, puncturing fuel tanks and setting vehicles ablaze. Faced with such a withering attack, and hit by utter surprise, the enemy were barely able to mount the slightest response. Just minutes into the ambush the first of the makeshift 'pathetic white flags' were raised above the vehicles, but the fearsome onslaught, once started, proved far harder to stop.

Spying those flags of surrender, Farran began screaming at his men to cease fire. It proved impossible to make himself heard over the cacophony of several dozen assorted Vicker Ks, Brownings, Brens and Tommy guns unleashing hell. His was a decidedly multinational force, for many a non-Brit had been recruited across North Africa into the ranks of 2 SAS. One, a Frenchman called Durban, unloaded a whole belt of Browning ammunition upon the enemy with a 'tense, excited face', before eventually Farran was able to make himself heard.

Finally, the deafening racket stuttered to a stop. In the comparative silence that followed, Farran began to make his way down the line of shot-up and burning vehicles, in the front ones of which all were now dead. From within the thick pall of smoke a knot of German troops emerged, waving white flags. They'd taken cover at the convoy's rear. Still breathless from the adrenaline rush of the attack, Farran and his men began yelling at them to 'come forwards with their hands up!' In response, the enemy soldiers got on the move, led by a German officer who was bleeding heavily from an injury, and who was crying out for mercy for him and his troops.

Clearly, the enemy had not a shred of resistance left in them. Farran's greatest fear now was of some kind of response from Ginosa, where German forces were mustering. Aware of how his squadron 'had not sufficient strength for a pitched battle', he set about the most urgent priorities. Skeleton crews were put together to man the captured vehicles – valuable prizes, especially since the SAS were so short of transport. Once that was done the crowd of German prisoners were loaded aboard the trucks, which set off for Taranto. With that sorted, Farran and his men set about sabotaging any remaining kit, before hightailing it south for a good distance.

Eventually, his convoy of jeeps pulled to a halt. Curious as to the enemy's reactions, Farran set upon a ruse. Stopping a local farmer with horse and cart, he persuaded the man to take two of his soldiers up to the crossroads. They would bury themselves in the heap of hay that filled the cart, while making sure they got a good sight of the road junction. They returned a while later with a full report. Sure enough, the enemy had sent a heavy contingent of troops riding in armoured vehicles to investigate. Halting at the crossroads, they'd endeavoured to salvage what kit and equipment they could and to bury their dead.

They'd done so within an hour of the ambush, which meant that the enemy were proving swift and decisive in their response to any such incidents. Had Farran's squadron lingered after the attack they would have faced real difficulties, being heavily outgunned, and riding in their unarmoured, open-top jeeps. The decision to make theirs a shoot-'n'-scoot attack had been entirely the right one, Farran's assessment proving tellingly accurate. In other parts of the peninsula, British forces were taking some punishing casualties.

Even as Farran and his men had been battling the enemy, so a second SAS squadron had motored out of Taranto, heading into the gathering gloom. Or rather, half a squadron, for the remainder possessed no jeeps in which to get on the move. Bill Stirling's second in command was in charge of A Squadron, and he rejoiced in the splendid name of Major Oswald Aloysius Joseph Cary-Elwes. As Stirling himself was banned from deploying – he was viewed as being too valuable to risk at the coal face of war – Cary-Elwes had been dispatched to Taranto, to act as his eyes and ears.

Stirling had good reason to send Cary-Elwes. Bill and his brother David Stirling had been good friends with Cary-Elwes at Ampleforth, the celebrated Catholic boarding school, where the latter had excelled both at rugby and boxing. More to the point, Cary-Elwes was a longstanding career soldier who had compelling reasons to fight. The youngest of eight children, he'd signed up to the British military in 1933, in memory of his elder brother, Wilfrid, who had been killed in action in 1917, aged eighteen. That same year, 1933, another of his brothers, Columba, had been ordained as a priest at Ampleforth.

Hailing from a long line of champagne merchants, Cary-Elwes spoke fluent French, was a fierce Francophile, and could act the 'perfect Frenchman', which would prove mightily handy for what was coming. Oddly, considering his background, he'd first been dispatched to West Africa, to soldier in one of the war's lesser known conflicts. Finally making it to North Africa, he'd jumped at the chance to try for 2 SAS. Being all of thirty years old – a comparative elder in such a unit – he'd thrown himself into the training with gusto, after which he'd cut his teeth on a series of raids, news of which was carried home to his family by none other than Randolph Churchill, the British prime minister's son.

A sometime soldier sometime journalist, Randolph had been

one of the first to report on the exploits of the SAS. Getting word home was important to Cary-Elwes, for in 1939 he'd married Pamela Brendon and they had one infant son, Charles. The Cary-Elwes family traced their roots back to William the Conqueror, at which time the name was spelled the Norman 'Helewisa'. It also appears as 'Helwys', and may well have been of earlier, Viking origin, with *Hel* meaning 'big' and *Wys* meaning 'wisdom'. The Elwes clan had since added French and Cornish blood to its lineage, and boasted a string of senior military figures in its line.

Coming from a family steeped in tradition, Cary-Elwes wore it surprisingly lightly. In fact, there was much of the maverick and the buccaneer about his bearing. The recruitment of Corporal Charlie Hackney to the SAS was a case in point. Having volunteered for Special Service, Hackney ended up getting deployed to North Africa in 1941, serving in an armoured regiment, the 4th Queen's Own Hussars, with whom he saw 'a brief but bloody spell of fighting'. Promoted to sergeant, he was given command of a Crusader tank, but it was hit in action and set aflame. Discovering that all of his crew had been killed, Hackney bailed out and hid in some scrub, before he was picked up by friendly troops.

Commanding his second Crusader, he again spied 'an orange-coloured flash of flame' up ahead – the signature of a German 88mm gun firing – and his tank was hit. This time his driver was killed instantly, his wireless officer mortally wounded and his gunner badly injured. Again, Hackney was the only one to escape relatively unscathed. Luckily, a dispatch rider was able to pick him up, while his injured gunner was 'propped up in great pain in the motorcycle's side-car'. On arrival back at their lines, Hackney was ordered to take out another Crusader without delay. He was 'unshaven, dirty, exhausted from lack of sleep, and his clothes were in tatters'. He point blank refused.

Hackney was placed under close arrest and confined to a tent guarded by a pair of soldiers with fixed bayonets. Reflecting upon his dire predicament, he realised he very likely faced a court martial and might well be shot for 'cowardice in the face of the enemy'. At this juncture a tall, ramrod-straight figure boasting a spectacular moustache appeared. Introducing himself as Major Oswald Cary-Elwes, the newcomer inquired of the prisoner why he was under arrest. Hackney explained. He also added that he'd volunteered for Special Service early in the war, was commando trained, and had taken part in Operation Claymore, the Lofoten Islands raid. The major's response was to make an offer to Hackney that he 'in his right mind would have been foolish to reject'.

Cary-Elwes explained that he hailed from a unit called the SAS, one that the prisoner clearly had never heard of. Having outlined a little of what they were about, he told Hackney to be outside with his kit in double-quick time if he wanted to be whisked away from a world of trouble. Hackney did as suggested and joined Cary-Elwes, along with two other fresh recruits that the major had garnered. So began a journey of over 1,500 kilometres by jeep, crossing the Great Sand Sea of the Sahara Desert, via the Siwa and Kufra oases, to reach the SAS's isolated training camp at Kabrit, Egypt. Upon arrival, Hackney and his fellow recruits were told to pick a tent and to 'fight it out for possession when the two occupants returned from the desert'.

Cary-Elwes advised Hackney that a strict condition of joining the SAS was to lose a rank, so he would have to 'take down his sergeant's stripes'. This Hackney did on the spot, tearing off the relevant insignia. Noting the gesture, Cary-Elwes's good nature seemed to get the better of him. He disappeared, returned with a needle and thread, and told Hackney to sow back on the one stripe, making him a lance corporal. Hackney's intensive training had only just started when a letter arrived, ordering him to be returned to his parent unit to face a court martial. Believing Hackney 'was worth more alive than dead', the SAS founders ignored the missive. As far as they were concerned, if the 4th Hussars wanted Hackney so badly they could come and get him.

They never did.

Over a year later, in Taranto, Hackney was serving in Roy Farran's D Squadron, while Cary-Elwes, his recruiter, was commanding A Squadron. In the hours after making landfall, Cary-Elwes pushed his jeeps some 35 kilometres north-west of the port city, making for the town of Mottola. The squadron had taken possession of their vehicles only shortly before departing for Italy. They had been forced to test-fire and zero-in the gas-operated Vickers K guns during the drive from their SAS camp to the port of Bizerte, using rocks and other desert features as makeshift targets.

Even so, when battle was joined the men of A Squadron shot first and bit hard. The squadron's War Diary takes up the story as 'Major Cary-Elwes' patrol ran into an enemy section just outside of Mottola.' The SAS proved decisively quicker on the draw. They 'killed three and took three prisoners, without suffering casualties'. Having broken off contact, a second patrol, commanded by Lieutenant Huggett, one of Cary-Elwes's deputies, 'ambushed and attacked an enemy transport column'. In the thick of the firefight a jeep conked out, leading to three of Cary-Elwes's men being taken captive.

As the SAS major concluded, their work here was turning into 'a stalking match, which is won by the quickest man on the draw'.

Chapter 5

FASTEST MAN ON THE DRAW

Despite such losses, the SAS was well up in the battle tally. But while probing at and cutting through the enemy's lines, the 1st Airborne Division had been struck a mighty blow. The terrain pushing up the boot of Italy was markedly rugged, and it favoured the enemy. Having accepted the Italian surrender in Taranto, the commander of the division, Major General George 'Hoppy' Hopkinson MC, who was never to be found far from the action, led an advance in the same direction as Cary-Elwes. He and his men reached an enemy roadblock and an attack was launched. In the ensuing melee Hopkinson was hit and mortally wounded.

Hopkinson was 'very much a frontline general, and any brigade or battalion in trouble would very soon find him in the midst'. He was a driven, inspiring, endearing character, and he would end up being the only British airborne general to be killed during the war. His epitaph would read: 'Who is the happy Warrior? Who is he that every man in arms would wish to be?' His loss was an immense blow. Into the void created by his death stepped Major General Ernest Down. In light of Hopkinson's untimely loss, there could be no formal hand-over of command nor any managed transition.

Fortunately, in Down – a craggy-faced Cornishman, nick-named with great affection 'Dracula' by his men – there could have been no better individual to take up the cudgels. A talented rugby player, Down was no desk-bound staff officer. With his 'pugnacious countenance', he openly admitted to hating such duties. Taking up where Hopkinson left off, he would prove to be a brilliant and unorthodox leader, and was revered by his men. In many ways Down was the perfect individual to oversee SAS operations here, especially as the grinding warfare began to bite, and considering all that was coming.

A third one of Bill Stirling's SAS squadrons was heading into the thick of the action, and it consisted of one of the most un-orthodox and unusual gatherings of men ever drawn together by war. In founding 2 SAS, Stirling had left no stone unturned in terms of where to find suitable recruits. Described in the SAS War Diary as 'a man from the shadows', Bill had helped David, his younger brother, shape and form the original SAS in the summer of 1941. But in truth, his role in Britain's elite forces went back to the very earliest beginnings. In the summer of 1940, he'd played a key role in founding the Special Training Centre, better known as the 'Guerrilla Warfare School', at Inverailort House, in north-west Scotland. Inverailort was the crucible in which the first Special Service recruits were forged, and thousands would pass through its training portal.

Inverailort would form such a standout centre of unorthodox excellence that when William 'Bill' Donovan, the founding father of American special operations, wanted to experience how to form a similar American unit, he would put himself through a course at the Guerrilla Warfare School. Donovan would take what he learned there back to the States, at which point British know-how and tradecraft became the foundation stone of all such American outfits, in the form first of the Office of Strategic Services (OSS), which would later become the CIA.

From Inverailort, Bill Stirling went on to command 62 Commando, a unit that specialised in daring cross-Channel raids, aiming to spread a campaign of terror along the enemy coast. After his brother David's capture by the enemy in North Africa in February 1943, he was charged to form the 2nd SAS Regiment. He took as his core cadre the battle-hardened men of 62 Commando, the vast majority of whom he brought into his new unit. Hungry, ambitious, driven, Stirling had come across an unexpected source of recruits in North Africa, plus an exceptional figure to lead them, a rare breed of soldier even in a time of war.

Lieutenant Raymond Jack William Couraud was a dual French-American national, who'd spent half his life in Paris and half in Pennsylvania. His mother, an American actress named Flora Leebowen, had married a Frenchman – a shadowy but beguiling arms-dealer figure – who had died when Couraud was young. At age eighteen he'd volunteered for the French Foreign Legion, using a fake Belgian identity in order to do so, for no Frenchman is allowed to serve in the Legion. That said, it was quite possible to reinvent oneself and without too many questions being asked, as Couraud had done. The Legion offered anonymity, protecting the identities of those who served.

During training, Couraud experienced the Legion's iron 'march or die' discipline, plus the promise that in the Legion everyone's past was forgotten, the slate wiped clean. He thrived within its ranks. General Pierre Langlois, one of the unit's foremost commanders, would assess Couraud thus: his 'adventurous spirit' had served him well in the Legion, while his 'intellectual abilities' put him well above the average recruit.

At war's outbreak Couraud had volunteered for service in the defence of Norway, along with Johann, an Austrian driven by hatred of the Nazis, who had stolen everything from him, 'his family, his possessions, his country', and Garcia, a Spaniard who'd been fighting fascism ever since the Spanish Civil War, plus Nielsen, 'a tall, pale-eyed Dane', a hard-drinker whose country had likewise fallen under the Nazi jackboot. Ill-equipped, out-gunned and hounded by the Luftwaffe, Garcia would sum up the Legion's lot in Norway with his catch phrase: *Por la mañana, mierda* – 'In the morning, shit'. In the coming actions Couraud would be awarded a Croix de Guerre for storming a German machine-gun nest, after his friend Garcia had been gunned down.

Evacuation, retreat and defeat in France had followed, after which Couraud had deserted the Legion, being unwilling to serve under the Vichy puppet regime, immersing himself in the milieu of the Marseille underworld instead. In that French port city the ex-legionnaire-turned-gangster met and fell in love with a gorgeous, glittering and wealthy American socialite, Mary Jane Gold. With his devil-may-care attitude and battle-hardened demeanour, Couraud won Gold's heart. She gave him the nick-name 'Killer' Couraud. More to the point, Couraud brought his very particular skillset into the clandestine work that Gold was then orchestrating, for she was a key link in an underground network smuggling Jews out of Nazi-occupied Europe.

Together, Couraud and Gold would help rescue some two thousand such souls from all-but-certain death. But Couraud remained haunted by Norway and defeat in France, and he hungered to return to the fight. At one stage he cornered and murdered a Nazi informer. At another, he was arrested and tried by the Vichy authorities for being a deserter from the Legion. With her influence and her cash Gold managed to cajole and bribe officials to release him. But eventually, their network was penetrated by the Gestapo. Hunted, Gold – a high-profile citizen of what was then a neutral nation, America – was relatively safe. Not so Couraud. He executed a dramatic escape across the Pyrenees and into neutral Spain.

There he was arrested again, this time by the Spanish authorities. His release was secured only after the personal intervention of Colonel Robert Drummond-Wolff, Britain's assistant military attaché in Spain, and a former instructor at a top French military academy. Drummond-Wolff, a formidable giant with a bristling moustache, demanded the captive's release and got it. Shipped to the UK aboard the SS *Leinster*, Couraud arrived at Liverpool dock on 13 October 1941, to be interrogated by MI5, the British domestic intelligence service. Their conclusion regarding the mercurial, feisty and war-bitten Franco-American was: 'Wants to go to Russia in the Tank Corps. Makes a good impression.'

Via his connections to Gold – his sometime fiancée – Couraud was given a free pass into Britain's high society. He met and charmed Lord Louis Mountbatten, who at that stage was the Chief of Combined Operations, an inter-service body that planned, prepared and executed special military projects. Mountbatten in turn introduced Couraud – fluent in both French and English – to the SOE. In his thickening file held by MI5, Couraud's case was declared as being 'too inflammatory to be discussed by telephone'. Noted one MI5 luminary, 'The less ventilation given to such cases the better.'

Within both MI5 and SOE, Couraud began to be referred to as 'Jack Lee', a cover name for a supposedly British national. His recruiters at SOE included Major Maurice Buckmaster, the head of its French Section, and Major Lewis Gielgud, the actor Sir John Gielgud's brother. Both concluded that Couraud possessed 'qualities which we believe we can turn to good account'. Dispatched to Scotland, training in SOE's dark arts followed, including stints at the 'shooting house', in which agents had to burst in and 'kill' dummies positioned around the rooms, while fresh sheep's carcasses were hung at entry and exit points, to ensure trainees emerged covered in blood.

Using dummy explosives, rail sabotage was executed along the West Highland Line, while at other times Couraud was ordered to travel the length of Scotland with no money, by fair means or foul. The problem was solved by hijacking an express train at gunpoint and arriving in style. At one point, fellow French trainees would decide to steal the Duke of Buccleuch's prize trophy, a set of saddle bags that had been taken off Napoleon at Waterloo. It was typical of Couraud – who would go on formally to adopt British nationality – to take up the cause. The duke hailed from one of the oldest and noblest Scottish families, as Couraud well appreciated, and he had offered his estate for special duty training. Working himself up into a 'holy anger', Couraud ensured that the precious saddlebags – a trophy of war – were 'miraculously' returned to their rightful owner.

Couraud's training was in preparation for a very particular role: he was to be the only Frenchman on Operation Chariot, the daring March 1942 commando raid on the heavily defended dry dock at St Nazaire. His mission was so secret that even he was not to be allowed to know the true identity of his parent unit. He was sold a lie – that he was serving with 'MO1 (SP)', which supposedly stood for Military Operations 1 (Special Projects). In truth, MO1 (SP) was a myth created to provide a pseudo-military cover for a secret, deniable outfit which had been formed to break all the rules of war – SOE. In other words, without knowing it Couraud was serving as an agent of SOE.

On the night of the St Nazaire raid the vessel that Couraud was sailing in was raked by fire, as were many of the assault ships. Hit and badly wounded in the legs, Couraud was lucky to make it out alive. He was hospitalised in the UK, his handler writing to his boss that the secret agent who 'took the boat to St Nazaire . . . did not know that he is an SOE officer, and therefore I am not reporting the casualty. You in fact are the only person in possession of the facts.' Even Couraud's injuries were top secret. He recovered. After a whirlwind romance he married an English beauty called Kathleen Davies, and was dispatched on a series of clandestine SOE missions, during which he was assessed as being a 'lion . . . full of enterprise and courage', but too indiscreet for much of SOE's work.

Characterised as being a 'lone wolf', MI5 advised that Couraud be retained for solo operations 'of a dangerous character'. His final SOE mission, codenamed Snowdrop, was to southern France as an assassin. Flown to Gibraltar, he crossed secretly into Vichy France, made his way to Marseilles, entered a café where two Gestapo informers were known to be playing cards and shot them both dead; they were cut down 'without a shout'. An innocent bystander was also killed, for Couraud had been told there should be 'no witnesses'. Making his escape, he ended up in a shootout with Vichy French police, killed two, and risked a further gunfight with the Spanish authorities. He'd also managed to burn through a small fortune in French francs during the process.

In short, while it was mission accomplished, Couraud had left a trail of corpses and potential diplomatic incidents in his wake. Assessed as being 'irresponsible', but hugely capable, and blessed with seemingly 'limitless personal courage', SOE turned to Mountbatten to decide what to do with Couraud. As Bill Stirling was forming 2 SAS, Couraud was dispatched to join him, supposedly with an appropriate health warning. There was no sign that Stirling found the twenty-three-year-old Couraud anything other than prime SAS material. Noting his 'excellent record of service', he tasked Couraud with scouring North Africa for recruits, including as many French Foreign Legionnaires as possible.

As matters transpired, Couraud was sowing his seed on very fertile ground. Outside of France, North Africa was the home of the Legion. Its headquarters was in Sidi-bel-Abbès, not far from the SAS's base at Philippeville (today's Skikda). At first under Vichy French control, its members had been kicking their heels for months on end. Even with the arrival of the Allies, little had changed. Initially a clandestine venture, in which willing recruits were forced to desert the Legion in order to join the SAS, Couraud's efforts eventually won the grudging blessing of the Free French Forces. Some fifty legionnaires were recruited, among the first of which was his very able deputy, Louis de Sablet, who was as unlike Couraud as chalk is to cheese.

They christened their part of the SAS's Algeria base 'Camp Jeanne d'Arc'. Of average height, and with dark, wolfish looks, Couraud began to train his men relentlessly. Though his demeanour was often sarcastic and abrasive, he would never leave anyone 'bereft of help' in a crisis. While Couraud was very much a man of the people, de Sablet, by contrast, was a high-born aristocrat who luxuriated in the name of Louis Gabriel Saltet de Sablet d'Estières. He and Couraud formed an unlikely but effective partnership, as they licked into shape what became known as the SAS's French Foreign Legion Squadron.

In his downtime, Couraud was drawn to Farran, and vice versa, as the former took the latter on tours of the local bars favoured by the men of the Legion. Birds of a feather, they would go on to have innumerable adventures. But before any of that, General de Gaulle would make a last-ditch effort to claw back the SAS Legionnaires into the French fold. Officially, de Sablet commanded 2 SAS's French Squadron. Couraud could not be seen to do so, for a whole raft of reasons: he'd been formally tried as a deserter, he'd taken British nationality, but worst of all he'd served with Britain's secret services, which was seen as being a black mark for any Frenchman, who should be serving with de Gaulle's Free French equivalent, or so the argument went. On the ground, Couraud was in command, of course, but this was the necessary deception.

In the spring of 1943, General Henry Giraud, then commander-in-chief of Free French Forces, wrote to senior British commanders, noting how a French unit, led by Lieutenant de Sablet, has been 'seconded' to the Special Air Service at Philippeville, receiving 'very thorough instruction'. Giraud requested their return, so they might train similar elite units of the French military. As there was little response, Giraud wrote again, this time in more strident tones, identifying the forty-strong 'group of Frenchmen in 2 SAS' whom General de

Gaulle believed 'should not be retained in a British unit'. He asked for their return forthwith.

By then it was too late. Couraud and de Sablet had deployed to Italy with their SAS Legionnaires, on Slapstick business.

With his fluent French, Cary-Elwes had a secondary role to fulfil around Taranto. While the French Foreign Legion welcomed allcomers, regardless of background, past or nationality, the one iron rule was that all recruits had to learn French. It was the Legion's lingua franca – the language that served to decode a multitude of otherwise unintelligible tongues. Of course, Cary-Elwes was a natural to play the role of 2 SAS's liaison with Couraud, de Sablet and their men. For what was coming, it would prove pivotal. Cary-Elwes and Couraud had also served together before on SAS missions, most notably when the former had helped defend the latter from false accusations of cowardice. A good deal of trust had been established between them.

In the hours after the Taranto landings, Couraud managed to commandeer an ancient bus as his squadron's makeshift transport. With that battle wagon crammed full of his former legionnaires, Couraud struck out west, serving on the left flank of Cary-Elwes and Farran's more northerly advances. In the squadron's War Diary, written up by 'Sergeant Chef Meronane, French Detachment', he recorded how the bus-borne raiders encountered the enemy '3 kilometres short of Palagianello'. The German troops were armed 'with automatic weapons and mortars'. The small town of Palagianello lay on a high point, amid rough, dry, craggy terrain, some 30 kilometres west-north-west of Taranto.

As Couraud and his men edged ahead on foot, they caught sight of a demolition team about to blow up a road and rail bridge, which was defended by machine-gun posts and anti-tank guns. In the adjacent vineyard a figure was spotted, disappearing 'like a rabbit'. One of Couraud's men gave chase, slamming him to the ground in a rugby tackle. They'd captured a local youth who seemed to have been spying on the enemy. Surrounded by Couraud and his men, the captive had 'panicked eyes' as he faced the squadron commander's questions.

Did he know a way around the enemy position, Couraud demanded. And without being seen? Couraud's intention was to outflank the German defences and hit them from the rear. After a brief moment's hesitation, the teenager nodded a yes. He knew a way to slip past.

Would he act as their guide, asked Couraud.

As the youth hesitated, his captor, legionnaire Sakri, made sure that the barrel of his weapon pressed deeper into the captive's ribs.

Yes, the youth answered. He would guide them.

The column set out, with that young man at the fore, leading a line of heavily armed troops into an adjacent valley. It was more like a chasm hewn into the earth, as rainstorms turned this dry watercourse into a raging torrent. Choked with low, thorny trees, it had all the characteristics of Maquis, the typical thick and tangled vegetation that cloaks the lower slopes of the mountains fringing the Mediterranean.

Couraud was accustomed to this kind of terrain from his time in and around Marseilles. The sun beat down remorselessly and their progress proved painfully slow. Suddenly, a yell of alarm rang out from the front of the line, followed by the noise of crashing branches. A legionnaire dashed back to Couraud.

'The little shit!' he gasped. 'He ran away, my Captain.'

No one was to shoot, Couraud warned. If they did, the enemy was sure to be alerted.

One moment their guide had been there, Couraud's man explained. The next he had dropped into a thick clump of trees and had vanished. Cursing their renegade guide, Couraud's main worry was whether he had run away to warn the enemy. Who knew on what side the young man's allegiances might lie? If they had been betrayed, the ravine they were following would prove a death trap. The enemy could rain down fire from above. Couraud gave the order for a fast march to exit the gorge as quickly as possible.

Climbing up to the lip of the ravine they discovered a vineyard, which offered a modicum of cover. As they had all but circumvented the enemy position, Couraud urged his men on. Slipping from tree to tree, they must have been spotted. An enemy gunner sent a first burst of machine gunfire whipping through the trees. Rounds tore into the olive grove, kicking up small bursts of dust in the dry soil. The German troops were positioned a few hundred yards away, and it was only a matter of time before they would find their range and their aim.

Couraud ordered an about-turn. Pursued by a storm of lead, he and his men doubled back the way they had come.

'The little bastard sold us out!' someone yelled, as they made their dash for cover.

The first to be hit was legionnaire Felger, but he was only lightly wounded. Then, while making the leap into the ravine, Bellanger, one of Couraud's youngest, was cut down by a burst of fire. Couraud dragged the wounded man into the cover of the gorge. Bellanger's groin was soaked with blood, the femoral artery no doubt severed. Slapping a bandage onto it, immediately it was stained red. As Couraud fully appreciated, Bellanger needed an ambulance and urgent surgery if he was to live.

There was nothing like that around here.

Jamming his hand deep into the wound, to try to stem the flow, Couraud's gaze met that of the wounded man. 'Hold on,' he urged. 'We'll get you out.'

But Bellanger's eyes were already glazing over. He managed a faint smile. 'No need for you to tire yourself, Captain. It will soon be over.'

With their faces streaked in sweat – or was it tears? – they carried the dead man out of there. Once they were safely away from the enemy's range of fire, they dug a shallow grave in silence and buried the fallen man.

A while later they reached an isolated farmstead. A few goats and chickens wandered about. An elderly man welcomed them with water, figs and olives. He had an air of stoical resignation about him, and Couraud guessed they were not the first troops to pause at his outpost. He called for his wife. Some chickens were caught and a meal prepared.

Sometime later, a cry rang out from one of Couraud's men. 'My Captain! I've got him! The little bastard from this morning!'

While searching a hayloft for eggs, their 'guide' from earlier in the day had been discovered, cowering beneath some hay. Brought before Couraud, the SAS commander ordered two of his men to take the captive to a patch of open ground. 'Make him dig a hole. His own hole.' This time, there was to be no escape.

At dusk, the grave was declared ready. Couraud approached. He took out his revolver and cocked it. The young man fell to his knees, sobbing. Pleading for mercy.

'Tell him to say his prayers before he dies,' Couraud announced, via one of his men who was fluent in Italian. 'We are avenging Bellanger, who he had killed this morning.'

As he went to raise his weapon, a cry of distress rang out. The old couple from the farmhouse came hobbling over. They protested, tearfully. What was their son – for this was their son – accused of? What had he done?

Couraud explained.

'Talk to the Germans? Never!' the farmer protested. 'Look what they did to him yesterday.' At that he ripped his son's shirt apart, to reveal a back that was red, bruised and bloodied. The father explained how German troops had visited the farm the previous day and assaulted the boy savagely. They had whipped him, accusing him of being a deserter from the Italian military.

By way of answer, Couraud sheathed his weapon. He eyed the young man. 'You are lucky you have a father speaking up for you,' he declared, plus a mother who cooked chicken stew 'just the way I like it'.

Couraud's French Squadron were a man down with little concrete to show for it. But they had made a crucial discovery. As they'd pressed inland, they'd found that the main routes of ingress – the key road and rail junctions – were going to be intensively defended.

Somehow, they would need to find another means to break through.

Chapter 6

THE GHOST OF NO-MAN'S-LAND

Even as Couraud had forced that hapless Italian youth to dig his own grave, so McGregor and his men were preparing for a special mission. They were about to head a dozen kilometres behind enemy lines, on foot and at night, to ambush an in-bound enemy convoy. According to intelligence reports, it was expected through Palagianello at dawn. That was where they had to get to in order to strike. The country they would have to cross was similar to that which Couraud and his men had fought through: a patchwork of 'orchards, vineyards, hedgerows and walls'. In fact, Couraud and his French Squadron had been hit during their own advance towards Palagianello, being stopped well short.

McGregor and his force set out at just before dusk, slipping through their own lines – held by the forces of 1 Airborne Division – and into the unknown. As 'the darkness closed in' they knew they'd have to move fast to reach the ambush spot in good time. They hit their first problem when clambering over a wall. One man vaulted onto the far side, only for there to be a 'terrific crash of broken glass'. Suddenly, 'all the dogs from Rome to Taranto' seemed to be barking, and McGregor and his men froze. That hapless individual had landed in a greenhouse. Bit by bit he had to extricate himself from the shattered glass, every move causing a nerve-jangling tinkle.

Finally, the six got moving again. Pausing to check their maps by the moonlight, they realised they were nearing Palagianello. Arnold and Sutton were forming the rearguard, and as they followed the path of a sunken lane, aiming to skirt around the nearest houses, a torch beam pierced the darkness. It flashed in their direction. Arnold and Sutton crouched down, hoping that they'd be mistaken for 'a couple of bushes' in its light. The moment the beam swept away, they hopped over the wall that fringed the road, following after the others. Behind them, footsteps rang out. Voices speaking German were heard. 'They passed us and went on down the lane.' That had been close.

Arnold and Sutton now had to find the others. Hurrying on, they reached a patch of woodland. As they scanned its dark interior, Arnold spied a figure standing motionless in the cover of a tree. It was too dark even to see which way he was facing. As Arnold provided cover, Sutton set off through the woods to approach from the flank. Arnold watched him flit closer, a silent, wraith-like form among the trees. Finally, Sutton crept right up to the mystery figure and whispered: 'Boo!' At last, the statue-like form moved. He turned around to face Sutton. Both men laughed. It was Dellow. He'd come back to search for them and to guide them to the rest of the stick.

With Dellow leading the way they pressed on, rejoining McGregor and the others in the cover of a hedge. Up ahead lay a large country house. Sentries were prowling the grounds. It had to be some sort of German HQ. They marked it on their map. Prime intel to hand over to their own headquarters. Skirting that house, finally they reached what seemed to be the perfect ambush spot. It was just after 4.00 a.m. If the convoy came at dawn, as expected, that was two hours away. Time to snatch some rest. With a sentry rota set, those not on watch curled up on the ground and were soon fast asleep.

Snatching a kip just prior to launching an ambush while behind enemy lines – the coolness of McGregor and his men typified their collective spirit. More to the point, they had trained relentlessly for such night operations, until they were masters of the craft. One of their final 'missions' during 2 SAS selection had been to execute an assault on their own camp. Not only that, they had to steal a certain set of papers. Driven over a hundred kilometres from their base in a covered truck, so no one could check where they were going, they were dropped off with no maps or compass, and precious little food or water, and would be forced to navigate by sun and stars.

The SAS camp was surrounded by rolls of Dannert wire – coiled razor wire. The defenders would only use blanks and flares, but they were also armed with 'flaming onions' – a type of flash grenade that would 'burst into an enormous flame'. Jeep patrols would be on the search and their guns would be armed with live rounds to fire warning shots. It took four days to trek to the camp. Several times they were chased and fired upon by the SAS jeeps. Once there, McGregor and his men lay up in hiding, studying the camp's defences. As Arnold noted: 'It is one of the advantages of special ops that you can get right up to the enemy's doorstep . . . and watch him at his daily routines.' Like this, they noted guard changes, mealtimes – and when vigilance seemed to grow slack.

They split into four groups to make their assault, going in at

2.00 a.m. Someone must have been spotted, for weapons started firing. But McGregor, Sutton and Arnold made it through the wire undetected. From there they headed for the cook house to execute their cunning plan. Picking the lock, they slipped inside, then proceeded to change into a set of chef's 'white overalls, aprons and caps'. Thus disguised, they stole across to the Operations Hut. Spying their kitchen attire, the sentry seemed relaxed enough, until he was pounced upon, tied up and gagged. That done, Sutton removed his chef's clothing, to reveal his uniform beneath, and took over as if on sentry duty himself.

The door to the Ops Hut was firmly locked. Shortly, Sutton hissed a warning. Someone was coming. With McGregor and Arnold in hiding, Sutton took a few steps of 'his' sentry beat, even as the newcomer arrived at the door to the Ops Hut. In a flash the three impostors had pounced upon him, with McGregor's pistol at his back. They had captured the 2 SAS intelligence officer. He was persuaded to unlock the door, whereupon they scooped up the necessary papers, before leaving the two captives bound and gagged on the floor. As Arnold recalled, they 'locked the door' and 'keeping the key' they made their way out of the camp, 'mission accomplished'. One of the other teams had actually got into Bill Stirling's tent and bound and gagged him, before tying him to his bed.

Those who had managed to pass SAS selection had done so by dint of far more than sheer physical toughness. Mental strength was the key: 'it needed willpower and great strength of mind . . . to keep you going no matter what the situation even when you thought your body could not take any more'. McGregor and his men had decided to celebrate with a raid on the nearest RAF base, which lay some six kilometres away. Getting in at the dead of night proved child's play. They proceeded to chalk and paint the aircraft, to let the RAF know their security had been breached. 'Wrote all kinds of things on the planes,' Arnold observed, 'some of which I would not like to repeat. The most prominent being "Kilroy Was Here".'

Getting back to their camp undetected, they had a few drinks before crashing out. The next day they awoke to the howl of aeroengines, as RAF warplanes roared across the SAS base at just above tent height. As all took cover, 'an awful smelling stuff fell down on us'. The pilots had emptied their latrines onto the base. That was followed by a second airstrike, this time unleashing 'slops from the cookhouse, stinking meat, old cans, rotten vegetables'.

Thankfully, there was to be no such rude awakening behind enemy lines here in Italy. McGregor and his men roused themselves to discover a thick and silent ground mist cloaking the landscape. Just before 6.00 a.m. they heard 'the rumble of trucks in the distance'. As the mist began to lift, the first of the canvas-backed trucks hove into view. It nosed ahead, the driver seeming oblivious to the hell that was about to be unleashed. Lying in hiding at the head of his men, McGregor was the first to open up – the thunder of his Tommy gun signalling for all to do likewise. Hit by his barrage of fire, the lead truck skidded to a halt just below Arnold and Sutton. 'We sprayed the canvas top with bullets, and heard the screaming of the men inside as the holes appeared,' noted Arnold.

The second and third trucks ground to a halt. Dellow and a fourth of McGregor's men, James 'Geordie' Laybourne, were onto them in a flash, hurling grenades into both of the vehicles.

Those German troops not already dead or wounded piled out of the vehicles, trying to make for the cover at the sides of the road, 'but they were still in our line of fire, poor bastards', as Arnold observed. 'The air was filled with the screams of the wounded,' plus the yelling of orders in German, as the officers tried to muster some kind of response. Finally, McGregor hurled a last grenade, which sailed right over the lead truck – the agreed signal to cease fire and make good their getaway.

They'd set their route of escape beforehand: it followed a path leading over a nearby hill, to a prearranged rendezvous point. But Arnold and Sutton still had to dash past the line of trucks to get to the start of the escape route. Arnold yelled for Sutton to go first. They'd each slung their weapons over their shoulders and had a grenade gripped in either hand, with the pins removed. First Sutton and then Arnold sprinted down the line of shot-up, burning vehicles, hurling their grenades – 'that kept the Germans' heads down' – enabling the two men to break away. They hurried up the slope as sporadic fire broke out from behind them, but the surviving enemy clearly couldn't see the SAS among the ground mist, for none of the rounds came anywhere close.

They reached the rendezvous point and all six were reunited. So far so good. McGregor led them on in what was now a race to reach their own lines. The day was dawning, and all were painfully aware that most of the escape and evasion would need to be executed in broad daylight. Suddenly, the last of the mist blew away, and the raiders found themselves in an open field, 'feeling as naked as plucked chickens'. There were walls on three sides. Above the far one there appeared a German helmet. McGregor crept forward, his knife drawn. Just as he was about to rise up and strike, the German sentry moved away a few strides.

McGregor stole across to his new position. But once again, just as he went to use the blade the enemy soldier moved on.

'If the situation had not been so tense, I could have laughed at the look on the boss's face,' Arnold remarked, 'mingled with surprise and annoyance.' Finally, the sentry turned and walked away, blissfully unaware of how close he had come to death that morning. On the far side of the wall lay Palagianello, the village they had passed during the night. Skirting around it and sticking to the cover of vineyards and patches of thick woodland, McGregor led his men back towards their own lines. The first sign of friendly forces was some airborne troops, dug in beside a road and manning a machine gun. Approaching with maximum caution, McGregor let it be known they were British forces coming through.

Shortly, an ancient Fiat truck came 'clattering down the road' from the direction of Taranto. An SAS man was at the wheel. McGregor and his team piled aboard. A few minutes later they rounded a bend, only for the truck to be met with a 'hail of bullets and then two loud bangs'. All bailed out as the 'old Fiat went careering down the road on its own, until the German fire caught up with it', at which point it left the highway 'in a mass of flames'. Unwittingly, they'd driven into a German position, which was all too easy to do with the ever-changing, shifting patchwork of enemy and friendly forces. Luckily all had bailed out safely. On foot they made it back to their own lines.

Returning to their headquarters, they reported on their mission. As noted in the SAS War Diary, for the night of 11/12 September: 'Went out on night patrols in the area south of Castellaneta. Lt. McGregor penetrated German lines near Palagianello . . .'

In the process of executing his mission, McGregor had spoken to the town's stationmaster. He'd revealed that German forces were advancing towards his location, aiming to dig in around the station itself. The enemy were busy running 'railway carriages down the line', which were rushed through Palagianello itself, but the stationmaster couldn't confirm what they were carrying. Clearly, the railways were going to prove key arteries of the war that was being fought here.

As well as reporting on such intelligence, McGregor handed over the coordinates of the country house and suspected German HQ that they had discovered during their night patrol. Later, it would be raided and a valuable prisoner seized. But by then, McGregor and his men would be earmarked for other pressing business – for up ahead there lurked an untold evil, and the SAS had a date with destiny.

Having probed, pricked and stung the enemy, the SAS consolidated, establishing a makeshift headquarters at Chiatona town, just to the west of Taranto, and basing themselves in the deserted railway station. 'Settled in at Chiatona,' the 2 SAS War Diary noted, simply. By now it was 13 September, some 72 hours after the USS *Boise* had made landfall. In the interim, Farran's squadron had launched an abortive attack on Gioia del Colle aerodrome – the enemy had just vacated it – and several of the other squadrons had managed to commandeer some barely serviceable vehicles.

In their desperation, C Squadron, commanded by Captain John Gunston, had grabbed a clapped-out 1916 Renault truck in an effort to join the Gioia del Colle airbase raid. But as their entry in the War Diary records, the Renault had a 'maximum speed of 10 m.p.h. The woodwork was just capable of bearing the weight of 15 men with automatic weapons.' En route to their target, their valiant steed 'was overtaken by a somewhat faster lorry . . . contact was not made with the enemy.' Thwarted, Gunston and his men had chugged their way back to base.

Then a very odd thing happened.

A mystery figure appeared from the no-man's-land beyond Chiatona. Dressed as a civilian, he introduced himself as being Zeljko 'Zelcko' Ljubo. Zelcko was his nom de guerre, for he had originally served as a partisan – a guerrilla fighter – in the then Yugoslavia. In April 1941, Yugoslavia, lying across the Adriatic Sea from Italy, had been invaded by Italian and German forces. Overwhelmed, the Royal Yugoslav armed forces were obliged to surrender, but many fighters had taken to the hills, and a lengthy and bitter insurgency had begun. As Zelcko related, he had been captured by Italian forces and shipped across the Adriatic to be imprisoned on Italian soil.

The very day of the Allied landing at Taranto, Zelcko had broken out of his place of incarceration. He'd done so in the company of one other prisoner, Antonio Fragasso, an Italian and staunch anti-Fascist. Stealing an Italian Bianchi S5 police car from the local guard force, they'd sabotaged the other vehicles so as to prevent any pursuit. They'd also equipped themselves with fake identity documents, 'duly signed, countersigned and properly stamped' – the Yugoslav prisoners were the past masters at such forgeries – to speed them on their way. With the camp's rigid surveillance systems, and with its borders being intensively policed, past breakouts had almost always been thwarted, the escapees being 'easily tracked down in the surrounding area'. Zelcko and his comrade's attempt had been 'prepared down to the smallest detail'.

Having slipped free of the camp, the two escapees had separated to maximise the chances of one of them getting away. While Fragasso had headed in one direction, Zelcko had made a beeline for Allied lines. Under a burning sun, and badly weakened from the long months of incarceration, he'd made impressive progress. En route, some of the locals – troglodyte farmers who lived in caves – had sheltered and succoured him. In just three days he'd covered the one hundred-plus kilometres separating the camp from Taranto, braving a route that was far longer and more challenging when moving across the punishing, hilly terrain.

Zelcko's sense of urgency had driven him on. He insisted he speak to the senior Allied commanders, for he bore what in his view was vital intelligence. By coincidence, General Down's signals officer was an SAS veteran of sorts – Captain Anthony Deane-Drummond. In February 1941 he'd served as the second in command on Operation Colossus, a daring mission executed by 11 Special Air Service Brigade to blow up a freshwater aqueduct in Italy. Formed in the autumn of 1940, in response to Winston Churchill's call for airborne Special Service troops, 11 SAS was the forerunner of its future namesake. Indeed, David Stirling had been advised to adopt the name and mantle of 11 SAS when founding his North African unit.

Captured in the aftermath of Colossus, Deane-Drummond had escaped, but been recaptured as he tried to cross the border into neutral Switzerland. Hospitalised, he'd escaped again and this time was successful. Upon his return to the UK, he was awarded a Military Cross in recognition of his gallant actions. Posted to the 1st Airborne Division, he had a natural affinity with the Stirling brothers' SAS, as did General Down himself. They shared that audacious, leftfield mindset so deeply embedded within the Special Air Service, and the sense that, when blessed with the calibre of men that they commanded, nothing was impossible.

Brought before the commanders of 2 SAS and 1 Airborne Division, Zelcko revealed all. His story, in equal measure shocking and borderline unbelievable, plumbed the depths of human degradation, epitomising all that the Allies were fighting against in this war. High in the Italian hills set back from the coastal plane was a tiny settlement called Marconia. It lay a dozen kilometres from the nearest railway station, at Bernalda Scalo. There, the locals had become accustomed to seeing Fascist Italy's desperate and condemned – resistance fighters, partisans, Italian priests, anti-Fascists and Jews – spewed out of overcrowded and stinking cattle carriages, to be marched south . . . into hell.

Zelcko had escaped from 'La Colonia Confinaria di Pisticci', better known as 'the First Italian Concentration Camp'. Established in 1939, complete with watchtowers, gun-emplacements and barbed wire, Pisticci was the Fascist mirror to the Nazi Holocaust. Hundreds of Europe's so-called *Untermenschen* – sub-humans – had been corralled there, including Yugoslav and French freedom fighters, plus those Italian noblemen, artists, opera singers, politicians, writers and intellectuals who had had the courage to resist Mussolini's iron-fisted rule. There was even a group of Spanish Civil War veterans incarcerated in the camp, plus a bunch of Poles who had served in the French Foreign Legion.

As one of its inmates, Zelcko had witnessed it all.

Chapter 7

WITNESS TO HELL

To those listening, Zelcko's tale appeared utterly fantastic. At this stage in the war, September 1943, few Allied commanders knew the slightest thing about the Nazi and Fascist concentration camps. Zelcko spoke of a 'prison-factory' built by die-hard Fascist industrialist and profiteer Eugenio Parrini, which was designed to work prisoners into the ground. It was a tale of hundreds being delivered by train in cattle cars, after weeks on the move in inhuman conditions and with little food or water. It was of locals – women, children and the elderly – spitting at and pelting the new arrivals with rocks and rotten fruit, while screaming at them, 'Robbers! Rebels! Murderers! Criminals!'

The new arrivals were emaciated, unshaven, dishevelled and shell-shocked. The Italian soldiers supposedly providing escort did little or nothing to safeguard them. When some of the prisoners tried to retort that they were 'freedom fighters' and 'fighting against 'fascism', the words seemed to have little effect, despite the fact that many were genuine partisans and resistance forces. The locals had been brainwashed by Mussolini's virulent Fascist propaganda, which had been all-encompassing.

In Yugoslavia, Italian troops had burned villages, executed

hostages and rounded up 'Slavs' for deportation to the camps. Captured French and Greek resistance members were likewise shipped to Pisticci, as were 'racial groups' that Mussolini warned were 'dangerous' to the Fascist cause. The Pisticci internees were defined as being 'undesirable elements full of hate against totalitarian regimes'. Food was so scarce that camp inmates hunted stray dogs and rifled through garbage heaps. Across Italy, thousands had died in such camps, one of which at least would be declared worse than Buchenwald, the notorious Nazi concentration camp. Cemeteries overflowed with the dead.

The area that had been chosen for the Pisticci camp was a largely uninhabited, malaria-ridden, godforsaken tract of land far from any major towns or cities. The earliest work for those housed there had been to hew cultivable land out of the wilderness. Engaged in that back-breaking labour, Pisticci had been designated as a 're-education camp' – in Nazi terminology, an *Arbeitserziehungslager* – one designed to 'cure' prisoners of their democratic, freedom-loving ways. Once some two thousand acres of land had been tamed, the inmates were set to work in brick kilns, chicken farms, shoe-making factories and weaving sheds, becoming accustomed to the daily 'discomforts of solitude, the obsessive presence of the guards, of hunger'.

With a layout like barrack blocks – serried rows of buildings arranged around a central square – and sentry boxes on all corners, the camp commandant Colonel Ercole Suppa's quarters lay to one side. Suppa had around a hundred mixed carabinieri and troops under his command, backed up by the notorious Black Shirts – Italy's Fascist militia. Mobile patrols travelling by motorcycle and truck helped ensure that any escapees were quickly recaptured. Those duly tracked down disappeared into other, worse places, like the notorious 'Pain Villa' in Trieste, a place of 'heinous torture' menaced by the OVRA – the Organisation for the Vigilance and the Repression of Anti-Fascism, Italy's equivalent of the Gestapo.

One of the youngest dissidents held in Pisticci was fourteen-year-old Domenico Rocco Giannace, a young anti-Fascist who had become the camp's de facto 'mascot'. Colonel Suppa's iron control at Pisticci was extended to the dozens of previously venerated priests who were held there, including prominent anti-Fascists Don Francesco Maria Giua, Don Francesco Brambilla of Cremona, Don Guiseppe Pinfari of Mantua, Don Nazzareno Lombardi of Perugia, Don Giovanni Gorzegno of Cuneo and more. Together, the clergymen had built a tiny chapel, set to one end of the camp, dedicated to the Blessed Sacrament – the body, blood and soul of Christ.

Over time, they had decorated the chapel's interior with beautiful ecclesiastical paintings, including one striking image in oil depicting Jesus Carrying the Host. Inside the entrance a flight of free doves formed a striking mural, one of the birds bearing a ribbon inscribed with the following Latin inscription: *Florete flores quasi lilium et date odorem et frondente in gratiam* – 'Bloom flowers, like the lily, and spread perfume and make graceful leaves'. It was a thinly veiled reference to the hopes the inmates nurtured that one day, freedom might once again be theirs. Such a place of beauty in the heart of hell.

The chapel housed one very unusual inmate. There, Prince Filippo Andrea VI Doria Pamphilj, one of Italy's foremost aristocrats, was lodged. A diehard opponent of Nazism and fascism, in 1938 the prince had had the courage to refuse Adolf Hitler entry into his famed residence in Rome, the thousand-room

Palazzo Doria Pamphilj, which housed a priceless art collection, including works by Titian, Caravaggio and Raphael. His anti-Nazi stance had been stiffened via his marriage to Gesine Dykes, a Scottish nurse who he'd met in Switzerland when undergoing medical treatment. The prince had been educated at Magdalen College, Cambridge, and British spouses were something of a Doria Pamphilj family tradition.

The prince listed among his forebears Pope Innocent X, numerous nobles, plus an illustrious Italian admiral and some-time pirate. In keeping with the family's Anglophile roots, he had petitioned his cousin, the Italian king, not to ally their nation with Nazi Germany, and he and his wife had refused to donate gold to the Italian Fascist cause. With the prince absent from the palace, his wife, Princess Gesine, had been forced to face down a mob after the family had refused to abide by a diktat to fly the Fascist flag. As they stormed up the stairs six abreast, Princess Gesine blocked the way, dressed in a flour-dusted apron, for she'd just been baking. Having smashed a few windows, the mob departed when Princess Orietta told them to leave.

Forced out of Rome on Mussolini's orders, Prince Filippo went into hiding, before smuggling himself back into the city in 1943, and becoming known as the 'underground governor of Rome'. Amongst his many secret activities was the covert funding of the escape lines – routes by which downed Allied airmen, escaped POWs, and the wider enemies of the fascist state could be spirited out of Italy. Harold Macmillan, the future Prime Minister of Britain, had met with the prince during the war years and would remark that he had the demeanour of a 'medieval saint'. All of the above seemed to have qualified Prince Filippo for confinement at Pisticci.

Being Italy's first concentration camp, Pisticci was the model for those that followed. Eugenio Parrini, its progenitor, became the grand architect, as seventy such camps sprung up across Italy. Amid such a 'universe of concentration camps', along with the Jews, the Slavs had faced the very worst abuses. As Zelcko revealed, some seven hundred Yugoslavs – nearly all fellow partisans – were held at Pisticci. With the Allied landings on Sicily and then mainland Italy itself, unrest had exploded across the camp. As the inmates sensed the imminent end of Fascist rule, there were hunger strikes and riots. A guard had been beaten and his weapon seized, as the prisoners tried to arm themselves. Colonel Suppa responded by a show of strength, the guard force being boosted to some two hundred strong. He also set up armed roadblocks and increased the mobile patrols.

The same would happen across Italy, as German forces took the lead in clamping down upon the so-called enemies of the Reich, resulting in a series of horrific massacres. But that wasn't the worst of it. The very worst was the threat now hanging over Pisticci. With the Allied landings at Taranto, plans were afoot to spirit the inmates north by train. On 1 September orders had been issued to ship north 350 of the Slavs – a first consignment – 'to the Concentration Camp of Chiesanuova', a stepping stone to Nazi Germany itself. Indeed, on 10 September the Germans had 'occupied Chiesanuova camp, and by way of two train convoys' had emptied it, transporting the prisoners north via the Bremmer pass to Austria, making way for a new influx of prisoners.

All anyone was waiting for at Pisticci was an available train. With Allied warplanes pounding Italy's rail network, that was the chief cause of delay. On 13 August American warplanes had hit Bernalda Scalo railway station itself, 'targeting the enemy's military outposts', while a strike on a rail tunnel had caused more casualties. The concentration camp had not been targeted, for the Allies mistakenly believed it to be a hospital. But British aircraft with 'dragon's teeth markings' had attacked the nearby airfield, shooting up German warplanes. It was the RAF's 112 Squadron who had first painted those famous markings on their aircraft, the Curtiss P-40 Warhawk, an American fighter-bomber christened the 'Tomahawk' or 'Kittihawk' in British service.

Yet as much as the Allies were determined to paralyse Italy's rail network, so the Germans – along with their Fascist Italian cohorts – were determined to keep it running. In short, the future was bleak for all at Pisticci camp should they be forced to board those trains. (Many such prisoners would be transported to Nazi Germany, ending up in places like Auschwitz.) That was why Zelcko had come. There was one chance to intervene, and it was relentless and urgent. If the forces gathered at Taranto could somehow get to Pisticci in time, they had a chance to release the inmates and strike a mighty blow in freedom's cause.

The question was, who present might take on such an audacious and risk-laden mission, especially since freeing those prisoners served no military purpose. Pisticci concentration camp lay dozens of kilometres from any major rail network, roads or towns. There was nothing notable about its location, barring its sheer isolation. Seizing it didn't gain the Allies significant territory, and raiding it didn't take out any key military targets. In short, a mission to liberate a concentration camp lying deep behind enemy lines just wasn't within the remit of most of the forces based at Taranto.

But on the other hand, perhaps it did tick all the boxes for Bill Stirling's 2 SAS.

Audacity was their calling card. So was doing the utterly unexpected. Thinking the unthinkable and then putting it into action was the bedrock of SAS operations. If you could think of a way to attack the enemy that they might never conceive of, then by definition you would strike in a manner least expected ... and by utter surprise. Time and again, it was those kinds of missions – impossible-seeming and therefore the least defended-against – that had won the day. As a case in point, their operations in North Africa had been shaped and defined in this way.

As those gathered at Taranto considered Zelcko's proposition, they set their minds to thinking if there was a similar way in which to hit Pisticci, with that same kind of audacious spirit to the fore? In a sense, one man had prior form in terms of masterminding such a mission. During the brave but doomed May 1941 Allied defence of Crete, Roy Farran had suffered multiple injuries and been captured. Imprisoned in Greece, he'd masterminded an escape despite his heavily bandaged legs, which entailed him commandeering a caique – a local wooden-hulled fishing boat – and navigating it from Greece to North Africa, to reach Allied lines. Shortly after doing so, he'd 'walked into "A" Force Office to volunteer to go back to Greece'.

The enigmatically named 'A Force' was a top-secret body established under the auspices of MI9, the British escape and evasion specialists. Their remit was simple: to get their hands on escaped Allied POWs as soon as possible, to see if they would be willing to return to the country whence they had fled, to help others do the same. Taking the bull by the horns, Farran had wandered into A Force's Cairo office and volunteered his services. As their Cairo commander, the inimitable Lieutenant Colonel Anthony Simonds, noted, Farran's 'story is symbolic of the courage of this young officer and his determination to escape'. At the time Farran was just twenty years old, and one of Simonds's first acts was to ensure that he received 'a well-earned MC'.

Simonds had welcomed Farran with open arms. During his escape from Greece, their caique had run out of fuel, due to the skipper – a local Greek retained by A Force – selling the diesel on the black market. Later in the voyage, things were so desperate that Farran was forced to 'shoot two Greeks who tried to grab the water supply'. One of his first missions with A Force was to ensure 'steps were taken to deal with the Greek caique skipper'. After executing a deal of fruitful work in Greece and further afield, Farran eventually left A Force in the summer of 1942. The reason he had given Simonds was that A Force work wasn't 'exciting enough and he didn't get to kill anybody'.

Here in Italy was perhaps a chance to do both: to spring those in dire need of rescue at Pisticci, and to deal with the concentration camp guards and commanders as surely they deserved. But by anyone's reckoning, the challenges were legion. The Pisticci camp lay deep inside enemy territory, especially using the convoluted route that any raiding force would have to take. If the SAS's experiences over the last three days were anything to go by, the terrain would be closely guarded and hard fought. But the greatest challenge of all was this: even if they could get to the concentration camp and blow open its defences, how on earth were they to spirit the hundreds of prisoners back to Allied lines?

As Zelcko had made clear, few would be capable of attempting such a journey on foot. More to the point, such an endeavour would be highly visible and slow. Hundreds of concentration camp escapees moving through enemy territory under their own steam would present all too easy a target. They would be at risk of recapture or death. Shepherding such a highly vulnerable flock could also expose the SAS to untold dangers. And with the very limited transport they possessed, there was no way to evacuate the escapees by vehicle. With a handful of purloined trucks, plus a few dozen SAS jeeps, there just wasn't the capacity to free the kind of numbers held there.

Despite all this, the men of 2 SAS were determined to go. Some had distinctly personal reasons. For Oswald Cary-Elwes, Bill Stirling's deputy, it was all about his concern for 'the people imprisoned there'. Cary-Elwes's Roman Catholic faith provided his moral touchstone, and his innate 'compassion for others' was triggered 'in times of war'. As one possessed of a 'great "sympathie" for the French', the idea of the French resistance fighters held at that camp being sent to their doom in Nazi Germany rankled. Cary-Elwes also had 'the ability to think laterally, to come up with unorthodox ideas that were not by the book, but driven by imagination and daring,' plus he was a 'shrewd assessor of the potential and quality in those he trained . . . he observed and he listened.'

In the French Foreign Legion Squadron, Cary-Elwes knew he had an outfit that had the dash and the flair to undertake such an impossible-seeming mission, and they had compelling reasons to do so. For a man like Raymond Couraud – for all of those in the French Squadron – the idea that former legionnaires were at risk of being shipped to the Nazi death camps was unconscionable. Plus Couraud, of course, had previous form in such endeavours – he'd played a key role in rescuing two thousand-odd Jews from Nazi clutches in Vichy France. Among those that he commanded there was another strong pull – the shared sense of national identity with those in the Pisticci camp.

One of Couraud's stalwarts was Wladislas Cieslak, a Pole by birth who'd run away from home aged eighteen to join the Foreign Legion. Volunteering to serve in the defence of France, he'd manned a 25mm anti-tank gun, taking out several German tanks and blocking their advance at the French village of Void-Vacon. For his actions Cieslak was awarded the Croix de Guerre, but that did little to take away the sting of being ordered to surrender, as France threw in the towel. Capture and ill-treatment had followed. Marched into a POW camp at Dusseldorf, Cieslak had vowed to break free. He'd done just that, crossing Nazi Germany in an epic escape and evasion, and finally making his way back to North Africa and the Legion.

But there, all he'd done was 'playing at soldiers . . . a waste of time'. When Couraud had appeared, looking for volunteers, Cieslak was 'first in the queue'. Five foot seven inches tall, broad and strong as a bear, he'd taken the French name of 'Lucien' when serving in the Legion. That was how all knew him now. One of twelve legionnaires recruited en masse, he'd endured the strictures of SAS training stoically, being 'thrown off moving lorries like a sack of potatoes . . . pitched from cliffs into sand-pits, dropped from balloons . . .' Rock-solid, calm, implacable, his philosophy with SAS operations was 'what is there to be scared of?' There were fellow Poles held in that concentration camp. For Cieslak and the other Polish SAS, there was no question but to go.

As Cary-Elwes fully appreciated, the ideal SAS commander 'presented the task at hand to his men and asked for their opinions as to how the objectives might be achieved. The final plan was the distillation of the best of what they came up with.' The SAS major did just that right now, as he and his men contemplated the Pisticci conundrum. It is uncertain who first came up with the audacious suggestion. To many of those present, it would – counter-intuitively – have seemed like the only natural course of action. Whoever's it was, the plan they set upon was to 'commandeer a train' and to steam it 'through hostile territory until they reached the concentration camp'.

In the 2 SAS War Diary, such a momentous decision was recorded simply as: 'A special train was assembled, manned by French Squadron, and Lieut. McGregor and his troop . . . with the object of releasing internees from a concentration camp . . . The camp was in German-occupied territory and was guarded by Italians under a Fascist Colonel.' That was Colonel Suppa, of course, the man who had seen fit to double the guard and stiffen the camp's defences.

'Lieut. McGregor' was very much a kindred spirit with those who had volunteered to man the rescue train – chiefly Couraud and his French Squadron. A real man's man, McGregor would go on to see service himself with the French Foreign Legion as a special operations instructor. McGregor and his troop were ordered to join 'the French Squadron on their railway expedition', as the War Diary recorded it. In co-opting McGregor and his men, Cary-Elwes had just made a fine addition to Couraud's team.

Being last-minute additions to the train raid force, McGregor and his men were given a hurried briefing on what was, even by their standards, a most unorthodox kind of mission. They were told they would be heading 'by train to a prison camp', to liberate those held there. 'Our job was to get them onto the train and get them back to Taranto,' Arnold noted, simply. They were ordered to get 'all the occupants if possible', and to target in particular 'the prison officers and governor'.

With his rescue force sorted, all Cary-Elwes and his men needed was to find their train, and someone to drive it, for no one then present had prior experience of handling a locomotive. Subsequently, they would make 'driving a locomotive one of the skills we learned in the course of SAS training', as Cary-Elwes would observe. But not quite at this early juncture. As no Italian engine driver was found who was 'willing to face the adventure', the word was put out: the SAS needed a volunteer to drive a 'special train'.

There being no immediate takers, a delegation set out by jeep to visit the men of 261 Field Park Company, an engineering unit that it was hoped might prove fertile recruiting ground. Part of the Airborne Division since January 1942, the 261 had become its 'experimental manufacturing unit', tasked with conjuring up whatever pieces of kit or equipment might be required. Only a 'very select few' had made it through jump training, to deploy at the sharp end of operations. The first such task of 261 Field Park Company RE (Airborne) had involved a dozen men joining Operation Freshman, the ill-fated mission to blow up the Norsk Hydro heavy water plant in Nazi-occupied Norway, a component of Germany's fledgling nuclear programme.

Operation Slapstick was their second such deployment. Under their commanding officer, Major John Chivers, they'd landed at Taranto 'in the first wave', making certain that 'such essential kit as a battalion sewing machine and one case of whisky' were included in their load. Having no motorised transport, and little idea where the enemy might be, the men had lashed themselves to some old carts and pulled them out of Taranto laden with their kit, and with one or two riding on purloined bicycles. On the city fringes they'd found an abandoned 'winery', unloaded their bottles of whisky – 'distinctly necessary' – requisitioned an ancient bulldozer, and got to work repairing roads and rail tracks.

The main line leading out of Taranto was blocked. A locomotive lay on its side, jammed in a tunnel, with carriages 'scattered higgledy-piggledy roundabout'. Before they could be cleared, the 261's sappers – their explosives experts – had to check the mountain of debris for any booby-traps or mines. After Herculean efforts, the wreckage was declared free of explosives and the line was cleared. The nearby station was re-opened and christened 'St. Pancras for the North', for it was to form a hub by which to resupply the advancing British troops. The men of the 261 had just finished all of that, and were queuing for tea with 'knife fork and spoon', when Cary-Elwes pitched up in his SAS jeep.

The SAS major accosted the nearest officer, who happened to be a Mark Henniker, a battle-hardened airborne commander who'd already been awarded a Military Cross on earlier operations. In short order Cary-Elwes outlined exactly why he'd come. The SAS intended to 'send a platoon by train into German-occupied territory . . . about one hundred miles north of Taranto', to liberate the Pisticci camp. As Cary-Elwes explained, 'It was hoped that it would be only a matter of minutes to get the prisoners on board . . . and bring them back to Taranto.' All the SAS were short of was a man to drive their rescue train. Could Major Henniker possibly help?

While Henniker felt certain he 'ought to try', he was determined to avoid any repeat of the Operation Freshman disaster. In November 1942 a pair of Halifax bombers had towed Horsa gliders into Norwegian airspace, packed with the men of the 1st Airborne Division, charged with sabotaging the Norsk Hydro plant at Telemark. All had either died when the gliders crash-landed, or were captured and subsequently executed by the enemy. Several of the dead were from 261 Field Park Company, and to Henniker, Cary-Elwes's train-rescue mission had the hallmarks of being an equally hazardous mission. Indeed, he reckoned it was a 'hare-brained enterprise with a lot of SAS desperadoes whose competence . . . I could only judge from appearances'.

Fortunately, Henniker liked the cut of Cary-Elwes's jib. He was 'clearly a first class officer'. With Major Chivers's blessing – a man who understood that with the wartime SAS, 'rules didn't mean a damn thing; they were a whole different breed' – Henniker and Cary-Elwes went in search of a couple of 'ex-railwaymen from the Great Western Railway' who were known to serve in the unit.

The 261's company sergeant major yelled out an order: 'Fall out anyone who can drive a train!'

A 'somewhat surprised young man' stepped forward, saluting smartly. Sapper Dennis Elkin was a former train driver who'd worked on the Cornish Riviera Express, the line that runs from Penzance, on the far south-western tip of England, all the way to London. An 'enterprising type, wide awake and all for the adventure', the twenty-two-year-old was promptly persuaded to 'volunteer' for what was coming. Elkin's one misgiving was 'lest a railway collision occurred in the process'. By way of answer, Cary-Elwes promised to put an Italian railway inspector on the locomotive, to 'interpret the signals' for Elkin as he drove the train deep into enemy territory.

That safeguard agreed, Henniker gave the green light. Having 'bolted his tea', Elkin was quickly transferred onto the jeep, so that he could be whisked off to front up what the SAS themselves were now referring to as their 'pirate train'. Cary-Elwes and his men had their train driver. They had an objective and a mission plan. They had a guide of sorts, in Zelcko, though he of course hadn't ridden that route by train. By rights they needed a local military man, someone with the kind of stature and clout to lend them an edge.

They found it in Colonel Usai, an Italian Army officer, who, as a 'good Italian' now allied to British forces agreed to ride in the locomotive, along with Zelcko, Couraud and McGregor, with their newly recruited chauffeur, Sapper Elkin, manning the footplate, the large metal platform where the driver and fireman stand in order to operate and fuel the engine.

Now all they needed was a suitable train.

Chapter 8

THE PIRATE TRAIN

From the SAS's earliest beginnings trains had been objects of desire. When the sixty-odd SAS originals – the earliest recruits, drawn together by David Stirling in the North African desert – gathered, two among them were Blair 'Paddy' Mayne, the Ulsterman who would go on to earn untold renown as the SAS commander par excellence, plus his great friend, the southern Irish Catholic Eoin McGonigal. Once training was under way, they were charged to carry out a dummy mission as proof of concept. It involved crossing a vast tract of desert by whatever means possible, to assault a well-defended RAF airbase. Of course, rather than bombs they were to attach stickers to warplanes that read variously 'BOMB' and 'BANG'.

In trailblazing style, McGonigal, then a lieutenant, had done the utterly unexpected. Instead of marching across the empty desert, as most patrols intended, he and his men had staked out the nearest railway line at night. Swinging a red lantern beside the track, they'd managed to stop an approaching train and had 'persuaded' the driver to speed them to Cairo. From there they'd 'borrowed' transport from the local military headquarters, driven to the fringes of the target, lain low for several days keeping close watch, before executing their mission. Despite causing some serious ructions on high due to missing HQ vehicles, McGonigal's actions had embodied the very spirit and ethos of the SAS.

Several months later, SAS commander Alexander 'Sandy' Scratchley – 'pining for action' – had endeavoured to put a variation of McGonigal's train mission into practice. He was selected to lead a patrol charged to blow up a heavily guarded fuel dump deep behind enemy lines. Scratchley's plan of attack involved 'jumpin' a train' at a deep desert station, and 'ridin' the rods' as far as the target itself. Scratchley had set off in his convoy of jeeps in search of their train, but events overtook them. British forces had broken through the enemy defences, and as battle raged all around Scratchley and his men had been forced to go to ground in the desert.

At around this time, another SAS patrol had seized an enemy-occupied railway station at the port of Mersa Matruh, and blown the place to smithereens. And back at the SAS base camp, men were undergoing instruction with an officer from Egyptian Railways, advising them on the best means to derail a train. Later, an SAS contingent would even prepare a locomotive packed full of explosives as a last-ditch DIY means to take the fight to the enemy. But all of this fell a little short of commandeering a train to serve as a Trojan Horse, to gain access to a concentration camp, the guard force of which were in any case *expecting* such a means of conveyance to arrive to ship out their prisoners.

One of the biggest challenges facing Cary-Elwes and his men was the unknown state of the rail tracks, or what kind of defences the enemy may have mounted along the way. As Allied intelligence reports would note, 'Railroad stations are guarded and should be avoided . . . Mining of bridges and tunnels has been a policy of the enemy since the Sicilian campaign . . . Bridges should be avoided because of guards . . .' This was all well and good, but not when riding on a train. Even as the enemy were keeping close watch and booby-trapping key locations, so the locals were growing desperate; there were reports of them ripping up railway sleepers to use as fuel for cooking.

When that pirate train set out, there was also going to be the very real danger of 'friendly fire'. With the Allies enjoying air superiority in the skies over southern Italy, any transport seen moving – especially outside of the Allied bridgeheads – was assumed to be that of the enemy, which made it fair game. By necessity, the rescue train would have to steam forth after dusk, and attempt to execute the entire mission under the cloak of darkness. As a final layer of uncertainty, no one seemed to know for sure if the railway station at Bernalda Scalo was still operational. Even if it was, from there to the concentration camp was a twelve-kilometre schlep. Somehow, they would have to seize transport to convey those they rescued from the concentration camp to the waiting train.

Another major challenge arose, as the SAS studied their maps and whatever local intelligence they could garner. The railway to Bernalda Scalo curved west as it left Taranto, hugging the coast and the low-lying terrain. It carried on in that vein all the way to Crotone, the next major settlement, some 250 kilometres along the coast. Long before that, the line to Bernalda Scalo branched off north, at the tiny costal hamlet of Metaponto. From there it carved a route inland, climbing all the way, the rail station itself lying at over 1,000 feet (300m) of altitude. That vital Metaponto rail and road junction would have to be seized, for the SAS would have to ensure that the points could be switched, to enable their pirate train to steam through to the target and back again.

The plan was evolving rapidly. It would now need to be a twofold operation. Long before the train set off, a jeep-bound force would have to slip through the lines and speed west to the Metaponto junction, so as to take it and then hold it at all costs. With Couraud and McGregor commanding the special train, Cary-Elwes decided it was in the very finest of hands. He would command the jeep-bound mission, taking with him all of C Squadron's available vehicles, plus as many troops as they could carry. Equipped with five heavily armed jeeps, and with ten men riding in them, he hoped that his 'light but formidable scouting force' would have the firepower to punch through.

As one final modification to the plan, Farran would push his squadron north-west in an effort to drive back the enemy's forces, to keep them away from the main operation and the route the train would take. That way, as a bonus he would get exactly what he had told A Force's commander, Simonds, that he most hungered for: *excitement, and the chance to kill the enemy.*

With Sapper Elkin's help, a locomotive and carriages were begged, borrowed and stolen from in and around Chiatona railway station, which was proving itself to be a fortuitous location at which to have established the SAS base. There, Elkin, plus Couraud's piratical force, got busy trying to acquaint themselves with 'the Italian rail engine controls', for, of course, they 'cannot have been familiar with them'. One thing was clear, as they got to know their engine and carriages: no way could any such train evacuate all who were held at Pisticci. Once the camp was taken – if it was taken – any number would have to be told to 'head for the hills' to await the Allied advance and final liberation.

Recognising that he'd had very little action so far on this deployment, Cary-Elwes selected Captain Gunston, a long-experienced soldier, to serve as his deputy on his side of the mission. The twenty-four-year-old John St George Gunston was the son of Baronet Derrick Wellesley Gunston, a Unionist MP, and educated at Harrow and Trinity College, Cambridge. Joining the jeep force, no longer would the son of the baronet need to content himself with dawdling along in an ailing Renault truck of 1916 vintage.

On 14 September, five days after making landfall at Taranto, Cary-Elwes's heavily armed force set out, pushing west from Chiatona into bandit country. Their orders were crystal clear: 'to hold the crossroads and railway crossing until 0130 hours, 15th, to enable a special train manned by French Squadron to steam through and liberate prisoners in concentration camp at Pisticci'. As they advanced to seize that vital 'road/rail crossover point', they found themselves heading into a dry, scrubby land-scape interspersed with 'well-ordered olive groves'. It was just the kind of terrain in which Couraud's men had been hit, and where legionnaire Bellanger had met his end.

At the same time, Farran's D Squadron were thrusting north-west into hostile territory. Knowing that the enemy had established a defensive line lying inland of Taranto, and that all roads were held by 'small sections of parachutists', Farran planned to take the route less travelled. His aim was to find a way through the enemy lines and hit them by surprise, striking from the flank and the rear. Steering his convoy off-road, he found it 'amazing how well our heavily laden jeeps travelled even over the most mountainous goat tracks'.

Oddly, at the first village they came across they were greeted as liberators, crowds of women and children throwing clumps of grapes at the jeeps, and crying out in Italian, 'Long live the Allied troops'. As Charlie Hackney pointed out, partly in jest, 'being hit in the face by a bunch of grapes was all right, but apricots and walnuts were liable to cause casualties!' Farran noted that the walls thereabouts were bedecked with the slogans 'DUCE' and 'REX', which were 'only crossed out with a single negligent stroke'. Mussolini had crowned himself The Leader – Il Duce – and Rex was an ancient title meaning 'king'. The local Carabinieri commander seemed not the slightest bit impressed by Farran's arrival, nor at the number of Allied troops landed at Taranto. The SAS commander didn't doubt that at the first opportunity he would betray them to the enemy.

Sure enough, even as the village square was thronged with well-wishers, so the first reports of gunfire echoed down the narrow streets. Unable to fight back for fear of civilians being caught in the crossfire, Farran extricated himself from the village in double-quick fashion, keeping 'one eye out for a withdrawal route to the open country to the south'. As he was painfully aware, 'it was all a cat-and-mouse game, for I dare not risk an involved battle with my slight strength'. Looping further west, he turned north again, trying to 'find a weak link in the enemy line' and aiming to 'twist the tails of the Germans'.

Eventually, the lead jeeps reached a blown bridge. Below it, the railway line snaked along a deep ravine, at the far end of which it disappeared into a tunnel. Farran sought intelligence from the locals. The ridge above the tunnel was heavily guarded, they told him. Pill-boxes and anti-tank guns lined the heights. There was no way through via the high ground. But perhaps there was a way to use the tunnel itself, Farran reasoned. Unwilling to commit his force to such a 'hazardous raid' without knowing the lie of the land, this called for a close-up reconnaissance. No better man to execute it than himself.

Creeping from boulder to boulder, Farran inched his way towards the tunnel entrance. Adjacent to the tracks there was a railwayman's cottage. Edging up to it, he found the place deserted, but scattered within were items of German military kit. Worming his way ahead, he approached the 'gaping black hole', finding that a 'heavy tree trunk had been dragged across the line'. By now, they had to be somewhere north of Bernalda Scalo, the station to which their pirate train would be headed. At this juncture, certainly, the railway line was blocked, which made him wonder why, and what might lie beyond.

Stepping around the felled tree, he stole into the tunnel. By the time he was halfway along it, and could see the bright daylight at its far end, there was the harsh rattle of gunfire, 'as if someone were dragging chains along sheet tin'. As it had come from behind, he figured his men had to be in trouble. Hearing the rapid rasp of Vickers K guns and the answering bursts of the enemy's MG 42s, that confirmed it. Dashing back the way he had come, he found that bullets were 'whistling across the cutting, bouncing off the rocks on the far side'.

Using a steep gully as cover, Farran rejoined his men. Sure enough, the jeep convoy had been spotted from the heights, and the gunners on both sides were exchanging bursts of fire. Pulling back until they were out of range, Farran outlined his plan. Big Jim Mackie would take a patrol on foot through the tunnel, under cover of darkness. Choosing a force of twelve, he'd leave two to guard the tunnel, after which he'd check out the enemy's strength and positions. That done, he was to 'kill as many as he could with a few surprise bursts', before withdrawing the way he had come. At present the tunnel seemed unguarded. It might not remain so. They had to seize the moment.

While Mackie was readying his men, one of Farran's satellite patrols returned from a separate attempt to probe the lines, and bearing an unexpected prize. Lieutenant David Huggett, another of Farran's trusted deputies, had driven into the nearest town, not realising it was firmly held by German troops. But equally, the last thing the enemy had been expecting was a small unit of SAS to come thundering into their midst. With surprise on his side, Huggett's patrol had got the drop on their adversaries, gunning down several in a brief but bloody street battle, before making off with the 'office truck of a German parachute battalion'.

In addition to the fabulous intelligence that the truck contained – it was stuffed full of papers – Huggett had captured the 'German Orderly Room Under-officer' who came with the truck, plus a deal of loot. As Farran noted, the 'cigarettes and food were most welcome', for by now they were running short of supplies. Having handed around the goodies, Big Jim Mackie's patrol set off to penetrate the tunnel. While they were engaged on that mission, Farran got some old telegraph poles dragged over to the demolished bridge, and by laying those across the gap, and with concrete railings and sods of earth scattered on top, they cobbled together a repair of sorts.

As Farran was painfully aware, if Mackie and his men hit real trouble, the only way to race to their aid was via that bridge, hence the need to mend it, albeit temporarily. Once they were done, one of his men 'stuck up a crazy sign' bearing the words: 'S.A.S. Bridge, Sept., 1943'. As Farran noted, 'there was surely nothing that could stop us now.' The bodged bridge proved just strong enough to bear an unloaded jeep. The first of the vehicles inched across, then raced ahead, only to return shortly with some good news. The road beyond had been blocked by an anti-tank gun, but the SAS had been quicker, and 'made hay of its crew before it could come into action'.

Meanwhile, the operation to liberate Pisticci concentration camp was building up a head of steam. First into action had been Cary-Elwes and his jeep-bound force, as they headed for the Metaponto junction. In the C Squadron War Diary, the entry for 14 September reads: 'Capt. Gunston and eight men were taken out in Jeeps by Major Cary-Elwes to crossroads west of Metaponto and east of Pisticci in reported enemy occupied country . . .' With a top speed of 65 mph, and with the clock now ticking, the jeeps 'shot off' westwards, their pivot-mounted machine guns menacing the terrain to all sides.

Deep, jagged gullies cut the slopes to their right, their depths cloaked in shadow. 'Tension among the drivers and gunners' was at fever pitch, as the jeeps raced along the coastal road, 'not knowing when the enemy might strike'. In large part this was all about sheer bluff and daring now. More often than not, if a military convoy drove along a road acting as if it had every right to be there, the enemy would presume the same thing. Later in the war, Cary-Elwes would be depicted with 'his rifle balanced on his shoulder, like a real huntsman . . . tall and very slim, bright-eyed and with a fresh complexion, he had a dazzling smile . . . and was glad to be alive'. His jeep convoy adopted the same spirit and poise right now.

It was typical of Cary-Elwes's bearing behind the lines, where he was often to be found whistling 'Oh My Darling Clementine' as if he hadn't a care in the world. He acted as if he had every right to be there, as if embarked upon a 'proper adventure'. An SAS buccaneer at heart, it was in that same spirit that his squadron of jeeps tore along the coastal highway, heading for Metaponto. By the sheer audacity of that convoy's thunder run, Cary-Elwes's force 'enjoyed a clear go at it', arriving at their objective without a shot being fired. It was a marvellous start to the wider mission.

Having set their defences 'on both sides' of the junction, the long wait began, for they would need to hold their position overnight, to allow the train to pass through and return. Not content with seizing that core of vital territory, Cary-Elwes decided to push out a patrol on foot, 'forward of the crossroads and railway bridge', to seek out the nearest enemy positions. It 'revealed no Germans for at least 3 miles down the road'. So far, the coast seemed clear for the pirate train to steam through, with its 'band of well-armed French SAS' riding shotgun.

As the bulk of Cary-Elwes's men 'guarded the railway and road crossing', his foot patrol edged west in search of the enemy. One of Captain Gunston's most experienced NCOs (non-commissioned officers) was his Squadron Sergeant Major, John Alcock. Known as 'Jack' to all, Alcock had fought in the 1940 defence of France, taking part in the desperate rearguard action that had enabled the evacuation of more than 300,000 troops from the Dunkirk beaches. An early 2 SAS recruit, one of his key roles had been to accompany Bill Stirling on his whirlwind recruitment drives, as they'd endeavoured to draw in the kind of individuals they sought for 2 SAS.

Here at Metaponto junction, Alcock led that foot patrol west, with two others in support. Up ahead they spied a series of farms, set atop a ridge. They commanded an ideal vantage point for any enemy who might be keeping watch on the coastal railway and road. By agreement, Alcock and his fellows decided to search those farms one by one, alternating who would take the lead, so 'sharing the risk of an unexpected encounter'. That way, they could check if there were any German troops present, with their 'suspected machine-gun and mortar positions'.

The first two farmsteads, surrounded by their scrried ranks of olive groves, were found to be deserted. They approached the third, with Alcock in the lead. As they neared the farm building itself, perhaps a 'degree of complacency had set in', for both their jeep insertion and now foot patrol had turned up not a sniff of enemy resistance. As Alcock edged around a corner of the stone-built farmhouse, he literally bumped into a German soldier, and 'they bounced off one another'. With Alcock being right-handed, had he made a left turn around the corner of the wall, his Tommy gun would have been pointing away from the enemy. As it was, it was aimed right at his guts.

The enemy soldier had clearly been scavenging for food, for he carried a chicken in the one hand, while an MP 40 sub-machine gun was grasped in the other. One-handed, the German opened fire. Hampered by the chicken, his shots, though at close to point blank range, went wide of the mark. Alcock unleashed with his heavier Tommy gun, letting off 'a burst of rapid fire' that 'practically cut the enemy soldier in half'. Having searched the farmstead, and found no other troops present, they checked through the dead man's pockets for any papers or other useful intelligence. Clearly, he'd been sent out seeking provisions. There had to be a larger German force somewhere near by.

As Alcock was painfully aware, he'd been 'incredibly lucky to survive that encounter', for the German soldier had fired first. Earlier, during SAS training, he'd been one of those who benefited from Colonel Hector Grant-Taylor's instruction, which was designed to make their shooting more 'ruthless, systematic and so more effective'. At his 'school for murder', Grant-Taylor, a pistol and sub-machine gun expert, taught SOE agents, commandos and the SAS how to kill at close quarters. Nicknamed 'Tack-Tack', due to his insistence that the man wielding the weapon should fire in quick, short bursts, Grant-Taylor's initiation into his way of waging war had been memorable in the extreme.

Alcock and his fellow trainees had been waiting in a large hall, seated on hard wooden benches. Grant-Taylor was late and the men had grown restless. No one had met the comparatively elderly Grant-Taylor before, and they wondered what he might really be able to teach the SAS. Finally, he'd entered the room laden down with his kit. With his grey hair and thick spectacles, the figure known as 'the greatest British gunman' didn't quite look the part, and few paid him much attention. As the ruckus continued, Grant-Taylor made his way to the front of the hall, dumped his kit, and with absolutely no warning turned around, levelled his Tommy gun and proceeded to 'shoot out all the ceiling lights in the room'.

Plunged into sudden darkness, the air was thick with cordite fumes. The noise of the gunfire alone had sent his audience diving for cover. Tack-Tack sure had their attention now. He'd proceeded to teach them the priorities of killing. When entering an environment peopled by the enemy, the crucial thing was to shoot the first man to show any sign of movement or reaction to your presence. After that, you could gun them down in 'any preferred order'. Alcock doubted whether Tack-Tack would have approved of his reactions at the Italian farmstead.

But at least he had opened fire with a deadly accurate burst.

In September 1943, the Allies scrambled a force at short notice to take Taranto (above), the vital port on Italy's southern shore. With no aircraft available to fly them in, the SAS sailed at the tip of the spear, aboard the USS *Boise* (below), with their jeeps and other equipment lashed wherever there was space on the decks.

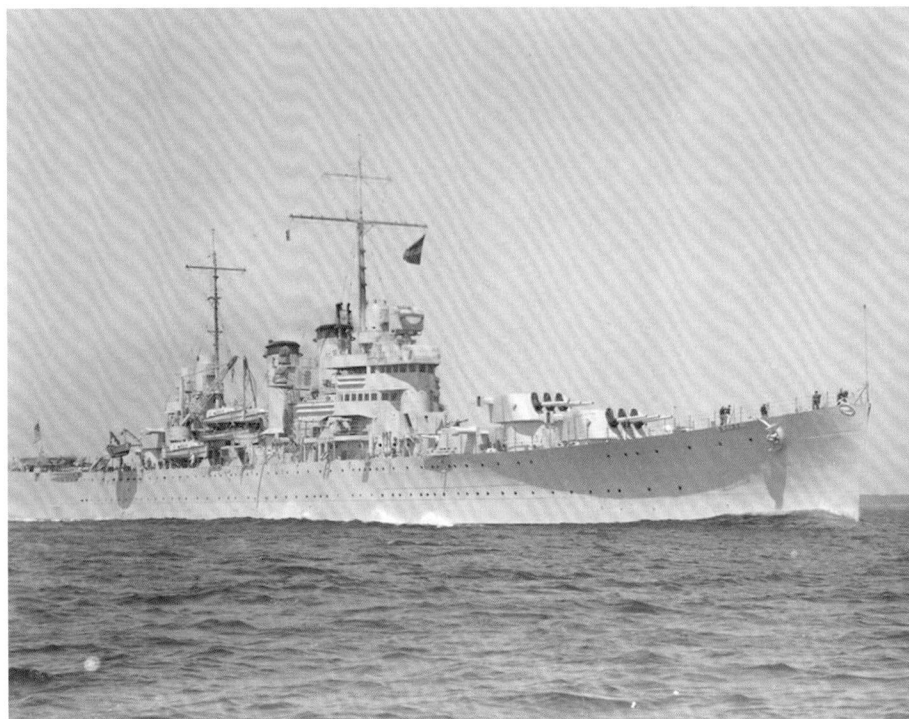

Where the USS *Boise* was supposed to dock, the minesweeper HMS *Abdiel* (above) took her place. A massive detonation sunk the *Abdiel*, killing many of her crew and the men of the 1st Airborne Division that she carried. For those of the SAS, like Corporal Charlie Hackney (below), a keen amateur boxer, it was a close call. Hackney and fellows were convinced a rogue Italian torpedo bomber had sunk the ship.

Major Oswald Cary-Elwes (above left), second-in-command of 2 SAS, together with his batman, Corporal Eric Mills. Having fought their way ashore at Taranto, Cary-Elwes was keen to mastermind 'Operation Loco' – the daring raid on an Italian concentration camp, after an escaped Yugoslav partisan alerted them to its existence. It was a race against time, before Italian and German forces moved the prisoners to Nazi Germany.

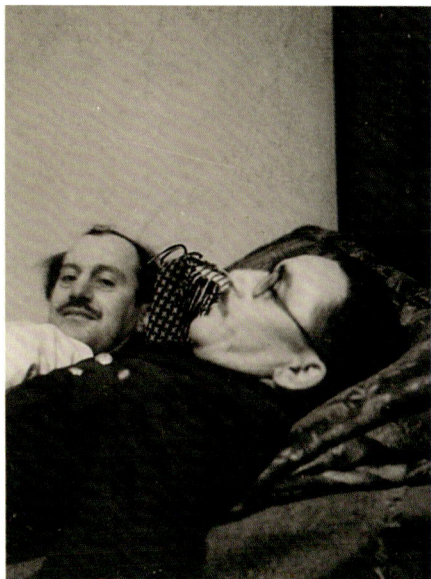

Cary-Elwes (above, far left), with Lieutenant Raymond Couraud, of the SAS's French Foreign Legion Squadron. Couraud (above right) had been charged by 2 SAS founder Bill Stirling to recruit Foreign Legionaries to the SAS (see below). The Squadron so formed would man the concentration camp rescue train, as it steamed deep behind enemy lines.

HRH King George VI visits the 261 Field Park Company (Airborne). At Taranto, the 261 volunteered one of their men, Sapper Dennis Elkin, to drive the SAS's 'pirate train'. At dusk the commandeered locomotive steamed forth from Chiatona railway station, with Sapper Elkin at the controls, on a rescue mission of untold daring.

Established in 1939, complete with watchtowers, gun-emplacements and barbed wire, the Pisticci concentration camp was a place of hell. It was guarded by scores of Italian fascist Black Shirts, soldiers and Carabinieri, while the entire Taranto region was defended by the battle-hardened troops of the German 1st Parachute Division.

Trooper George Arnold (above left), with SAS beret and wings, and right, after being commissioned into the King's Own Scottish Borderers. Arnold would spearhead Operation Loco, together with Wladislas Cieslak (below), one of the SAS's French Foreign Legionaries, who would be heralded in the British press as being 'the man with no fear.'

"Who Dares Wins"

The S.A.S. did amazing work behind the enemy lines in Italy. One of the most astounding stories concerns a squadron of the S.A.S. which had captured a train. They calmly drove the train deep into enemy territory up to a concentration camp. They quickly took control of the camp, released all the prisoners and loaded them and the Italian commandant into the train and steamed back to their base.

Amongst the hundreds freed from the concentration camp was Prince Filippo IV Andrea Doria Pamphilj, a foremost Italian nobleman and a diehard opponent of Fascism. Oddly, for such an audacious mission, there were no medals awarded to those who partook in the raid and almost zero publicity. It wasn't until 1968 that a short mention was made in the *Rover & Wizard Annual*.

Chapter 9

RAIDERS OF THE LOST CAMP

As Cary-Elwes and his men got to work, so too did the crew of the pirate train. With the afternoon shadows lengthening, Sapper Elkin began stoking up the locomotive's boiler, shovelling in the coal and building up just the right head of steam. From cold, it took around two hours to do so, which left Couraud and McGregor ample time to sort their defences. Or rather, to refine the rescue train's 'astounding' disguise and its bluff.

Once they were steaming through hostile territory, it stood to reason that any enemy who spied the locomotive and its carriages would presume it to be one of their own. Trains were on the move across Italy, speeding in reinforcements and war materiel, and on occasion shipping out those deemed to be the enemies of Nazism and fascism. So who would ever imagine that this one might be full of Allied troops, and engaged upon such an audacious mission?

To maintain the deception, Couraud had his French Squadron take up positions from where they could cover the train's progress, but remain hidden from view, McGregor doing likewise with his troop. As dusk descended over Chiatona they prepared to steam forth. One of their final precautions was to cut communications between the station and all points beyond. Oddly, it had even proven possible to put telephone calls through from Taranto to Rome. But with the war's shadowy, shifting allegiances, no one wanted to risk any 'Italian warning the camp commandant up at Pisticci' that a heavily-armed rescue train was on its way.

With forty-odd SAS manning the carriages, but keeping well 'out of sight', the funnel billowed black smoke, and the locomotive, enshrouded with steam, began to inch into motion. Hissing constantly, the slow, hollow, rhythmic whump of the engine echoed around Chiatona station, growing in tempo and volume with each turn of the wheels. Elkin leaned out of his cab to check that all the carriages were properly aligned, and his armed escort firmly in place. They were. Keeping one eye on the pressure gauge, all seemed well. Moments later, the train was surging forwards at ever increasing speed. Elkin worked his magic at the controls, flicking levers and switches like a conjurer, and darting this way and that as he nursed the engine into ever greater vigour. Gradually, it transformed into a snorting, living beast, or so it seemed to those aboard. It was well after dusk as the pirate train left the station, a long plume of steam enshrouding the length of her.

Steaming west along the coastal plane the train picked up pace as the engine came fully up to power. The plume from her funnel rose higher, making her visible for miles around amid the darkening sky. The guard force were well in hiding. All that mattered now was how the enemy might react, and whether Cary-Elwes and his force had been successful in seizing the junction up ahead. It was vital that they had switched the points, which would steer the train towards its objective. The locomotive would then have some altitude to climb, once she turned inland at Metaponto. The Pisticci region was sandwiched between the Cavone river to the west and the Basento river to the east, the three peaks which dominated the area being the Serra Cipolla, the San Francesco and Monte Como, each of which rose to some 1,000 feet in height.

They were making fine progress, but once the climb began they would slow to a crawl, making close-up study of just who was riding in the train far easier for any watchers. As an extra layer of cover, Colonel Usai, their Italian co-conspirator, was riding in the cab, resplendent in his full uniform. Couraud and McGregor were banking on the fact that the very sight of an Italian officer would give any would-be adversaries cause to pause, and in that moment the SAS would be able to seize the initiative, and overpower any potential resistance.

But most of all, the gathering darkness would prove their greatest friend.

Back at Taranto, one man was having a crisis of confidence. Major Henniker was filled with 'foreboding and gloom' regarding the train rescue mission. 'Suppose it all went wrong,' he asked himself? How could he possibly write to Sapper Elkin's wife or mother, 'with anything but shame that I had let him go?' After all, he hardly even knew Cary-Elwes's name, he reflected. 'All I could say was that he looked like a reliable man, and he was risking his own life on the journey too. I had acted on the spur of the moment,' Henniker lamented; 'now I felt I had perhaps been a fool.'

Tortured with such thoughts, Henniker's gaze alighted upon a church. Despite the blackout, he could see that there was a large congregation gathered within. Had he been embarked on the SAS's pirate train, Henniker knew for certain that he 'would have asked God's help . . . Perhaps it was not too late, even now.' His one doubt was whether he would be welcome in a Roman Catholic church. Just then, one of the Airborne Chaplains happened to pass by. Noticing Henniker's seeming confusion, he asked if perhaps he was lost?

'No,' Henniker answered, 'but I want to say a few prayers. It is OK to go into this Roman Catholic church?'

'Of course,' the Airborne Chaplain reassured him. 'There were Christians in Rome when our forefathers were still wearing woad.'

The Chaplain offered to accompany Henniker. Together they entered the church and knelt in prayer. Henniker felt his doubts begin 'to fade away. A feeling of greater confidence in the SAS Major who was in charge of the train suffused my mind.' That evening, instead of 'tossing and turning in mental anguish', he slept like a log, even as the rescue train steamed deeper into enemy terrain.

Meanwhile, well to the north, Big Jim Mackie's patrol stole through the tunnel that their commander, Farran, had tasked them to infiltrate. Once they reached the far side they made sure to leave two men to guard their escape route, after which they crept forwards into the dark terrain beyond. Before long they found themselves in the midst of an entire German battalion. Mackie spent a good deal of time noting the enemy's defences and positions 'at close range', before an extra-observant sentry finally got wise to their presence. The SAS lieutenant and the German guard each lobbed a grenade at about the same time, and quite suddenly the balloon was up.

The enemy, not knowing from which direction they were being

attacked, began to fire in all directions. Mackie, meanwhile, led his patrol back towards the tunnel entrance. But by the time they reached it, they found it blocked by a force of German troops, and there was no sign of the guards they had left there. With no other option, Mackie and his nine men had to fight their way through the mass of enemy. In a blistering assault, with 'grenades bursting in the cutting and tracer bullets winging into the darkness of the tunnel,' they broke through. Dashing down the tunnel all made it out alive, having had a 'skinful of adventure,' but only having escaped by 'the breadth of a hair'.

Mackie was 'furious with the two men who had abandoned their posts'. There was no excuse for them having 'fled back to safety'. Of necessity, discipline was harsh in such instances, for the SAS could not risk having 'a single weak link in the chain'. Farran held a 'short trial by my jeep in the olive grove'. While he found it all most distasteful, he told the culprits that they had behaved like cowards. It was made all the worse in that he had personally recruited the senior ranking figure. Though that man wept and pleaded to be allowed to stay, the SAS code was inflexible. He was expelled that very night on a captured truck – 'a broken, dispirited little man'.

Farran remained determined to push on. They needed a route to bypass the next chokepoint, the town of Grassano. If they could somehow push past that, they would have outflanked any forces around Pisticci, which would then lie to the south of their advance. On the approach to Grassano the convoy halted at a village. Once again they were mobbed by 'pretty girls, barefooted children, wizened peasants', as Farran described it, who 'fought each other for the honour of touching our equipment'. The usual complement of grapes, walnuts and bottles of wine were thrust into the liberators' hands, which was all well and good, Farran observed, 'but we were trying to fight a battle'.

At the height of the impromptu celebrations, a German truck drove into the far end of the village. There was no way the SAS could open fire, it being impossible to shoot through what had become 'a panic-stricken multitude'. Instead, Farran and his men managed to capture the truck intact. It proved to be loaded to the gunwales with sacks of flower, soap, and toiletries. As it was of little use to him and his men, Farran ordered it distributed among the villagers. He was tickled pink to see how his men gave 'the best items to the most attractive girls. Of such stuff are soldiers made.'

Big Jim Mackie was sent forward with two jeeps, to scout out the approaches to the town. He returned shortly with a 'miserable apologetic look on his face', and riding in a farmer's cart. Ambushed as he was approaching Grassano, he'd managed to withdraw without anyone being killed, but both his jeeps had been destroyed. The enemy had sited a pair of machine guns amid some thick corn. They'd opened up on the vehicles, and while Mackie and his men had returned ferocious fire, they were highly visible on the road, whereas the enemy were hidden among the densest crop.

Mackie was devastated at losing two of their precious jeeps. Farran blamed himself. Sending men and machines forward on open highways was a recipe for disaster. Impatience had got the better of him. There was clearly no way through this section of the enemy's defences. They were now around 130 kilometres in advance of the nearest Allied lines, and this was about as far as they could possibly get.

*

At well after midnight the incredible apparition came steaming through. To Cary-Elwes and the others holding Metaponto junction, it appeared like a ghost train, the one light at the front of the engine illuminating the way, as the otherwise darkened form snorted its way down the valley, spitting sparks from its funnel, which lit up the plume of smoke a fiery orange. The locomotive dropped its pace as Sapper Elkin prepared to negotiate the sharp change in direction. The deafening, rhythmic thud slowed in its cadence, the engine drawing level with Cary-Elwes's guard force, who were able to signal that all was well. Moments later, and with not a moment to lose, Elkin swung the train onto the righthand stretch of track, which would take them directly inland.

As the locomotive steamed away and began to climb, the onlookers could see the red-hot glow of the engine's firebox, into which more and more coal was being shovelled in an effort to deal with the gradient. The darkened carriages that ran on behind sung an eerie, high-pitched melody, as steel wheels gripped steel rails, and one by one the boxy silhouettes disappeared into the night. To the onlookers, there was not the slightest sign that this was anything other than a bog-standard night train. The deception seemed masterful and complete.

In fact, those riding aboard that ghost train were 'rather enjoying the trip'. As McGregor and his men noted, they were 'rocking along' nicely, with the driver trying to nurse 'all the speed he could from the old engine'. As the C Squadron War Diary noted: 'the Special train for the French Squadron ran through to Pisticci.' That was largely thanks to the sterling work of Cary-Elwes and his men, of course, for they had 'switched the points so that the train could run directly to the camp'. But in truth, there was no direct route to the concentration camp, and especially bearing in mind what lay ahead.

The part of the line that Farran had reconnoitred wasn't the only stretch to be blocked. Up ahead, as the tracks snaked and switchbacked toward Bernalda Scalo station, the damage caused by Allied bombing had yet to be repaired. In truth there was no way through. By that one light beaming out from the locomotive's blunt nose, Sapper Elkin, together with those riding in the cab, would have to spy the hazards that lay ahead. Half a mile out from Bernalda Scalo the engine was brought to a halt, to execute a 'listening watch'. Those aboard the train strained their ears and scanned the night 'to see if there would be any opposition. All was quiet.'

Elkin got them moving again. But soon enough the driver 'had to put his brakes on full', the locomotive screeching to a halt once more, and long before the sign announcing their arrival at Bernalda Scalo was visible. Even as it juddered to a halt, the locomotive crashed into a makeshift barrier – though 'the old engine went through with no bother'. Word went down the length of the train that *this* was the end of the line. 'Expecting a fight upon arrival', Couraud and McGregor tumbled out of the carriages, leading the charge. Up ahead, the bombed-out and darkened station appeared to be deserted. They had seized it 'without even a shot fired'.

Of course, they were still a dozen kilometres short of their objective, and it was now that the French Foreign Legion's famed 'march or die' ethos was to pay real dividends. When training in North Africa, Couraud had learned to march under crushing loads beneath a blistering desert sun, though plagued by thirst, pain and exhaustion, and to keep going no matter what, for the alternative was to be left to die. 'The Legion was brutally strict with its regulations – if one man in a patrol collapsed in the desert, he must be left behind. For the ruthless sun would get at those who lingered to give him succour.'

In the desert, the men of the Legion had been taught to 'witness blood and horror and not be afraid'. Some in the French hierarchy liked to brand those in the Legion as 'the scum of French society'. If they were 'scum' before joining the Legion, once there they learned to be so much more. In the Legion, Couraud had got to live and experience and embody the unshakeable bond; the meaning of true comradeship and camaraderie. He'd learned about true loyalty, wherein 'a legionnaire never abandons another, even at the cost of his own life'. This defined the Legion, and the Legion had 'become his family'.

Right now, serving in the British SAS, Couraud had another adopted family. He was acutely aware that with his French Squadron there could be no room for sloppiness of any kind; discipline was iron. The French were in the minority, which meant that at all times they had to strive to 'be the best'. As they formed up in line in the thick darkness, the non-legionnaires were about to learn what it really meant to march through the night hours. Farran himself would remark of Couraud's squadron, 'I have never seen a night patrol handled with such skill . . . His instinct for direction was uncanny . . . The men moved along noiselessly in widely spaced, single file, never putting a foot in the wrong place.'

If Couraud halted, so would all in turn, collapsing to the ground 'like a series of dominoes hit by a marble', Farran observed. 'At the snap of Couraud's fingers, a scar-faced legionnaire would double off on tiptoe through the trees to reconnoitre some suspicious object. The silent speed with which he moved over the ground pointed to a thoroughness in training unknown in the British Army.' But as Farran noted, most striking of all was the pace at which they could march, and tonight of all nights, speed was absolutely of the essence.

The road to the camp was known portentously as the Via Dei Confinati Politici – the street of the political prisoners. Well, on this night, 14/15 September 1943, it had become the way of the silent, night-dark assault. While there were forty in the SAS force, some had to be left to guard the train. The attackers faced some two hundred camp defenders, but the paucity of their numbers was more than compensated for by their sheer calibre. The camp lay on higher ground to the station. All began to climb. Moving up from lower terrain, the silent snake of men were swathed in the darkness, while the camp's defenders were silhouetted against the starlit skies.

Roadblocks supposedly barred the way. To either side lay marshy ground and a river. No matter. With a force such as this, those heavily defended barriers were easily skirted. Taking on those forces in full-on battle would only delay the attackers and risk alerting all in the camp to the coming storm. Circumnavigating those roadblocks, and moving along the night-dark highway, it took the assault force just over an hour to reach the outskirts of the concentration camp. Whenever those with less experience of moving silently at night stumbled over a root or branch, Couraud, or one of his men, cursed them into silence 'in the way only a Frenchman can swear'.

The first sign of the camp itself was a halo of light on the horizon. Designed to keep prisoners in, the defences seemed wide-open to an attack such as this. The four watchtowers loomed as stark, ugly silhouettes against the heavens. Each was armed with a heavy machine gun, complete with searchlights. Individual sentries appeared as stick-like figures, picked out in the harsh glare of the camp's perimeter lighting. But all eyes of the guard force were focused inwards – not out. As Zelcko had broken out of there just days before, he argued that he knew the best way in. There were also those inside – fellow partisans – who had managed to arm themselves for a moment such as this, when the time was right to make a break for freedom.

Couraud and McGregor paused. As both men appreciated, time spent in good reconnaissance was never wasted. The doors and windows to the individual brick-built blocks were secured with iron bars. No easy way through those. The angular silhouette of the water tower rose above the camp, its sides daubed in Fascist graffiti. Two buses were parked not far from it, each with their windows closed by iron bars. Those were the vehicles used to ferry the condemned from Bernalda Scalo train station to the camp itself. Normally. But right now, they would be perfect for operating in reverse – for ferrying those who had been freed to the waiting train. Even so, not all could be rescued that way. Those who were able to walk would have to walk. Those who were too sick to do so would be helped aboard the vehicles. Those buses had to be taken intact.

Having watched, studied and noted the defences, a plan of attack was set. A main barracks was located in Marconia village, some 2.5 kilometres away. It was crucial to seize the camp and overcome the guards, before reinforcements might be rushed in from there. Time was running. All would have to move with immense swiftness now. As Sergeant Chef Meronane noted in the French Squadron's War Diary, the next stage was a textbook operation: 'We attacked the POW camp containing Poles, Yugoslavs and Greeks. This attack was carried out under excellent conditions.' Indeed it was. As Couraud and McGregor led their men on a silent, lightning assault from out of the darkness, and with Zelcko acting as their guide, within seconds they were through the wire and into the heart of the camp itself.

The first barks of Tommy guns rang out, tearing apart the intense silence of the dead hours. Muzzle flashes pierced the gloom. Flares of tracer laced the night. Lights blinked out, their bulbs burst asunder by bursts of accurate fire. Taken by utter surprise, the camp guards seemed paralysed. Unable to comprehend what was happening, or to react. One was hit and he tumbled down, a bloody, twisted corpse. The first few figures broke free from the camp buildings, as those who were alert to the assault joined in with the fighting using whatever came to hand.

With the battle raging, the Polish prisoners were at the forefront of the melee. Seeing their captives breaking free, at last the camp guards seemed to rouse themselves into action. Two of the Polish prisoners were felled by fire, before the assault force gained the upper hand, and the battle for Pisticci was largely over. 'In a matter of minutes the camp was taken, the SAS seizing and disarming those guards who had not been killed, wounded or driven away.'

Those policing the camp had been utterly routed, especially since their commander, Colonel Ercole Suppa, 'an officer of the Italian Army', had been captured in his quarters, and in full uniform. With his hands tightly bound, Colonel Suppa was among the first to be marched out of the camp gates. As the fighting drew to a close, more and more prisoners 'came out of the huts towards us', noted Arnold. One of the interpreters shouted to them that a train was waiting, and that all who could manage it were to make their way towards the means of their rescue. Amid 'lots of shouting and running', the first figures made their move.

As the crowd of prisoners kept swelling, so a soaring sense of relief and exultation washed over the camp. It was followed by a surge of anger. The dead guard, Antonio Blancagemma, was a local man hailing from Pisticci. There were others who were wounded. But the sight of the dead and injured did little to assuage the prisoners' rage. Corralling their former guards and tormentors, they ripped off their insignia and slung items of uniforms and Fascist flags onto the camp's fences, as symbols of their oppressors' downfall and as a 'sign of their contempt'.

Among the freed prisoners, there were scores of Yugoslav partisans, Polish legionnaires and Greek resistance fighters. They saw fit to grab the guards' weaponry and ammo supplies, plus they emptied the contents of the camp safe. A Moto Guzzi motorcyle was seized, as were a dozen bicycles – more transport to the waiting train. Turning the tables, Couraud and McGregor got the newly armed former prisoners to corral the camp guards. Former captives were to stand armed watch over their former captors, just in case there were any who might have a semblance of fight left in them. But even as they began to get matters sorted, Couraud and McGregor were painfully aware of the ticking clock. Time was running, and they were far from out of this yet.

There was little time for a proper, coordinated search of the camp. A hurried check of the main blocks was organised. In one, the liberators stumbled upon a nightmarish scene; a 'hell of a mess, stinking men and women dressed in rags'. Old women lay immobile on their bunks, covered in sores and with only a threadbare, filthy blanket to keep them warm. Many seemed frozen into inaction, gripped by terror. After so long in captivity, they feared this might be some kind of devilish trap. When eventually they were convinced that the camp had been liberated and they were free, they were desperate to go with their saviours.

But of course, there was no way that the rescuers could take them all.

The weakest prisoners were loaded aboard the captured buses. Others were sent off to undertake the march to the station, with the SAS acting as escorts. As the ferrying got under way in earnest, somehow a means was needed to 'triage' the prisoners: to determine who should be rescued, and who should be dispatched into the surrounding countryside. With the latter, the SAS left what food, cigarettes and water they could, urging the escapees to take to the hills and go into hiding. Shortly, the main Allied forces would be there. Most importantly, no one was about to be shipped north to Nazi Germany on any death train.

In short, the hell that they had lived for so long was over.

Back at the station, those guarding the train were directing the new arrivals to get aboard. The carriages were 'quickly filled, some having to be placed aboard on makeshift stretchers'. The train was getting ready to steam home. 'Within a few minutes all the prisoners were loaded up', the carriages full to bursting. There would barely be room for their escorts to squeeze in. Having made certain that Colonel Suppa was safely ensconced in a designated carriage, McGregor, Sutton and Arnold mounted up, aiming to keep a close watch on the camp commandant.

When all were aboard the train got under way and 'headed back to Taranto'. Moving downhill now and with the greatest urgency, the 'locomotive rattled on, carrying scores of extremely sick and ailing people to a place of potential safety – something which none of them could have ever dreamed of just hours before'. As all aboard knew full well, they had been slated for deportation by train, north to Nazi Germany. Well, sure enough a train had come. Sure enough, they were being spirited away. But miraculously, they were speeding south-west, towards Allied lines and liberty.

McGregor and his men shared their carriage with one man who looked very ill. With typical solicitude, the SAS lieutenant asked if he was all right. In perfect English the man replied, politely, that indeed he was – at least now that he had been rescued. Shortly, they were to learn that this was none other than Prince Filippo Andrea VI Doria Pamphilj, the diehard anti-Fascist who had refused Hitler entry into his Rome palace when the Führer had wanted to visit his art collection. In view of the extensive looting of fabulously valuable artwork by the Nazis across Europe, the prince's objections would prove to have been prudent indeed.

There was also a very vocal individual in that carriage who sounded as if he was an American. No doubt he'd learned his English in the States, but as to his true nationality that remained to be determined. He kept yelling out expletives and 'shouting out his hatred for all Italians'. This struck McGregor and his men as being most unfair, not to mention infuriating. A lot of the Italians they had run into wanted nothing more than to drive out the Nazi occupiers. The finely spoken Prince Pamphilj Landi was a case in point.

McGregor and his men made it quite clear to the voluble 'American': either he would 'keep quiet' or they would 'throw him off the train'.

Chapter 10

LIBERATION DAY

Against all odds they had done it. Couraud, McGregor and their men returned 'in triumph through the lines'. Audacious bluff, daring and deception had once again been shown to be some of the greatest weapons in the SAS arsenal. Their 'Robin Hood system of operations against the German and Italian Fascists' had paid off, 'Cary-Elwes' concept of using a requisitioned train' proving to be 'a brilliant one'. This was yet another 'incredible tale of bravery and guile to add to the unit's legendary repute'.

There had been a last-minute glitch, even as the locomotive had steamed into Chiatona station. Racing to get there before sunrise, Sapper Elkin had the rescue train going like the clappers. 'The driver had a bit of trouble with the brakes,' as Arnold noted. 'However, we did stop after hitting the buffers at the end of the platform.' Despite their somewhat precipitate arrival, Elkin was the hero of the hour. On the platform stood Major Henniker, fresh from a sound night's sleep, and together he, Elkin and the SAS rejoiced at their incredible success. It was mission accomplished – with a real touch of genius thrown in.

As Sergeant Chef Meronane would note in the French Squadron's War Diary, 'We took all the prisoners back by train to H.Q. at 0700 hrs. The day was spent resting.' Only that day, 15 September 1943, was not to be entirely restful for Meronane himself. Cleaning his Tommy gun after the rigours of the night just gone, the legionnaire 'had an accident . . . and two bullets went into my shoulder'. Noting that it was 'only a flesh wound', he was dispatched to hospital. Two days later, on the 17th, he was flown out of Italy to North Africa for surgery. Shortly, others would follow.

Before all of that, there had been certain urgent matters that needed attending to. Some '180 internees of mixed nation- alities' had been crammed aboard that rescue train, complete with their escorts. Of course, there had been no way to turn the train around, so Sapper Elkin had had to push-shunt the line of carriages back the way they had come. Thankfully, it was mostly downhill. After their arrival at Chiatona station, 'Lieut. Hibbert and his troop escorted the internees into Taranto and got them billeted by A.M.G.O.T.' Lieutenant Grant Hibbert was another of Cary-Elwes's C Squadron deputies. With the rescue force having been engaged upon such a tense, knife-edge mission, it made sense for others to take charge.

The freed prisoners were handed over to the Allied Military Government in Occupied Territories (AMGOT), the system of martial governance to be established in those parts of Europe seized by the Allies. Of course, Italy was to be the first instance of AMGOT in action, and at the very outset of its tenure the SAS had delivered into their custody the very first individuals to have been rescued from a concentration camp. Indeed, Pisticci was the first such camp that Allied forces had encountered. It was now AMGOT's role to accommodate those so dramatically plucked out of the clutches of the enemy, and to deal with sick bodies and ailing minds. But as for returning them to their home nations, most, if not all, lay under Fascist or Nazi rule.

In truth, any number of those who had been rescued hungered for one thing only – to strike back. Indeed, several were to spurn AMGOT's overtures and guardianship, and instead step forward to volunteer for the SAS. Having seen Couraud and McGregor's men in action, and having survived the terrible privations of Pisticci, this was what they wanted – to soldier in a unit such as theirs. A handful were accepted on the spot. 'Enlisted 3 of the Poles rescued from internment camp,' noted the 2 SAS War Diary. One was Josef Lyczak, a former legionnaire who had been captured in 1940 during the fall of France. Lyczak, aged twenty-four and born in Radziejów, a town in central Poland, would prove a fine recruit to the SAS. Others slipped away quietly from Taranto, seeking to join the Italian partisans, who would do sterling work across Italy helping vanquish the forces of Nazi Germany.

Shortly after the rescue train's return to Chiatona, Cary-Elwes's jeep-borne force were back. 'Party returned to Chiatona,' ran the C Squadron War Diary entry for the morning of 15 September. And while it wasn't exactly cricket, and it remains unclear exactly who was responsible, Colonel Suppa, the concentration camp's commandant, was 'stripped of his uniform and badly beaten'. Having been interrogated for several days, he was eventually released by the Allied authorities, who had bigger fish to fry.

By then, Roy Farran's D Squadron had been busy mopping up Fascists around Pisticci, and they 'amused themselves lifting mines' – in other words, clearing minefields. In the process, they stumbled upon a satellite camp, consisting of a series of ramshackle wooden huts. The main concentration camp had consisted of a central brick and concrete structure, with scattered subcamps. This was one of them. The men, women and children freed by Farran 'feted us with tears running down their faces . . . Their main crimes seemed to have been "anti-fascist" sympathies or communism,' he noted, 'little enough cause for imprisonment over six years. It gave us a grand feeling of goodness to liberate these wretched people . . .'

Acting on the premise that if it had worked once, it would do so again, a second such mission was mooted. The day after the rescue train had steamed back into Chiatona, SAS Captain Simon Evan Baillie decided that he and his men could do with some of the same. Aping C Squadron's dramatic successes, Baillie, a thirty-three-year-old Scot hailing from Edinburgh, took four of his B Squadron men and boarded a civilian train, having crossed from Allied-held territory into that of the enemy. Stowing away in the guards van, they ran with it all the way to the city of Potenza, the B Squadron War Diary noted, which was 'then thought to be a large German H.Q.'.

In reaching Potenza, Baillie and his team had advanced 180 kilometres north-west of Taranto, into the southern reaches of the Apennine mountain chain. Somehow, he and his men managed to return by the same means, bringing with them '2 wounded U.S. airmen and much valuable information' – namely that the enemy had left Potenza and were withdrawing from the region, leaving it wide open to the Allies.

Closer to home, the SAS were busy linking up with advanced elements of the Canadian military, who were part of the Allied forces that had assaulted the toe of Italy shortly before the Taranto landings. Then, forty-eight hours after the Pisticci rescue mission, the SAS decided to expropriate yet another train. Pushing well beyond the Metaponto junction, the men of B Squadron, who'd yet to see much action, reached the Calabrian coastal town of Villapiana. There, they pounced upon a heavily laden 'Italian Army Supply Train' parked up in the town's station. The Italian colonel in charge confessed that it was of little further use to him, as all of his men had deserted, so the SAS may as well help themselves. 'Took 40,000 Milit Cigarettes, 20 lbs [pounds] sugar, 100 lbs rice and 100 lbs Macaroni,' the War Diary noted.

Oddly, for such a standout mission as the Pisticci concentration camp raid, there was remarkably little fanfare. Nothing was released to the media, and not a single medal would be awarded to any of the SAS, Cary-Elwes, Couraud and McGregor included. After the mission, Sapper Elkin typically returned to his parent unit 'as though nothing had happened'. Major Henniker would try to secure him a high valour medal, but it was turned down. Eventually, Elkin would earn a Mention in Dispatches for 'going off . . . with a platoon of the Special Air Service . . . by train into German occupied territory'. None of the men of the SAS were to receive any such formal recognition, and not a word leaked out to the press at the time. In truth, there was still a blanket ban on publicising SAS missions, but even that did little to explain the lack of medals.

It wasn't until October 1944, following the liberation of Paris, that the 'Dramatic secret of the war . . . the story of the Special Air Service (S.A.S.)' would be officially released to the world's media. This was the first time the SAS had been mentioned in the newspapers by name. Among the top stories were the bare bones of the Pisticci rescue operation. Under the bold headline, 'THE STORY OF BRITAIN'S MOST ROMANTIC, MOST DARING, AND MOST SECRET ARMY', the *Daily Express* reported, 'A

French squadron commandeered an Italian train and drove it through enemy country to a concentration camp, where they captured the guards, released the prisoners and brought the whole party back by train, including the Italian colonel commandant.'

In some articles, the iconic SAS mission would garner the peculiarly appropriate nickname 'Operation Loco'. But long before then, the ramifications of their mission, and what it portended for 2 SAS's fortunes, were to become crystal clear.

Even as the forces of Operation Slapstick had landed at Taranto, so a calamity was unfolding across Italy, one that could have been foreseen and should have been guarded against and prevented. It was well known that some 80,000 British, American and Commonwealth soldiers were held in prisoner of war camps across Italy, as well as around 100,000 French, Yugoslav and Greek troops. With the signing of the Armistice of Cassibile, marking Italy's surrender and exit from the Axis powers, those POWs should have been accounted for, and measures taken to bring them back into the Allied fold. Even as the secret negotiations for Italy's surrender were under way, Winston Churchill had declared that all efforts must be made to ensure the POWs' safety. He had himself been on the run behind enemy lines after escaping from captivity during the Boer War, and he felt this issue most personally.

As early as 26 July 1943, Churchill had cabled US President Roosevelt, declaring that 'an objective of the highest importance, about which there will be a passionate feeling in this country, is the immediate liberation of all British prisoners of war in Italian hands'. He added that it was a matter of 'honour and humanity to get our own flesh and blood back as soon as possible and spare them the measureless horrors of incarceration in Germany'. The message hit home. Shortly, Churchill and Roosevelt's joint declaration that all such prisoners were to be 'immediately turned over to the Allied Commander-in-Chief' had become part of the formal surrender document. 'None . . . may be evacuated to Germany.'

Roosevelt and Churchill would broadcast a joint message to the Italian people, noting that the Allies 'are carrying the war deep into the territory of your country. This is the direct consequence of the shameful leadership to which you have been subjected by Mussolini . . . your Fascist leaders sent your sons, your ships, your air forces, to distant battlefields to aid Germany in her attempt to conquer . . . the world. This association with the designs of Nazi-controlled Germany was unworthy of Italy's ancient traditions of freedom and culture – traditions to which the peoples of America and Great Britain owe so much.'

Noble words and sentiments, and the aim was crystal clear – it was to bring the Italian people firmly on side. But strangely, even as such measures were being put in place, one arm of the British state seemed to be working against all that Churchill and Roosevelt were striving for. In contemplating the plight of the Allied POWs, MI9 – with the War Office's connivance – somehow managed to take a contrary view. In one of the greatest blunders of the war, Norman Crockatt, the former head of the London Stock Exchange turned MI9 Chief – apparently, 'the right sort of chap' for the job – had decreed that no POWs were to attempt to break free from their camps. On the contrary, they were to 'standfast', remaining exactly where they were.

The order Crockatt issued, endorsed by the War Office, stated that 'officers commanding prison camps will ensure that prisoners of war remain within camp. Authority is granted to all officers . . . to take necessary disciplinary action to prevent individual prisoners of war attempting to rejoin their own units.' Crockatt's decision was predicated on two factors. One, the presumption that the POWs, after long months of incarceration, would be in no fit state to move. Two, that the Allies would sweep north through Italy liberating the camps. In truth, both assumptions proved woefully misguided. Due to Crockatt's order, the terrible situation would arise wherein POWs were prevented from leaving the camps under threat of court martial, and due to their fellow POWs standing guard on the camps' perimeters.

Once the Italian surrender was made public, predictably German forces moved in. Camps were surrounded and POWs seized en masse. By the time of the Pisticci concentration camp rescue mission, entire POW populations were being rounded up and shipped north by truck or train, just as Churchill had feared. Of those camps that adhered to the standfast order, 'the majority . . . were taken into custody by the Germans and transported to Germany', a report from the time noted. Some 30,000 POWs had ignored Crockatt's order, recognising it for the sheer madness that it was. They'd fled their camps and most were at large in the mountains. The rest had fallen into German hands.

When the grim truth became known, Churchill was aghast. How could one arm of the British state have acted against another, and against the Prime Minister's own wishes? He demanded immediate action. Special units would need to head deep behind the lines, to engineer the rescue of as many of those escaped POWs as humanly possible. Every effort would be made to bring them home. No stone was to be left unturned. No means was to be deemed too risky. The urgency of this was acute, for already the enemy had begun the hunt for the escaped POWs, and the winter weather would soon be closing in. In short, it was a race against time.

The man chosen to lead the rescue operation was none other than Roy Farran's former boss, Lieutenant Colonel Anthony Simonds. Under his A Force remit, Simonds was to be given all possible assistance from every branch of the Armed Services. A maverick and a free thinker, there was no better candidate than Simonds for the job. Indeed, and gallingly, Simonds had repeatedly tried to alert the powers-that-be to the disaster that threatened. In early July, with Italy's surrender under negotiation, he'd warned that it was 'obvious the Germans would make every effort to remove all POWs to Germany', and that the Italians couldn't be relied upon to safeguard the camps.

As the A Force chief in the region, Simonds had proposed an alternative plan – that all POWs should disperse into the mountains. Indeed, the gates to all camps should be opened '*the day before the armistice is announced*' (Simonds's emphasis), so as to outfox the Germans. In his plan, A Force parachutists would drop into each camp before the Armistice was announced, to lead the POWs to safety; 'these parachutists were to be trained and briefed to issue detailed instructions on the rendezvous and routes to be taken'. While his proposal had been submitted to MI9, the War Office and Allied high command, seemingly it had been ignored.

Frustrated and appalled, Simonds would note, caustically, that he had foreseen 'the Germans forcibly removing P.O.W.s from Italian camps immediately an armistice was announced'. His plan had been 'written to cater for, and to counter, this action'. Yet it had been ignored and Simonds himself had been frozen out of the process.

At one point during the Armistice negotiations, he had been dispatched to Brindisi, a port city on the Adriatic some 70 kilometres from Taranto, to negotiate the POWs' fate with the Italians. Dressed in civvies, and with the city thronged with German troops, he'd met with one of Italy's top admirals, to try to clear the way for the Royal Navy to evacuate the POWs from Italy's shores. Simonds had demanded full details of the minefields sown around Italy's coastline, plus the harbours and beaches that the POWs could be evacuated from, and the key German defences.

The admiral had bridled. 'Oh, that is top secret. I can't let you have that.'

Simonds repeated his request, with emphasis.

By way of response the admiral had opened a large safe, and removed a bulky, 'heavily sealed' envelope. He eyed Simonds. 'This was given to me by Mussolini, and see it has written upon it – "To be opened in case of grave emergency."' Simonds countered that 'as Italy had *lost* the war, it *was* a grave emergency'.

In short order he got what he'd come for. Armed with those documents, he'd met with Colonel Dudley Clarke, his immediate boss, and the brilliant architect of A Force's dual mission. On the one hand A Force was a POW-rescue outfit. On the other, it was a devilishly effective deception organisation. Sometimes – often – the two went hand in hand. Clarke and Simonds were of one mind. A comprehensive POW rescue plan was called for. They'd drawn it up with gusto, and shared it with all on high. But in the end, 'We received no support and apparently the extremely important problem evoked little interest. Nothing was done at all by Higher Command.'

With disaster unfolding across the camps, Clarke had been

summoned by 'all the top brass'. As Churchill was on the war-path, overnight the 'rescue of Allied P.O.W.s. was an absolute priority'. Clarke was duly informed that 'every effort must be made to stop 78,000 Allied soldiers falling into German hands'. While Clarke was assured that he was 'to have carte blanche' and enjoyed Churchill's absolute backing, it was all 'too little, too late!' As the final twist in the sorry tale, it was Simonds himself who would be charged to somehow pick up the pieces, and bring those thousands who had fled the camps safely home.

It was one hour before midnight on 23 September 1943 when Simonds received an 'Emergency Ops' order to mount 'operations to cope with the rescue and evacuation of large numbers of ex-P.O.W.s. believed to be at large in Italy'. That very night he held a planning meeting with his staff, to assess the challenges that lay before them. Self-evidently, due to the seventeen days that had elapsed between the Armistice and now, those 30,000 escaped POWs would be 'scattered all over Italy'.

His tiny staff could never cope with such a massive operation, especially at zero notice. They would have to beg, borrow and steal a team, cutting through any of the reviled 'red tape'. 'Men, aircraft and ships were required', of which they as yet had none. They would need 'parachutists and the necessary supplies and equipment . . . to rescue the ex-P.O.W.s. and to guide them to the coast', at which point extraction craft would need to be standing by. Aircraft for dropping supplies, and for flying reconnaissance missions would need to be found, as would 'fast naval craft, to carry out seaborne evacuations'.

As Simonds pointed out, organising all of that would require 'superhuman effort on the part of A Force', for none of it was in place on the night of 23/24 September. But one thing did play into his favour. After their Pisticci camp raid, the men of 2 SAS were prime candidates for such a mission, and shortly they were to be put at his disposal. After the SAS's Pisticci heroics, Simonds's boss Dudley Clarke had cabled high command suggesting, 'Best help you could give us would be loan of SAS personnel. Most grateful if you could signal One Airborne Div, to assist Simonds for loan of one troop with Motor Transport.' Clarke – and Simonds – were to get exactly what they had asked for.

Amid a whirlwind of activity, Simonds flew from his Cairo HQ to Bari, a city lying on the Adriatic coast about a hundred kilometres due north of Taranto. Two days after receiving his 'Emergency Ops' order, he gathered together the senior commanders of 2 SAS to give them their new mission briefing. They worked for him now, he told them, and with Churchill's direct blessing, on a mission codenamed Operation Jonquil (a jonquil being a type of small daffodil).

If the Pisticci raid was the SAS's calling card, Roy Farran's prior relations with Simonds were the imprimatur. They gathered at a deserted school – Simonds's makeshift base – to plan for all that was coming. But it was clear that certain figures were missing. After days of exhausting frontline operations, the men of 2 SAS had been pulled back to Taranto, supposedly to rest and recuperate. Yet Cary-Elwes himself had been obliged to fly out of Italy, with his squadron shortly to follow. He was needed urgently in North Africa. His boss, Bill Stirling, had been ordered back to Britain, for a major overhaul of Special Forces operations. In his absence, Cary-Elwes was to take over temporary command, the men of C Squadron overseeing the all-important 2 SAS selection and training.

Stirling's summons to the UK turned out to be mostly good news, for it enabled him to argue for the expansion of the SAS, and for his men to be used as he knew was best. While he still had powerful detractors among the 'more orthodox minded senior army officers', fortunately, in London, he was able to call upon the personal support of the British Prime Minister. For Churchill, 'commando style operations were always welcome', and Stirling was frequently allowed access to the Prime Minister, to argue his point in person.

With Churchill's backing, Stirling got nearly everything he wanted. But due to Crockatt's blunder and the dire consequences being felt across Italy, 2 SAS were about to land the kind of missions they craved in any case. Pursuing their A Force objectives, the SAS would be engaged in operations of audacity and daring deep behind the lines, being charged to do the utterly unexpected. In Simonds's view, nothing was off limits. As a potential downside, A Force's POW-rescue remit supposedly precluded offensive action. In other words, any teams sent in were there to rescue POWs, not to strike at the enemy.

But when had men like Couraud, McGregor or Farran ever adhered entirely to their orders?

Chapter 11

OPERATION LOCO

As noted in the War Diary, on 26 September elements of 2 SAS, including 'the French Squadron, passed under command of A Force'. With Cary-Elwes gone, Major Felix Symes was now in charge. Born in Italy to an illustrious family, and hugely well-travelled, Symes had experienced his baptism of fire following the Operation Torch landings in North Africa. Serving with the Irish Guards, in December 1942 his battalion had been pounded by enemy shellfire, before being outflanked by German forces. Three days of hand-to-hand fighting had ensued. Eventually, the unit had found itself completely cut off. Breaking into smaller groups to escape and evade, only a third of the men made it back to Allied lines. Symes's response was to volunteer for the SAS.

As per Simonds's Bari briefing, the SAS were tasked with 'rescuing Allied P.O.W.s who had escaped from their camps and were now at large'. The means were brutally simple. Small teams were to be parachuted into the mountains or dropped ashore, blind (i.e. with no reception parties), to locate and shepherd the POWs towards Italy's eastern coastline. There, rescue ships would be ready and waiting to whisk the escapees back to Allied lines. As Simonds was so desperately short of personnel, he'd accepted an offer from the Americans with open arms. Eighteen men from the Office of Strategic Services (OSS), the US equivalent to SOE, had volunteered for 'a joint operation with the British SAS', and were to join the POW-hunting mission.

The American codename for their side of the things was to be Operation Simcol. The OSS operators hailed from their newly formed 'Operational Group' (OG). The unit consisted of American nationals whose heritage harked back to the countries to which they would be deployed: in the case of Operation Jonquil/Simcol, they were all Italian-Americans. Each SAS party was to have one OSS member – an Italian speaker – embedded with them. Simonds was also counting on volunteers from 1 Airborne Division to boost his mission strength. In addition to all the usual kit and weaponry to carry behind the lines, both the American and British teams would be equipped with heaps of cash with which to bribe and cajole the locals.

With A Force combining SAS, OSS and 1 Airborne troops, they decided to shoot for the stars. From intelligence that Simonds had been able to garner, 400 escaped POWs were known to be hiding out around the Chieti area, a hundred kilometres to the north of Termoli. They would need to be 'guarded and guided down to the coast, and embarked'. Some three thousand escaped POWs were known to be hiding in the 'mountains south of Sulmona', 170 kilometres inland of Termoli. They would need to be found, contacted and steered to the coastal pickup points. But some of the SAS were to be held in reserve, for they were earmarked for missions inspired by Operation Loco – the Pisticci raid. They were to 'attack the camps of POWs', for two had been identified holding some 15,000 prisoners, and they were to be sprung.

Privately, those American OSS teams were also serving in

a secondary, top-secret role. The Operations Groups had been founded, SOE-like, to raise guerrilla armies and resistance forces among the populations to which they were deployed. The Italian-Americans were tasked to do exactly that here in Italy. Once they'd winkled out the POWs, they were to use their cash and resources to foment uprisings behind the lines. There were no firm plans in place in terms of how they were to withdraw, at mission's end. They were either to remain with the guerrilla units they'd raised until the enemy collapsed, or make their own way back through the lines. In that sense, their missions and those of the SAS were markedly different. Simonds's A Force operations were scheduled to last just a few short weeks. The OSS were in there for the duration.

With no time to lose, the first teams were to be dropped by 2 October. That left precious little time for planning and preparations. Even so, as all agreed, there was time for 'a night out in Bari'. A last drink before deploying. It would prove an evening to remember. Leaving their precious jeeps under guard, Simonds led his SAS compatriots to the newly 'liberated' Hotel Imperiale. They 'staggered in armed to the teeth' to demand a meal. 'Looking around, we saw the dining room was full of Italian Army Officers!' Simonds observed. 'We were the only British there.' Fortunately, the head waiter had worked in London before the war, as the 'Deputy Head Waiter at the Savoy Hotel'.

They were duly served a meal, which, while not quite up to Savoy standards, was washed down with copious quantities of Asti Spumante, 'the Italian champagne'. Having eaten and drunk their fill, they were presented with the bill, which Simonds 'meekly paid', though he doubted if 'German officers in a similar situation' would have done the same. After dinner he requisitioned a wing of the hotel for all who needed rooms. As there was little or no fresh water in Bari, the Germans having 'blown up the entire water supply', they 'made do with Asti Spumante for our ablutions and consumption'.

While Simonds and his new A Force commanders were carousing at the Hotel Imperiale, the rank and file had likewise been partying hard. Bari was known as the queen of southern Italy, and the SAS had been among the first Allied troops to arrive there. They'd rolled into this ancient, beautiful city riding in 'our motley collection of trucks, jeeps and busses', Arnold recalled. 'To the Italians we must have looked a scruffy lot, with our somewhat dirty clothes and most of us wanting a shave, loaded down with our guns and ammo belts and all kinds of paraphernalia . . . like some sort of mafia that had just escaped from the hills.'

They established themselves in a large building in the city centre that had once been a school, but recently served as a 'rest home for German officers'. Judging by the 'profusion of women's clothes, underwear and the appurtenances of love-making, it looked as if the Jerries had had anything but a restful time there'. Billeting themselves in what appeared to be a former brothel, they quickly realised that this was a city 'on the verge of starvation'. Before leaving, the Germans had not only dynamited the city's electricity and water supplies, but stolen all the food they could lay their hands on, pillaging the surrounding farms for good measure.

Despite this – or perhaps because of it – 'there was a good night life to be had', as Arnold noted. 'It is a peculiar thing that during war, a city that has just surrendered loses all moral sense and indulges in sex and fantasy . . . Nothing is real any more . . .'

For most, long months in the North African desert lay behind them, and all largely devoid of female company. This was a 'chance to have a hell of a time, for who knows what the future might be; would they be killed or wounded, or would the next few years be spent in a mouldy prison camp?' In Arnold's view, shared by most, 'this was a golden opportunity to make up for lost time; fun that would not be approved of by the wives and families at home was to them a relief from the rigours of war.'

Most partied like there was no tomorrow, seeking solace with 'a strange female that one meets for just one night in a foreign country that is still in the throes of war'. As Arnold remarked, 'Moralists might find it somewhat disgusting, but fighting a war in the heat of the desert and not knowing whether you are going to be alive from one day to the next rather weeds out the moralists.' Dispatched north with Swill Sutton in a truck packed with food, to relieve one of the worst famine-hit areas, Arnold came across an incredible sight: it was a five-piece band marching along the road, all playing their instruments, and all were young women.

One of them flagged the truck down. Arnold, who was driving, pulled over. The dance troupe asked for a lift and Arnold told them to hop in. He'd meant into the back, but in an instant two had piled into the cab, before Arnold and Swill managed to get the rest into the rear with their instruments. Even so the cab was decidedly cramped. As Arnold set off the young lady next to him kept trying to sit in his lap. The one next to Sutton had the 'gear lever between her legs and her skirt rolled up to her thighs. What a job,' Arnold declared. Whenever he had to change gear, he had to push the one off his lap, and reach over to a 'rather private part' of the other lady's body, in an effort to shift gear. Each time she proceeded to 'grasp my hand and hold it there while I was in a panic'. Each time Arnold feared he was about to crash.

Eventually, he stopped the truck and asked gear-stick-lady if she wouldn't mind moving 'her legs from the gear lever' and to 'put her skirt down'. By way of response, she stared into Arnold's face, before rolling her skirt still higher, and revealing her 'pink panties'. Recognising that 'there was no way that we were going to win', Arnold drove on. By hook or by crook they got back to Bari, and dropped the troupe at their destination. They were invited up to the ladies' flat for drinks. 'We had to refuse, worst luck,' Arnold observed, 'as we had to report to the school.'

At their school-cum-former-brothel, the SAS had orders to move. A Force was going to war.

After their night carousing at the Hotel Imperiale, Simonds set forth a little the worse for wear, with his A Force personnel riding in a mixed bag of jeeps and commandeered vehicles. The priority now was to speed north, to get within striking distance of their target areas, many of which lay hundreds of kilometres behind enemy lines. At first, Simonds rode in a jeep with his old friend, Roy Farran. He soon discovered what an unwise choice that was. They reached a blown bridge, which forded a small river.

Farran's response was to declare, impatiently, 'We will jump it!'

With that he put his foot to the floor and charged the broken bridge, the jeep sailing into the air, before plunging 'into the water, submerging ourselves and the jeep', as Simonds noted. Having dragged the waterlogged vehicle out, Simonds changed rides. They drove across Italy 'using lanes and side roads and meeting no Germans'. At midday, they reached a small town lying some 200 kilometres north of Bari. Their arrival was greeted by the town mayor with a stiff Nazi salute, and a 'Heil Hitler'. It was soon 'brought home to him forcibly that he was backing the wrong side!' While the mayor professed not to know where the nearest German forces might be, he argued that they were 'still winning'.

Moving on, they stopped for lunch beside a beautiful lagoon. While some of the SAS 'fished using hand grenades', Simonds picked apricots from the trees. Lunch was served. Afterwards, he and Symes strolled to the top of a nearby knoll to admire the view, only to be 'confronted by an astonished German sentry'. Having opened fire and missed, the enemy soldier ran away. They pressed on with a tad more caution, making for the Italian port town of Termoli, which lay on the same latitude as Rome. Termoli was the tip of the Allied advance, for a force of 1 SAS commanded by Blair 'Paddy' Mayne, together with British commandos, had seized it in a daring seaborne landing.

Checking his map, Simonds reckoned Termoli was not far away. He sent Farran on ahead, to scout out the lie of the land and to 'make the necessary administrative arrangements (accommodation, food, water etc)'. At dusk Simonds and the main body of the SAS rolled wearily into town. They made for the port area, a small, natural harbour improved with an artificial breakwater. The town clustered around the sea, the houses clinging to the hillsides above, tumbling 'over each other in typical ramshackle style'. Eventually, they found Farran standing on the flat roof of a house overlooking the port, with 'his arms around two pretty girls'.

'Roy,' Simonds shouted up at him, 'have you made the administrative arrangements?'

'Yes, Colonel,' Farran smiled. 'These are the administrative arrangements.'

While Simonds conceded it was funny, it was 'not the slightest bit of use!'

The Allied occupation of Termoli was barely forty-eight hours old, but the place seemed peaceful enough. Simonds established his HQ in 'a line of fisherman's cottages overlooking the tiny harbour'. Having liaised with the men of 1 SAS who were holding the town, Simonds got down to A Force business. Shortly, a pair of distinctive vessels nosed into port. Bizarrely, the ships – Landing Craft Infantry (LCI), well-armed ships, around 160 feet in length and capable of putting 200 men ashore – were showing lights.

Shells whistled through the air, cutting through the darkness. Simonds hurried down to the harbourside. As the lead vessel docked, someone flashed a torch all over the place.

'Put that bloody light out!' Simonds cried. More shells landed near by, underscoring his sentiments.

'Are you aware that you are talking to a brigadier?' came the answering reply.

'I couldn't care less,' Simonds countered. 'But if you want to remain a *live* brigadier you'd better put that bloody light out.'

The vessels were carrying a fresh contingent of commandos, and after Simonds's intervention the 'disembarkation proceeded quickly, and quietly, and in darkness'. The new arrivals brought with them good news and bad news. Among those coming ashore were Simonds's prized signals unit, who were charged with masterminding communications across A Force's fast-moving and widespread mission. The small team was commanded by none other than Captain Anthony 'Tony' Deane-Drummond, who'd been loaned to Simonds by General Down, the commander of 1 Airborne Division. Deane-Drummond – 'A very gallant, resourceful officer', as Simonds would appraise him – had already escaped once from Italian captivity, and he arrived with written orders that he was forbidden from operating behind the lines. 'Tony soon ignored that!'

That was the good news. The bad news concerned the LCIs. Assured of Churchill's absolute backing, Simonds had requested the loan of several such craft, for they would be perfect for plucking large numbers of POWs to safety. He had assumed that these were the first of his ships, but the LCI fleet commander was in receipt of no such orders. He was aware of a fleet of half a dozen caiques that were in-bound towards Termoli. They were crewed by the men of Couraud's French Squadron, and as far as anyone seemed to know they were the sum total of what was to be A Force's POW rescue fleet.

Those caiques were underpowered, unprotected and unarmoured. They were totally unsuited to extracting thousands of POWs from deep within enemy territory. This glaring lack of any proper rescue craft was just one more thing that Simonds would have to deal with. He was familiar with the caiques and their capabilities. At the height of his A Force work, he'd run a fleet of seventy such boats out of Cyprus. Manned by British officers and local crew, that A Force armada had possessed a certain piratical dash and flare. So much so, that the Admiralty had been forced to intervene.

'It has been brought to the attention of the Admiralty that personnel of your organisation are sailing armed boats in the Eastern Mediterranean, flying a flag the insignia of which is the skull and crossbones . . .' wrote the Admiralty. 'This practice by your organisation will cease forthwith.' Simonds's response was to ask the magician that A Force employed, Jasper Maskelyne, to conceive of a flag that would appear entirely Jolly Roger-like, but was 'technically not the same'. His design showed the British crown over two crossed swords, 'which at a distance looked just like the skull and crossbones'. That became the 'A Force flag and insignia'.

In due course Simonds got a '"rocket" from the War Office', but by then their work was done. At around that time, he had been assessed by high command in the following terms: 'This officer is a Pirate: only useful in times of War.' It was a top secret appraisal, one that Simonds was never supposed to see. When he did finally get sight of it, he wholeheartedly approved. His Cyprus-based fleet had been perfect for the job at hand, which was running one or two former POWs back into those territories from which they had escaped, and plucking the odd few out again. Here in Termoli, with thousands needing rescuing, it was a whole different ball game.

Simonds led the new arrivals back to his makeshift head-quarters. There, Deane-Drummond tried to take stock of his surroundings. Or more to the point, just who he was to be working with. Simonds made a bizarre apparition, with a bandage wrapped tightly around his head and under his chin, 'leaving a small shock of sandy hair sticking out the top'. That was what happened when you let Roy Farran drive you half-way across war-torn Italy.

Seated at a rough wooden table covered with maps, and with a cigarette dangling out of the corner of his mouth, Simonds briefed Deane-Drummond. 'You have joined an unconventional army here. The gangster who showed you in is a Yugoslav agent and we have another as our Officers' Mess cook.' Deane-Drummond had indeed been shown to his quarters by a 'swarthy-looking ruffian who mumbled in a strange language and wore a mixture of

American and British uniform'. In tried and tested style, Simonds had started to hoover up escapees from across Italy, recruiting them as A Force agents. 'Our fleet consists of . . . Italian fishing boats equipped with ancient diesel engines,' he observed. 'What have you brought with you?'

Deane-Drummond explained that he came equipped with a wireless base station, to be set up thereabouts, and several 'suitcase wireless sets', which were to be dispatched with teams into the field. Getting a sense of Simonds's style, Deane-Drummond was introduced to a tall, distinguished-looking individual, who turned out to be the former Polish ambassador to Italy. Along with his son, he was another of Simonds's recruits. They had been used as forced labour by the Germans. Their presence now was fortuitous. As they had been employed laying mines around Termoli harbour, they were charged by Simonds to map them all, so that his caique fleet could avoid getting sent to the bottom.

Simonds's Termoli HQ became the 'scene of strange and bizarre arrivals'. It was a magnet for anyone 'who had made their way through the German lines'. A major issue would be security and the vetting of new arrivals. But Simonds had developed ways and means. He'd been blessed to have as his senior commanders Brigadier Dudley Clarke, and before that, Major Orde Wingate, 'the two most individualistic and original soldiers of our day and age'. With Wingate he'd first seen action during the East Africa campaign, in 1940, as part of Gideon Force, in which some seventy British officers, commanding 1,500 troops of the Sudan Defence Force plus a hodgepodge of local irregulars, had vanquished Italian forces 30,000 strong. They'd done so using audacity, bluff and daring, and with only a camel train to convey their supplies across supposedly impossible country. Time and again the Italians had ended up bewildered by Gideon Force's hit-and-run tactics, and their ingenuity at creating makeshift weaponry.

In six weeks, thousands of the enemy had been captured, along with an immense amount of war materiel, as Gideon Force had liberated an area the size of France. At a time when Britain was desperate for victories, Simonds and Wingate had sought to act as the evangelists for irregular warfare, with Gideon Force as their calling card. But as they had quickly discovered, 'nobody wanted to know, and nobody displayed the slightest interest'. Their reports had been buried by headquarters, to ensure they never got into the hands of those that mattered – General Archibald Wavell, then in command in the Middle East, and his successor, General Claude Auchinleck. They'd grown 'fed up and disgusted' at all the 'intrigue and attempts to denigrate our successful victory over the Italians', which had been won against impossible odds.

Before the war, Simonds had read T. E. Lawrence's *Seven Pillars of Wisdom*. He'd retraced many of Lawrence of Arabia's key camel routes. Irreverent, unconventional, iron-willed – a born guerrilla fighter – Simonds had endured. Installed at his Cairo A Force headquarters, an order had been circulated that staff must carry at all times a 'Special Identity Card' to get access to official buildings. Clarke's 'forgery section' duly produced a card marked: 'Name – Adolph Hitler. Height – 3'. Any marked characteristics – Walks on all fours.' It was used for months to enter General Headquarters in Cairo. So much for mindless bureaucracy.

As the SAS had discovered, unconventional, irregular operations were rarely to prove popular with high command. Sadly,

Simonds would face more of the same here in Italy. As the SAS War Diary noted for 2 October 1943: 'Caiques arrived Termoli 17.30 hrs and were shown billets.' Or as Roy Farran would write, more poetically, of their tiny fleet's arrival: 'They came in just as the sun was setting in a golden ball to the West, casting a gilded sheen on the water. Four little caiques heeled over against the wind led in by a tall schooner. I envied the others their opportunity to play pirates.'

Farran's envy was well founded. The caique fleet was manned by Couraud and his French Squadron, plus McGregor and his men. They had done their best to appear like Italian fishermen: 'swarming all over the rigging and the decks were the men of the SAS ... There was not a scrap of khaki on them.' In fact, Simonds's crew were 'dressed in the brightest colours ... bright blue bell-bottom trousers, red pullovers and silk cummerbunds', with 'gaudy silk scarves around their necks or on their heads ... they all had a knife or pistol in their belts'. One of the most striking of all was Lieutenant McGregor himself, 'with his long dark hair and dark features', who 'looked the perfect pirate'. As even Simonds was forced to conclude, they looked 'a wild and unruly group of fighters'.

While sailing north along Italy's eastern seaboard in their requisitioned fleet, they'd pulled in at Manfredonia, a town lying 120 kilometres to the south of Termoli. Being the first Allied troops ashore, they'd come across an enemy headquarters containing 'a cache of gold sovereigns, silver etc. looted by the Germans'. Couraud and his men had proceeded to seize the lot, loading it all aboard their caique fleet. They'd also brought with them the three Poles recruited following Operation Loco, plus some of the Americans forming the OSS contingent.

As Simonds surveyed his fleet, the challenges before him appeared legion. He'd just been made aware of who had blocked him from getting the LCIs that he'd requested. The Admiral of the Fleet, Sir John Cunningham, had cabled a message stating that Simonds 'is to be given every assistance, <u>provided no ships of H.M. Navy are used</u> [Cunnigham's emphasis]'. In other words, he was to be given no assistance at all. As Simonds fully appreciated, this was outrageous, especially since Churchill had personally asked Cunningham to assist and been given assurances that he would. Once again, the potential for irregular operations was being stymied by those on high.

Simonds carried with him a letter, dated 28 September, which confirmed that he had been 'ordered by General Eisenhower, AFHQ, to carry out the rescue of several thousand Allied ex-prisoners of war now at large ... You are requested to give Lieut. Colonel Simonds every possible facility and assistance to carry out his task that he may require.' It also stated that he 'carries authorisation from General Alexander that Army commanders are to give him what help he needs to carry out his task'. (Alexander was Eisenhower's British opposite number.) Simonds waved it under the nose of the local Royal Naval commander at Termoli, who offered him an olive branch of sorts.

In addition to the requisitioned caiques, Simonds was offered the use of three Italian Navy boats and their crews. Those vessels were *Motoscafo armato silurante* (MAS) boats, the Italian equivalent to British motor torpedo boats (MTBs). With a top speed of 45 knots and armed with twin torpedo tubes and Breda 13.2mm heavy machine guns, they were fine craft in their own right. But they were far from ideal for collecting thousands of POWs. More to the point, as Simonds fully appreciated, the Italian crews 'up to a few days previously had been fighting against us!'

Taranto had been designated 'Advanced A Force HQ'. It was a grandiose name for a handful of harbourside cottages, a skeleton staff and a cobbled together rescue flotilla. More to the point, Simonds was dealing with 'the stress and urgency of this large scale escape operation', including 'non-stop work, flat out, with almost no staff or resources behind me. Items like transport, fuel, rations, equipment, parachutes, maps, money etc. all had to be produced in 48 hours, involving much hasty improvisation.' But there was worse to come.

Shortly after the caique fleet had tied up, Termoli harbour became the target of a fierce enemy counterattack, with shells falling with 'disconcerting accuracy' and enemy warplanes swooping from the skies. In no time one of the vessels, the schooner *San Vito*, was hit and sunk, a stick of bombs landing 'astride the jetty'. As the SAS War Diary recorded, '4 dive bombing attacks by Focke-Wulfs on harbour . . . HQ Schooner hit . . . (1 killed and 5 wounded). Shelling of town began . . .' The wooden hulled craft had taken a real pounding, splintering apart, and the vessel had sunk like a stone.

Witnessing the calamity, Simonds rushed to the harbour. Seeing bubbles rising from the depths he dived in to rescue whoever might be in such distress. He emerged having retrieved a rucksack, but nothing more. Farran also took the plunge, but having forgotten to remove his heavy 'German jackboots', they filled with water, and he himself had to be rescued. The dead man turned out to be Trooper Arthur 'Digger' Dench, married, with two children. Dench had only volunteered for the SAS three weeks earlier, having served in a regular unit prior to that.

By rights, he shouldn't have been on the *San Vito* at all. Part of 2 SAS's headquarters unit, he'd only gone aboard in search of some stores.

Among the *San Vito*'s injured were two OSS operators, Sergeant Dominic Balbi and Corporal James Inglima, who were 'acting as interpreters with British 2 SAS', as their OSS records noted. Inglima had been thrown bodily into the air, as the *San Vito* had been hit. Knocked unconscious, he'd come back to his senses even as the vessel was 'sinking rapidly'. Injured, he'd searched for his OSS buddy, Balbi. He'd found him with a 'big "V" gash in his forehead, plus other wounds in other parts of his body'. At first Inglima thought Balbi was dead, but when he realised he was still breathing, he and other survivors had dragged the OSS sergeant to shore. They got off 'just before the boat went down'.

Both men would be hospitalised but survived their wounds. They were awarded Purple Hearts, the medal given to American military personnel wounded while in service. There were also two Italians among the wounded, including one called Bruno, whom Couraud had recruited as the ship's cook. As the *San Vito* had contained much of the treasure that the French Squadron had retrieved from the German's Manfredonia headquarters, Couraud and his men spent hours 'diving to recover their looted gold'.

Though Simonds and Farran were not to know it, the sinking of the *San Vito* signified that the siege of Termoli had begun. Galled by the loss of this strategic port town, and the ability it gave the Allies to leapfrog German lines, an enraged Hitler had ordered Field Marshal Albert Kesselring, his Italian commander-in chief, to retake Termoli at all costs. Kesselring had dispatched several *Kampfgruppen* – battlegroups – of the war-hardened 16th Panzer

Division (Wehrmacht), to throw a ring of steel around Termoli and close for the kill. All that stood against them were the men of 1 SAS, together with those of Nos. 3 and 40 Commandos, along with a few assorted other units.

Mustering their forces for the defence of the town, 1 SAS would suffer a terrible blow. Their convoy of trucks was targeted by deadly accurate shellfire. Eighteen men were killed outright and many more injured. In response, they launched a house to house search of Termoli. It seemed obvious that someone 'with a wireless set was spotting for the German artillery . . . as the shooting and correction was very accurate'. Shortly, that SAS hunter squad discovered a pair of German officers together with a radio set, sequestered in a church tower that overlooked the town. Clearly, it had served as their observation post. Tempers were running high and those two enemy officers were shot dead.

As the battle for Termoli raged, there was a very real danger that the town might be 'overrun, or cut off'. With Simonds's blessing, Farran took twenty men and six Bren guns and dashed off to plug a gap in the frontline. While Termoli held out, Simonds was determined that his mission would continue. Escapers were pouring into his base. Each faced 'a quick interrogation, to get news of other escapers, P.O.W. Camps, and German dispositions'. After that, they were asked if they were willing to serve as A Force agents. Volunteers from the Italian Army also flocked to the call. One proved 'particularly useful', as he was the former 'Italian Army Commandant of a British P.O.W. Camp'. Another, a leader of a group of Italian partisans, was put to work by Simonds 'harassing the Germans'.

Though Termoli was under siege, Simonds figured he could still get his teams out. There were ways through even the most constricting of traps. First off were three of Simonds's own 'Jeeping Parties', each consisting of an A Force officer and sergeant, with an Italian partisan serving as their guide. Using jeeps on back roads to penetrate the lines, they pushed 'way ahead of the invading British and American armies'. Equipped with loud hailers, they would 'drive up, unseen, near a column of prisoners and urge them to escape the line of march, where to hide up and where to make for'. Such a simple ruse would prove remarkably effective, for thousands of POWs were on the move, as the enemy sought to relocate them further away from the Allied advance. Often, a few words of encouragement and instruction broadcast from a loud hailer were enough to make many break away.

Next up would be those of Simonds's men who would parachute deep behind the lines. While those going in by caique would pose as fishing crews, no one held out any great hope that such a ruse would pass muster, especially as their ships would be crammed full of highly visible POWs. With A Force's seaborne means of insertion looking decidedly dodgy, everyone wanted to go in by air. As the SAS War Diary noted, there would be 'four parties of six, to go by boat, and a party of one officer and six men to parachute, along with four Italo-Americans. Capt. Power, Lieut. McGregor, Lieut. Hibbert drew lots for who would parachute; Lieut. McGregor won the draw.'

McGregor, the Operation Loco veteran, was parachuting in, and wherever he went, trouble for the enemy was sure to follow.

Chapter 12

UNLEASHED

McGregor's drop would be plagued by bad luck and trouble. Leading an eight-man team, which included his old regulars, plus OSS operator Corporal John Nicolich, their deployment was to prove a horribly rushed affair. In the final briefing, McGregor and his men learned that theirs was supposedly a short-duration mission and a piece of cake. 'Everything was easy, they told us . . . The job was to last ten days and on the tenth night we would board a Navy boat . . . Mr. Churchill himself had ordered the job, and if we brought it off successfully we would be thought of highly by him.'

Bidding farewell to 'the rest of the boys, saying we would see them in a few days', the eight men went to board the waiting aircraft. Nicolich, the patrol's newcomer, was a 'young lad, six-foot tall, built like a bloody horse', as Arnold observed. Originally a Yugoslavian, 'Nick', as they'd christened him, was a naturalised American who'd worked as a longshoreman in the New York docks before the war. As a bonus, he was fluent in Italian. As Arnold followed Nicolich across the airstrip, 'ambling in that Yanky fashion', he was struck by the newcomer's 'broad shoulders, and open, honest face. I thought he would be a handy bloke in a tight corner.' So matters were to prove.

The eight men had decided to deploy wearing US army over-alls, for they doubled as makeshift jump-suits. With copious quantities of pockets and pouches, they were also perfect for behind-the-lines guerrilla operations. Dark green in colour, as opposed to khaki, they complemented the men's US Army hav-ersacks, plus their high, rubber-soled parachute boots. Each man also carried a Tommy gun or carbine, '.45 pistols, fighting knives, escape kit, soap, towel, razor, brush and as many cigarettes and chocolate as we could scrounge', plus escape maps, compasses and the all-important bundles of cash.

Preparing for take-off in the late afternoon of 2 October, the location of their DZ had only been determined shortly before they boarded the waiting plane. When McGregor queried this, the aircraft's navigator had assured him that he was 'certain of this D.Z. on the map and . . . could drop the stick on a sixpence'. Somewhat reassured, McGregor and his team had clambered aboard the waiting Albermarle, those much-reviled warplanes being all that was on offer. They were to be released at the 'foot of some mountains 30 miles inland', offering them a vast tract of isolated terrain in which to disappear, and across which to search for the POW-escapees.

They took with them four cylindrical drop-containers packed with rations, explosives, ammo and 'comforts for P.O.W.s'. They were to be released between jumpers number 5 and 6, with the intention of them landing somewhere in the midst of the stick. It was just after 4.00 p.m. as the aircrew prepared to take to the skies. Though they had a flight of over 400 kilometres ahead of them, it struck McGregor as being far too early to get airborne, for their intention was to drift to earth under cover of darkness. But when he'd been slated to be sent back to Britain, months

160

earlier, and had instead jumped from that speeding train, he'd done so because he hungered to get into the action. Right now, he was serving at the vanguard of A Force, and as he'd learned during Operation Loco, sometimes the prize justified the most extreme risks.

Their present mission was codenamed Operation Begonia. As with Jonquil, Bill Stirling had been fond of selecting botanical names for 2 SAS missions, after those plants that grew on the Stirling family estate, in Keir, Scotland. Stirling was the laird (lord) of Keir, and Keir House, the family seat, epitomised the formal grandeur and elegance of the Victorian era. In the spring of 1942, he'd opened the grounds so that a war-weary British public might marvel at the 'narcissi, alpines, flowering shrubs and ornamental trees' that thrived there. With the proceeds from admission fees, plus charges for tea and buns, he'd raised money for nursing associations and the building of a new warship.

The pilot of the Albermarle fired up the engines and the air-craft took to the skies. The Operation Begonia team slipped into their gear, shrugging on their parachutes, plus their backpacks, which were lashed to their chests 'with bits of string', and with carbines or Tommy guns strapped on top. The pilot had warned them the journey in would be an exercise in 'low level hell'. They'd turn out to sea and head north kissing the very wavetops, in an effort to avoid detection by the enemy. As the Albermarle headed for the Adriatic, so McGregor passed around chewing gun, 'as was his habit'. Moments later they were over the sea. 'It was bloody frightening, we were so low the bloody spray was wetting the windows.' What would happen if they ran into an air pocket and 'the props hit the water'?

Thirty minutes into the flight the pilot warned them that an enemy warplane had been sighted. The Albermarle was flying so low that he believed they'd slip through undetected. As no enemy rounds came tearing through the fuselage, those riding in the hold figured the pilot's low-level tactics had to be working. Above the roar of the engines, the men swapped stories of 'the time we had in Bari, the girls we had met, the drinks we had had, and the good times we were going to have when we got back, that is, of course, if we got back'. Then the aircraft began to climb, and all sensed that the jump would be coming shortly.

Standing, each man checked his parachute harness, and clipped his static line – the canvas strap that pulled the parachute out of its pack – to the wire running the length of the aircraft's ceiling. One by one they checked the man in front's hookup, 'to see that it was safe'. The Albermarle began to circle, and McGregor and his men assumed they were over the DZ. The aircraft's dispatcher – the member of the flight crew responsible for getting them, and their containers, out of the plane – ripped open the jump hatch. Moments later he was 'shouting get the bloody hell out, and as each of us got to the door he pushed us out'.

Typically, McGregor was first to leap through the Albermarle's yawning jump hole. But very quickly his worst fears were realised. As he tumbled through the aircraft's slipstream, his 'chute being dragged free by its static line, before erupting in a mushroom of canvas high above him, he was struck by how bright it was. The time was just after 5.30 p.m., meaning sunset was a good hour away. Within a matter of seconds a dozen further parachutes had blossomed in the sky, each a shining, silvery dome burnished by the evening sun. As a report on Operation Jonquil would note, McGregor and his team had been dropped 'half an hour too early in broad daylight'. They 'floated down to earth', the SAS lieutenant and his men, plus their drop-containers, being visible for many miles around.

Once his 'chute had stabilised, McGregor was hit by a second shocking realisation, like a punch to the guts. They'd been released in entirely the wrong location; in fact, the worst kind of place that he could ever have imagined. Spread out below him lay the ancient city of Chieti, 'a mass of roofs and streets' dominated by its ornate cathedral tower, and with the snowcapped peak of Gran Sasso – the highest in the Apennines – rising in the background. Surrounded by the rugged terrain of the Apennines to the west, and bordered by the Adriatic Sea to the east, Chieti was the site of a notorious POW camp, PG 21, which had been overseen by a cabal of die-hard Italian fascists. Overcrowded, unheated, with little food or running water, there had been many escape attempts, including tunnels and even efforts to swim through human sewage.

Upon the Armistice being signed, the camp's senior British officer, Lieutenant Colonel William Marshall, had abided by the standfast order to the letter, appointing his own men to guard the watchtowers, and threatening 'that any man found attempting to escape would be court-martialled for desertion'. Soon after, German paratroopers had marched into the camp, corralling the prisoners, some 1,300 of whom were shipped north to Nazi Germany. But scores had managed to conceal themselves in and around the camp, using half-built tunnel systems, sewers, roof spaces or even water towers in which to lie low. Once the enemy had removed the bulk of the POWs, those in hiding had emerged and slipped away into the surrounding hills. It was those kinds of escapees that McGregor and his team were here to rescue, but right now they looked set to land in the depths of hostile territory; in the heart of this enemy-occupied city.

As McGregor studied the lie of the land, he figured they were coming down on top of the bridge that forded the Pescara river, which lay on the western fringes of the city. Worryingly, he could see the ant-like forms of German soldiers rousing themselves for the hunt, 'coming from the Chieti area to meet us', as he would report. The enemy troops mounted their fast motorcycle and side-car combinations, and sped out of their barracks, with more vehicles in hot pursuit. McGregor fought with his 'chute against the prevailing drift, in an effort to steer himself further west and away from the city. Eventually, and with the wind gusting strongly, he came to a crashing halt on some rough ground on the outskirts of Villanova, a suburb on the city's western outskirts.

Even before his feet hit the earth, McGregor was aware of a mass of people rushing towards the point at which he was going to make landfall. Unsure of their intentions, he was greeted by those who 'were shaking my hand before I touched the ground'. A group of seemingly friendly locals had witnessed the plight of the Allied parachutists, and by a stroke of good fortune they had got to McGregor and his men first. But only just; 'enemy troops were very close'. In a frantic rush, McGregor rolled up his stick, which had 'dropped in a large semi-circle', after which they dragged the containers into a nearby ditch. Stuffing their silk parachutes into the hands of grateful locals – they 'made excellent underwear' – McGregor was aware of the need to run and hide. The question was in what direction, so as to evade the enemy?

One man was still missing: Swill Sutton. His 'chute had got tangled in some telephone wires, and he was desperately trying to cut himself free, sawing through the lines with his fighting knife. Moments after he'd dropped to the ground, McGregor and his men were waving and yelling, and Sutton dashed over to join them. Then a figure emerged dressed in a striking grey-green uniform. Whether German or Italian, no one could tell, and likewise whether friend or foe. As McGregor and his men confronted the newcomer, Corporal Nicolich, McGregor's OSS man, broke into a torrent of Italian.

It turned out that the uniformed individual hailed from the city's Guardia di Finanza, a paramilitary force similar to the Carabinieri, but with the remit to police smuggling rackets and financial crime. With the benefit of that man's warnings, Nicolich was able to alert all to just how close the enemy were – 'only a few yards away'. With the Guardia offering to lead them all to 'a safe place', and with 'no time to doubt his good intentions', McGregor signalled for his men to follow 'at the double'. Even as he did, a German motorcycle came roaring down the nearby road, followed by a military truck. Both vehicles ground to a halt adjacent to the patch of terrain where the SAS had come to ground.

'Let's go!' McGregor announced.

With the Guardia leading the way they dashed for cover, scrambling down the banks of the Pescara. The terrain on all sides was low-lying and swampy, thick with undergrowth. In no time the fugitives were up to their knees in muddy water. In the midst of such inhospitable terrain, McGregor ordered each man to crawl into the densest thicket that he could find and not to open fire unless 'absolutely essential'. The plan was to lie low until nightfall, when they'd make their getaway.

'If the Jerries do come and we get split up, we will meet at this map reference,' McGregor indicated, 'near the mountain.

Remember, it will be every man for himself, no heroics, and no one will give himself up unless he absolutely has no other choice.'

That sorted, the Guardia offered to return to the DZ, to check on their all-important drop-containers. He'd ask the locals to help him drag them into a place of proper concealment, after which he would return. No sooner was that grey-uniformed figure gone, than there was an almighty great explosion in the nearby bushes. It sounded more like a mortar bomb than a grenade, and the flash of the blast lit up the patrol's surroundings in the gathering gloom. Dusk was upon them, ushering in the darkness that should have welcomed their drop.

Another mortar round slammed into the marshy terrain. The wait dragged on and on. As McGregor was well aware, it had taken 'five precious minutes' for him to retrieve his M1 carbine from one of the drop-containers back at the DZ, for it had become 'lost amongst the rations'. It was a similar story with others. In future, all weapons would need to be carried on their persons, and especially when being dropped into the teeth of the enemy. Care in choosing DZs was critical, McGregor realised. Having Nicolich on hand with his fluent Italian was also proving essential. But right now they needed to get out of there, and into the kind of remote terrain that was supposed to have marked their point of arrival.

A while later, an indistinct figure emerged from the darkness. Even though they were menaced by 'pursuit by the enemy', they had no option but to move, the Guardia urged. He'd discovered a German guard standing watch on each of their flanks, clearly waiting for the SAS to break cover. One of McGregor's men was 'all for knocking off the nearest sentry with his fighting knife'. But as others argued, it would only be a matter of time before 'the Germans discovered the first body'. If they could last it out until well after nightfall, that would give them the best chance of slipping the net.

Eleven kilometres further west lay a remote farmstead, the Guardia explained. There the locals would harbour McGregor and his men, of that he was certain. That was the nearest place of sanctuary, and even then they must expect the enemy to launch 'an extensive search of the area' in order to hunt down the parachutists who had dropped into their midst. From now on they would be harried at every turn. Setting off with the Guardia acting as their guide, the silent snake of men flitted into the darkness. Climbing out of the swampland, they crossed a field and reached the road.

Crawling through a hole in the hedge that lined the highway, they got to a ditch and froze. From there they could see both sentries. Watching and waiting, they timed the enemy soldier's walks, scrutinising their every move. That done, McGregor explained his plan. He would flit across the road first, for beyond lay rural terrain in which they could lose themselves. Each man was to follow, singly. If any was to be spotted, those remaining would open fire, at which point it was time to scatter – 'every man for himself'.

One by one they stole across that expanse of open tarmac, and evidently none were seen. Slipping west through the ghostly forms of olive groves and scrubby forest that surrounded Chieti, they eventually reached a dense patch of trees. Stopping for a rest and a smoke, they took stock. They'd lost most of their food and cigarettes, for more than one container had been left behind. Their contents were 'probably in the German HQ' by now. But at least they had 'all our guns and ammo', as Arnold observed.

Under the unerring hand of their Guardia guide, McGregor and his men trekked on through that night, the clamour and crash of the hunt fading into the distance behind them. For now at least it seemed they had managed to slip the net. As McGregor was beginning to appreciate, it was 'far quicker and easier to procure guides than to rely entirely on Maps', especially since many Italians would prove 'willing to help in this way'.

It was well after midnight by the time they reached their end destination. Cresting a small hill, below lay the isolated farmstead. Leaving his men where they were, McGregor went ahead with the Guardia and Nicolich to check out the lie of the land. A while later a low whistle echoed out of the darkness. McGregor was signalling them all in. Climbing down the hillside, they reached a 'typical Italian farmhouse' consisting of 'cowshed, cart-shed, the stables and the pigsty all in the same building'. Inside, the farmhouse itself proved to be spotlessly clean – 'you could eat off the floor'. The farmer and his wife – well into their seventies – welcomed the newcomers with outstretched hands and tears in their eyes.

The farmer – 'a big man, very upright and broad shoulders; for all his age he looked very active' – pledged to do all that he could to help. Meanwhile, his wife told the newcomers to undress, for their overalls were soaking wet and caked in mud. She would clean and dry them all. As Nicolich explained, they were to address their hosts as 'Mamma and Papa', for it was now that the Guardia revealed that he was actually their son. His name was Roberto, and he was married with a family in Chieti. As he'd seen McGregor and his men drifting to earth, he'd 'watched for a few minutes', calculating where they would land, then rushed off to intercept the parachutists, in an effort to keep them safe from the enemy.

Having been fed, and dressed again in their dry clothes, McGregor went about setting a sentry rota, which should allow most of his men to grab some much needed rest. But Roberto and his father would have none of it. The British parachutists should sleep, they urged. 'My Papa and I will stay awake,' Roberto promised, 'and keep watch for any Tedeschi that might come near.'

Just after dawn the alarm was raised. McGregor and his men were woken, for 'on the skyline were some German soldiers'. They watched as the enemy troops entered a neighbouring farm. The hunters were close now. Clearly, there was nothing McGregor and his men could do to search for the POW-escapees while they were being pursued so relentlessly. The enemy would soon reach Mamma and Papa's farm, so Roberto led McGregor and his men to a nearby hideout. They should lie low, he explained, and return come sundown. They went to ground in a patch of mixed bushes and long grass, fringed by thick woodland on one side.

Sometime in the late afternoon they spied a fearsome sight. On the ridge above them emerged a long line of German cavalry. 'The sun was shining on their sword scabbards . . . The muzzles of their rifles could be seen over their shoulders as they were slung over their backs . . . It was obvious they were part of a patrol looking for us.' If they swept down into the grassland and bush there was nowhere that McGregor and his men could hide, and no way that they could outrun such mounted troops.

A trumpet sounded. The extended line of horsemen switched smoothly into a tight column and began to descend from the ridge. To Arnold, himself a former cavalryman, it sent shivers up his spine, but predominantly they were ones of fright, not of excitement. Moments later the horsemen were lost from view behind the adjacent woodland. There were a few beats of tense silence, as all wondered what they should do. It was broken by McGregor, who argued that their best option was to stay put.

'If they come in here they will have to dismount, and we can easily pick them off,' he reasoned. The bush they were hiding in was just too thick to allow mounted men through.

'Yes, but sooner or later we'll have to get out of here,' Arnold countered. 'It's not so easy to escape from cavalry as it is truck-bound troops.' Enemy troops in vehicles were constrained to the roads. No such issue when on horseback.

'That's true,' another voice piped up. 'Why don't we space out in a long line. Then, if one of us is seen, in the confusion the rest might be able to get away.'

The discussion went back and forth for a while longer. This was one of the great things about McGregor. Even in moments of high tension and danger, he remained keen to have all voices heard. Finally, they decided to spread out in line, and see what action the enemy cavalry might take. They'd just completed that manoeuvre, when a familiar figure appeared. It was Roberto and he came with a grim warning: the enemy troops were riding down the nearby track, towards McGregor and his men. Arnold happened to be closest to that roadway. McGregor came to join him, to keep watch.

Together, they lay in hiding, eyes and ears straining to detect the enemy's next move. Hooves rang out on the 'rough gravel' of the track. They could hear the riders talking. The two leading horsemen came into view, mounted upon 'fine black mares', as Arnold described them. Noticeably, they now bore their weapons at the ready. Heavily outnumbered, there was no option for the SAS but to keep their heads down and hope for the best, as the enemy column streamed past. Shortly, it became clear where they were headed – to Mamma and Papa's farm.

Two figures went inside the farmhouse. A while later they re-emerged, mounted up and the entire column turned back towards where McGregor and his men were hiding. They pulled to a stop where the road lay nearest to the concealed British troops. An order rang out. Two figures fell out of the column and turned their steeds towards the hidden men. The nearest horseman rode directly towards Arnold and McGregor's position, until it seemed impossible that they would remain undiscovered.

But just when the rider and steed were only a few yards away, the 'old mare would have none of it' and refused to go any further. The bush ahead was too thick and inhospitable for any horse and rider. They turned away, the rider backing out, and moments later he went to rejoin his comrade. A while later the column was spied going at a fast trot and heading off to search another area. 'It was a close one,' as Arnold recalled, simply.

At sunset Roberto emerged from the gathering darkness. They were to follow him to a farm lying about seven kilometres away, he explained. Hopefully, the German dragnet hadn't reached it yet. When they got there, the owners proved to be hugely welcoming, but they bore a warning. The Germans were on the hunt, and most farmers had been given pamphlets informing them that anyone found harbouring the Allied parachutists would be shot. Still, McGregor and his men were sheltered and fed and watered. Early the following morning, they were discussing what should be their next move, when a young boy came running into the house. Apparently, there were three 'Inglese' walking along the nearby road.

McGregor dispatched Arnold and Sutton to investigate. Hiding in a hedgerow, they let the trio pass, and could overhear them talking in English. Breaking cover, they started to follow the three men. When one turned and noticed that they were being tailed, he appeared horrified. As one, they broke into a run, dashing into a patch of nearby trees. Arnold and Sutton gave chase, but beyond the woods lay an isolated farm and the trio seemed to have vanished. They approached the farmhouse, finding the lady farmer inside. By the look on her face, it was clear that she thought they were German troops. By the time they'd got her to understand that they were British, she had tears of relief streaming down her face, and was crying out 'Benvenuto' – 'welcome'.

With no common language between them, she gestured at a door. Arnold and Sutton went through it, only to see distant figures making for a haystack. They yelled out that they were British. The running figures came to a halt. As if in slow motion they turned and stared at Arnold and Sutton, before raising their hands into the air. The two SAS men approached. They began explaining exactly who they were and their A Force remit. Staring at Arnold and Sutton in disbelief, it was as if the trio could not believe what they were hearing. Then; 'grasping hold of our hands and furiously shaking them, they demanded, "Why the hell didn't you tell us that when you first saw us?"'

Arnold and Sutton took the POW-escapees back to McGregor. There, they revealed all about 'their life in the POW camps and of their friends who were still in captivity'. In an utterly surreal moment, the newcomers realised that they recognised one of McGregor's men – Corporal James 'Geordie' Laybourne. They hailed him by his Christian name, and soon they were all embracing one other. They'd served in the same unit in North Africa, before the trio had been captured, and before Laybourne had stepped forward to volunteer for the SAS. Here, deep behind the lines in Italy, they had been reunited.

In truth, there was precious little time to indulge in such emotional scenes. Furnishing the POW-escapees with kit and money, they were told to head for the beach rendezvous where Couraud and his French Squadron would be waiting. From there, an A Force boat would whisk them back to Allied lines. Using their maps, McGregor and his men plotted out the route east to the coast, and identified the exact spot at which the trio would find the SAS beach party. 'We saw them off more happy than they had been for a long time,' Arnold remarked.

Ten more POW-escapees were rounded up from nearby farms and dispatched in the same fashion, before the enemy closed in again. McGregor and his men were woken in the night by their farmer host, who was 'visibly trembling'. Enemy troops were searching the neighbouring buildings. The last time they'd visited, they'd warned him that they would find the British parachutists and that they had 200 men on the hunt. 'It looked as if Jerry was really after our blood.' With a tearful Mamma thrusting parcels of food into their arms, McGregor and his men got out of there only just in time. As they left via the back door they heard a German motorcycle unit pull up at the front.

McGregor led them inland, into the foothills of the mountains, hoping to shake off the enemy. But a 'march in hostile county in the dark with all the lanes and roads being guarded was not going to be easy'. In addition, one of their number was suffering from an attack of malaria, and 'to top it all it had started to rain'. Come daybreak, all were sopping wet and freezing cold. They tried to wring out their sodden clothes, but dare not light a fire. For two hours McGregor and Arnold lay shivering on a ridge, and watching enemy patrols scouring the terrain thereabouts.

As was clear to all, 'The hunt was still on.'

Chapter 13

BEHIND ENEMY LINES

Hiding up in thick vegetation, a German patrol passed perilously close to McGregor and his men. Later, they heard movement. Sutton and Arnold went to investigate, discovering two POW-escapees in utterly desperate straits; 'in an awful mess, their clothes were soaking wet and their boots were falling apart'. Once again, they equipped the pair as best they could and sent them on their way. With trucks pulling up on the nearest highway and enemy troops disgorging, McGregor got his men on the move. The malaria victim 'swayed like a drunken man' as he tried to march, the next few hours being sheer 'hell for him'. Finally, it was clear he could go no further, and again they found shelter at a 'small house tucked away on a hillside'.

McGregor's stick had been released by the crew of the Albermarle scores of kilometres short of their intended drop zone. Worse still, being dropped in broad daylight had alerted the enemy, unleashing the hunters. Once they seemed to have shaken off their pursuers, the eight men pressed on, making for the area around Castignano, 150 kilometres to the north-west of Chieti. The terrain was challenging in the extreme, for they were trekking through the spine of the Apennine mountains. Even so, by the night of the 6/7 October they had made it, slipping into an area of dense pine forests, plunging ravines and knife-cut valleys, surrounded on all sides by peaks that topped 1,500 metres.

It was little wonder that those POWs who had escaped the camps had made for such a region as this: it was a mountain fastness, offering innumerable caves and crevasses in which to hide, not to mention scattered and isolated farmsteads. With reports of 'many hundreds of ex-POWs there', McGregor set up a 'Command Post' sited in a farm, and he set his men to work. Divided into teams of two, they were dispatched to all points of the compass, charged to round up as many escapees as possible and to channel them through his farm-headquarters.

Over the next seven days, some three hundred fugitives were brought in. While most were in a very sorry state, they seemed overjoyed to see the SAS team and to learn of their mission. In executing their flight from the POW camps, many were close to exhaustion, and they were clearly suffering from exposure to the tough mountain conditions. Dressed in the threadbare uniforms in which they had been captured – often North African desert kit – their clothes were no match for the October cold. By now, many had been on the run for a month or more. Any number were 'very poorly dressed' and 'without shoes'. But as McGregor reported, 'all were willing to go'.

Since they had deployed with thick wads of cash, courtesy of Simonds, McGregor and his men had the means to purchase better clothing and kit from the locals. Having equipped the escapees as best they could, they began to pass them along an escape line, aided by local guides and making for the coast, which lay some fifty kilometres due east of their farmstead head-quarters. There, at the pre-arranged rendezvous, Couraud and his French Squadron would be ready and waiting. With all they shared the pre-arranged password: 'Jack London'. If they gave that to the French Squadron, all would be well.

As McGregor and his men cast their net far and wide, they became more confident and brazen in their actions. At first, they'd made sure to move only at night, and 'cross-country'. But McGregor realised that was 'over-cautious', for it was 'easy to pose as Germans if necessary. Many Italians ignorant and easily fooled,' he noted. More to the point, when they began to move 'by day along roads' they were 'twice waved at by German truck drivers'. It seemed that pretty much anyone they came across – whether Italian civilians, or the enemy – automatically took them for German troops. In a sense it was hardly surprising: who else would be moving through Italy some 400 kilometres behind the frontlines in full uniform and well-armed?

While they remained low-profile – a secretive rescue force – they were automatically taken for German soldiers. Only those who knew the truth were any the wiser. It might well be different if they broke cover, or engaged in any offensive action. For now at least, they were hiding in plain sight and it was all too easy to pose as an enemy patrol. By the end of the second week of October, McGregor figured their A Force task was complete, their orders being to 'Land . . . on night 2nd of October . . . contact and rescue 400 British Other Ranks in hiding . . . These 400 Other Ranks will have to be guarded and guided down to the Coast and embarked.'

As far as McGregor saw things, it was mission accomplished. But there had been no confirmation from Termoli headquarters. Frustratingly, while McGregor's patrol was supposed to have radio contact with Simonds and his team, there was no sign of the party carrying their signals kit. It was hardly surprising, bearing in mind how wide of the intended DZ McGregor and his men had been dropped. In Operation Begonia's footsteps, a second A Force team had been slated to deploy. It consisted of Lieutenant Peter Sauro of the OSS, and nine of his men. McGregor and Sauro had intended to rendezvous at a prearranged meeting point, to enable joint operations and share the use of the suitcase radio set that Deane-Drummond had entrusted to Sauro's team. But there had been no sign of that OSS unit nor any means to make contact.

The lack of radio communications had potentially dire ramifications. In theory, McGregor should have been able to call in supply drops of ammo, weaponry, rations, clothes and kit, plus cash. As it was, they were forced to survive with what little they carried on their person. But as each POW-escapee was being given a fistful of Italian lire to fund his onwards escape, sometime soon McGregor's coffers were bound to run dry. After that, they'd need to find other means to fund their activities. It also begged the question of how they would signal their own need to withdraw at mission's end.

But McGregor figured they'd worry about that when the time arose.

By chance, Lieutenant Sauro's OSS team had dropped into a far better situation than had McGregor's. In the same spirit as Simonds's top secret 'This officer is a Pirate' dossier, Lieutenant Sauro's OSS file is marked 'SUBJECT MUST NEVER SEE THIS FILE'. Via its exhaustive vetting procedures, OSS had probed every aspect of Sauro's life, to check where his true allegiances might lie – with the Allies, or the nation of his parents' birth.

Coincidentally, the thirty-two-year-old New Yorker had a father who had been born in Chieti itself. Sauro was obliged to provide five 'character references in the US', plus 'names of 5 persons who know you socially in the United States', plus the details of 'three neighbors at your last normal residence in the US'.

Educated at Nutley High School, a local grammar, he'd had to furnish banking details, three credit references, plus full employment history for the previous ten years. Prior to signing up, he'd worked as a tree surgeon, employed by the Essex County Park Commission. Under 'clubs, societies and other organisations', he'd listed the YMCA. Five foot six, lean and fit, he'd signed up to the military in 1941 and received parachute training. As he entered on his form under special qualifications, he had: 'Military training and experience for duty of Special nature where a combination of Military engineering and Parachute duty is required.'

Assessed as being a wholly patriotic American, the OSS obviously liked what they saw in Sauro. In May 1943, Colonel Huntington, commander of one of the Operations Groups, had written to Sauro's parent unit, requesting 'action be initiated to effect the transfer into the Office of Strategic Services PETER SAURO . . . presently attached to Parachute School, Fort Benning'. Dispatched to Italy that August, and dropped behind the lines on the same day as McGregor's stick, little did Sauro and his men know that some of them would be obliged to spend many months operating deep behind the lines.

Lieutenant Sauro's party had been fortunate enough to drop later in the day, as darkness descended. His sergeant, Frank DeLuca, jumping in the middle of the stick, had landed, only to be greeted by cries of 'Tedeschi!' Right away, they had been mistaken for German troops. Grabbing his machine gun, and not knowing who their reception party might consist of, DeLuca, a tough factory worker hailing from Chicago, found himself surrounded by '10–15 Italian civilians'. Quickly, he disabused them of the misapprehension that he was a German paratrooper. Having established his bona fides, DeLuca rolled up the rest of the stick, but their commander, Lieutenant Sauro, was nowhere to be seen. The last to jump, he would have landed furthest away.

The locals led them to a nearby house, where they claimed there was an Allied escapee. Sure enough, there was. An American POW was hiding there, and many more such escapees were 'scattered all over the mountains'. Shortly, a group of 'six English prisoners' were brought in by the locals. With Sauro having turned up – locating his men had proved tricky in the darkness – their work began in earnest, as they began to direct 'the English prisoners towards the boat landings'. Sauro decided to split his team into two. The escapees were scattered far and wide, and this way they could cover more ground.

Sauro's second NCO, Sergeant Arengi, would take half of the men and head on a north-westerly bearing, while Sauro and DeLuca would do the same in the opposite direction. During their first two days of full operations, Sauro's team rounded up some '200 to 250 prisoners', all of whom were given money and sent on the escape lines towards the coast. Finding them in scattered groups of 35 to 40, invariably the escapees proved incredibly wary. Spying approaching men heavily armed and in uniform, 'they would run for the hills, thinking perhaps that we were Jerries,' one of Sauro's men would observe.

Overnighting at a farm, come morning they were told that 'an English Major and four lieutenants' were based in the mountains around the village of Civitella, so not so far away. Though Sauro and his men couldn't know it yet, they were operating in the same vicinity as McGregor and his team. Having missed their intended rendezvous with the British patrol, Sauro had no easy way of making contact. It was frustrating, but the OSS lieutenant had other problems on his hands.

Sauro dispatched a team to speak to the 'English Major' and his men, but they refused to believe that the OSS team was genuine. Sauro and DeLuca went to see him, explaining again who they were and the nature of their A Force operations. The major, who gave his name as 'Gordon', was another escapee, as were his comrades. As he listened to Sauro explaining all, he acted as if he was keen to get involved. He suggested that he and his four deputies would join the escape line the following morning. But instead, he proceeded to set up a 'Command Post' some two hours' walk away from the OSS base, from where he began to do all he could to impede their efforts.

'As we directed prisoners, he impelled them to stay . . .' DeLuca would report. 'He contradicted everything we told the prisoners, telling them that he had no faith in the Allied operation.' It proved hugely dispiriting. Whose side was the 'English major' really on, they wondered? What game was afoot? Shortly, Sauro and DeLuca heard warnings that the 'Germans were coming after us'. Were the two connected? There was no way of knowing.

Right now, Sauro and his men were getting just a small taste of the dark rivalries and divided loyalties that would plague such behind-the-lines missions. As Sauro's men would soon learn, there was 'a reward on our heads of 10,000 Lire, and many Italians were set on collecting it'. The actual amount was far higher: it was 10,000 lire for an escaped POW, but 40,000 for any of the Allied parachutists. That went a long way to explaining the wariness of the POW-escapees, and the conflicted loyalties of many that the OSS team would encounter.

Leaflets were being scattered throughout the mountains. Written in English, Italian, French and Polish, they were addressed to: *'War prisoners who have evaded from concentration camps ...* REMEMBER! Should you be caught ... you will be considered franc-tireurs and ... will be tried in accordance with the laws of war. Why then, will you still put up with hunger, defy danger and suffer all sorts of discomforts?' *'Franc-tireurs'* was a term for guerrilla fighters who operated outside the laws of war. In other words, it was a thinly veiled threat. The leaflets urged all such escapees to hand themselves in, at which point the Italian Fascist authorities would again recognise them as 'prisoners of war'.

It was so hard to know who to trust. For now, Sauro ordered his signals specialist, Corporal Neal Panzarella, to make contact with headquarters. The OSS lieutenant sought to update Simonds on all that had transpired, and to seek guidance. But when Panzarella assembled his suitcase radio set and tried to place a call, he realised they had problems. 'As soon as I pressed down on my transmitter key I received an electrical shock,' he reported, 'and the receiver went dead.' Panzarella used his spares kit to give the machine a thorough overhaul. He 'changed tubes, checked wires, and tried the receiver, which was burned out ... I was unable to fix it.' As the radio set was of no further use, Panzarella took it apart and buried it.

In short, there was no way of making contact with anyone.

Chapter 14

ROADKILL

A few hours' walk across the hills, McGregor was beginning to sense the same as Lieutenant Sauro – that operations in Italy were going to prove incredibly insecure and fraught. While the OSS team had been busy rounding up POWs, so McGregor had sorted a second means of potential escape. A belts and braces approach, he'd pioneered a route south through the mountains to cross the German and Allied lines. McGregor's epic reconnaissance had taken him and his men south through 'Castignano, Torre, Popoli, Pratalo, Scanno, Alfedena', which amounted to a staggering 500-kilometre round trip. As McGregor noted, there were 'many more POWs roaming about'. En route they'd rounded up some three hundred, which they'd dispatched via this overland means, 'many of whom I believe to have got through', as McGregor would report.

Incredibly, his small patrol had still not been rumbled by the enemy, but all of that was about to change. Returning to their base near the hilltop town of Penne, to the south of Castignano, McGregor learned that 200 SS troops were in-bound, with the aim of rounding up those POWs hiding in the hills. It was becoming ever more challenging to move the escapees, for the winter weather was starting to bite. Some had thrown caution to the wind, 'enjoying themselves in local villages and taking no precautions against recapture'. They would prove easy prey for those SS troops, unless McGregor and his men could somehow intervene. Typically, the SAS lieutenant decided to 'create a diversion' to 'bring the attention of the . . . enemy upon ourselves'.

Of course, their A Force operational orders precluded any offensive action. McGregor and his men were there to rescue POWs. But in this instance McGregor felt that he could legitimately disobey his orders, for the action being contemplated was all to do with their POW-rescue remit. They would be acting as the bait in the trap, to prevent others far less capable of defending themselves from falling prey to the enemy. Of course, it would be ten SAS against two hundred SS, but regardless, McGregor rather fancied their chances.

Preparing to break cover in spectacular fashion, he sought a DIY SAS jeep, so as to launch hit-and-run attacks here in the Italian mountains. Having got hold of a *Fucile Mitragliatore Breda Modello 30*, an Italian light machine gun also known as the 'Breda 30' or the 'Alpine scythe', and a small Italian truck that they had 'commandeered off a local Fascist', they bolted the machine gun to it and set to work. But as the truck promptly broke down, McGregor figured they would resort to the simplest of ambush tactics – small groups, concealed in the thick roadside vegetation, mounting a blistering attack, before melting away on foot.

Accordingly, he split his patrol into two groups of four. One was led by McGregor, the other by his second in command, Sergeant Peter 'Pat' Mitchell, a Scot and another of his stalwarts.

Mitchell's interests in life, 'apart from fighting, were wine, women and song'. He was blessed with a wicked sense of humour, and had 'one of those smiles that both men and women found irresistible and in his voice there was a note of childish delight that made it impossible to dislike anything that he did or said'. But there was also a flip side to Mitchell: 'in a split second he could transfer himself from comic to a hardened killer.' After he had done his killing, Mitchell was wont to remark, whimsically, 'Ah well, it was'na sae bad.'

To add to their firepower, McGregor agreed to take along one or two carabinieri, who had decided to come over to the Allied side and help the SAS. Their first attack was laid with infinite care, as McGregor placed his teams in carefully concealed points of hiding. The road into Penne twisted and turned as it snaked through craggy peaks, with here and there an ancient, ruined castle clinging to the heights. In places, a thick cloak of trees lined either side of the route. Perfect ambush territory.

McGregor was hoping to hit a truck or a small convoy. 'Just think what we could do,' he ventured, 'if we could capture a German truck and get a couple of German uniforms . . . we could then go where we liked and no one would know who we were.'

It was a wild and intoxicating proposition, but as luck would have it, their first target was somewhat different. A German staff car rounded a distant bend in the road. As McGregor and his men studied the target, they realised there was only the driver in the front, plus a passenger in the rear. But still, taking out a senior German officer was sorely tempting. McGregor gave the nod, and upon his opening fire the rest of the patrol let rip, a storm of rounds tearing into that gleaming vehicle. In seconds, the unsuspecting driver and his equally oblivious passenger were dead. 'The Germans would be one officer short,' Arnold noted of the hit, which was all in a good day's work.

Day after day they menaced the roads, causing carnage for any motorised unit that might be out hunting for the elusive Allied POWs. Then there came a day when not a thing seemed to be moving on the highways. Maybe the enemy had learned their lesson. It was late in the afternoon and McGregor felt the urge to relieve himself. Having glanced at his watch, he remarked to his men: 'We'll give it another fifteen minutes. If nothing comes then I think we will call it a day. But first I must go and do my daily dozen.'

McGregor disappeared behind a bush, and Arnold could hear him trying to struggle out of his overalls, which were a tad too tight. 'His language was something not to be repeated.' Just then, he sighted a distant vehicle. As he grabbed his binoculars, he could see an ambulance, plus an army truck behind. With the Allies having air superiority, the Germans had taken to disguising their military vehicles as Red Cross transports. As an A Force team would report, 'Red Cross insignia on almost all vehicles, either a flag or painted on, but am sure they carry ammunition and troops . . . A bandaged soldier would sit in the front, but . . . trucks have been loaded with ammunition. 25 out of 30 trucks in one group had Red Cross insignia.' As all figured, this convoy was fair game.

Arnold glanced in McGregor's direction. He was squatting down reading a page torn from his bible. He'd brought it with him 'for this very purpose', McGregor arguing that it 'would last for ever', as long as only one page was used at a time. Indeed, each man in his patrol got 'a page from the Boss's bible' whenever they needed to relieve themselves. It had the added advantage that 'at times of stress and strain' you had the ideal reading material to 'ease your mind'. Arnold yelled across the details of the convoy to McGregor. He cried back that they were to go to 'action stations'. While Arnold and some of the carabinieri would shoot-up the lead vehicle, so trapping the truck, the bulk of McGregor's men were to attack 'the remaining passengers with Thompson sub-machine gun fire'.

'Okay, what about you?' Arnold queried of McGregor.

'I'll be there in a minute,' he replied from where he was crouched behind his bush.

Arnold's opening shots triggered the ambush. He and his cohorts struck like ghosts from out of the wildlands, taking the enemy by total surprise. Within seconds a dozen sub-machine guns and one Breda 30 sparked among the shadows, as rounds tore through the soft-skinned vehicles and cut down those inside. The first to judder to a halt was the ambulance – 'opened up on them; shot the driver' – though in McGregor's official report he would add, in a rare effort at diplomacy, that it had been 'shot up (by mistake)'. As the din of battle reached a crescendo, and a smog of cordite fumes mixed with the smoke from burning vehicles choked the narrow road, the second vehicle ground to a halt, rearing up the roadside bank at a crazy angle.

It was then Arnold spied something that unnerved him. Behind those first two vehicles was another truck and then another. Just how many were there? One of the attackers hit the driver of the third vehicle in line, and he tumbled from his cab, while 'trying to grab the door handle'. Arnold 'fired from the hip and saw his body jerk with the impact of the bullets and then sink to the ground'. Weapons were 'chattering away and everything was getting confused'. Arnold hurled a grenade towards the rear of the convoy, to catch anyone trying to get away. 'It went off with a shattering roar.'

The passenger in another of the lead vehicles managed to get out, uninjured. Arnold fired at him but missed, and then his gun jammed. As the truck door slammed shut, the German trooper turned towards Arnold and tried to draw his pistol, but the catch on his holster seemed jammed. Moments later a Tommy gun spat fire and the figure was flung against the vehicle's door, 'his body smothered in blood as he sank down'. Turning to see who had shot him, Arnold realised that it was Nicolich. He was standing there in full view, seemingly mesmerised by what he had done.

'Nick,' Arnold yelled, 'get down, you bloody fool.'

It was the first enemy soldier that Nicolich had shot, and he'd emptied a whole magazine into the target 'at a range of about six feet'. By now bullets were ricocheting off the tarmac, as more and more enemy troops jumped down from the rear of the trucks and joined the fight. A group of them went after Sutton, but they were caught in a hail of fire from several of the hidden SAS gunners. Arnold shouted for Nicolich to give him cover, so he could dash across the road. Just as he broke into a run, he heard the chainsaw rasp of a Spandau – an MG 42 – opening up. This was not good news.

A storm of bullets tore into the trees at the roadside. As Arnold ducked down, he spied yet more trucks coming around the distant bend in the road. A grenade exploded under one of those vehicles, which burst into flames. From the remainder, a phalanx of 'well-armed troops' bailed out, and they began to 'return our fire in a big way'. With the enemy 'opening up on us', it was clear to all that they had bitten off far more than they could chew, yet McGregor was still nowhere to be seen.

Someone yelled: '*Let's go!*'

Moving as one the ambushers broke cover, running along the roadside hedge, and then across a field. Pausing to do a head count, there was still no sign of McGregor. Then they spied a distinctive figure dashing after the way they had come, but stopping every now and again to fire at what had to be hidden pursuers. Eventually, McGregor caught up with them and they all took cover behind a thick hedge.

'There was someone following me,' McGregor panted.

He and Arnold spied a German soldier creeping through the grass. 'Another bullet from the Boss and one from me at the same time and the German rolled over, presumably dead.'

McGregor got his men moving once more. They were harassed by fire, as those German troops who had survived the ambush gave chase. The SAS made a beeline for the cover of a deep river valley. It was cloaked in scrub and thick olive groves, so there was a good chance they'd not be seen. Dashing into its depths, McGregor shouted at the others to follow. They made the riverbank unscathed. 'We could still hear rifle shots but none of them were coming our way,' Arnold noted. 'It looked as if the Jerries had lost contact.'

Tumbling down the slope and following the course of that mountain stream, McGregor and his men hurried along its depths, slipping away as stealthily as they had come. Or so they thought. But as they went to exit the valley, 'bullets came from the other side of the river'. They spotted a German soldier wading in. Arnold and McGregor fired and he went down. But more and more troops were streaming down to the river now, and McGregor and his men started taking accurate fire. Scattering, they dashed off in pairs, zigzagging this way and that, and seeking the cover of brambles and nettles in which to slip away.

On the far side of the valley, all rendezvoused in woodland. No one knew for sure if they had shaken off their pursuers. Moments later, German troops crested the top of the rise and the chase was back on. On the run once more, Arnold and the others swore that 'after the war we would never go fox hunting again'. For what seemed an age they charged through woods, over fields and along hedgerows, before finally they found a small, winding road. A van was seen in the distance coming in their direction. Seizing the moment, McGregor stepped into the middle of the road with his pistol levelled, and his hand signalling the van to a halt.

McGregor's men joined him, all guns levelled at the hapless driver. Nicolich had a few hurried words with the man behind the wheel, and then all piled in, the van taking off 'in the opposite direction to where we thought the Germans were'. McGregor and Nicolich were in the cab, giving directions to the driver, while the rest rode in the back. After covering some 20 kilometres, McGregor figured that finally they had shaken off their pursuers. Later, they saw four ambulances rushing past, clearly heading for the site of the ambush.

McGregor smiled grimly. 'We didn't do so bad,' he growled.

'That same night we got back to our farm,' McGregor would report. The ruse with the van most likely had saved them. Shortly, they got an update from a doctor contact who worked in Penne's main hospital. Officially, 'German casualties were 6 dead and 7 wounded, unfortunately no officers.' Rumours were that as many as 24 enemy soldiers were dead and injured. A senior German commander had vowed to the doctor that the 'British para-troopers must be caught, dead or alive and at all costs. Also that a special party of soldiers had been formed and were being sent out with the sole purpose of catching them.' Civilians had been warned about hiding McGregor and his men, or withholding information on their whereabouts. 'The punishment for any of these things would be death.'

McGregor's intention in breaking cover had been twofold. One, to divert attention from the POW-escapees onto themselves. Two, to seize usable vehicles for their own purposes. They had been spectacularly successful in the first instance, but equally the reverse in the other. All the vehicles they'd ambushed had been left as bullet-riddled hulks. Equally, such intense action couldn't be sustained without fresh supplies of weaponry and ammo, but there was no radio to call in any drops. On the one hand, McGregor was ambivalent about the lack of comms. 'Need of a radio, but restricts movements,' he would report. On the other, with such a target-rich environment he observed: 'valuable air targets are wasted through lack of information channels.'

By now it was early December and 'as yet we had heard nothing of the Americans or what they were doing'. All presumed that the OSS team had 'got back through the lines'. For a mission scheduled to last two weeks, they were now long overdue. Their sense of the state of the Allied advance relied upon rumour and gossip. They believed their forces had been halted somewhere just beyond Termoli, and that the enemy 'were fighting for every yard of ground before falling back'. The Germans and their Fascist Italian allies were said to have built a defensive line along the banks of the Sangro river, some 70 kilometres to the north of Termoli.

Since there were those in the immediate vicinity who had deserted from the Italian Army, there were always odd weapons to scavenge. They had already seized a 'couple of German tommy guns [MP 40s], a Luger pistol and an Italian Berretta'. But what they really needed was a bulk resupply of all kinds of ammo and arms. Fortuitously, McGregor learned of a Carabinieri marshal – commander – with a vast armoury of weaponry, at the nearby town of Collecorvino. He figured that was fair game.

In recent days McGregor and his men had got their hands on an ancient grocery truck, which they'd expropriated from a local Fascist. That same man had also passed McGregor a list of all the prominent Fascists in the area, with dates of when they had joined the party and their home addresses. That was going to prove most useful. While visiting him, McGregor and his men had got to meet the family. The teenage daughters had taught themselves basic English by reading English novels. Captivated by McGregor's romantic, piratical air, they'd confessed to Arnold, 'your leader is so handsome, he looks like a real Diavolo.' As Arnold noted, 'I laughed at her, likening the Boss to the Devil.'

For now, McGregor loaded himself and his men into the grocer's truck and off they set for the Carabinieri barracks in Collecorvino. With Corporal William 'Litre' McQueen at the wheel, they planned to get the truck as close as possible to the target, in order to execute a quick getaway. A Scotsman hailing from Grangemouth, McQueen was the next best driver after McGregor, despite the fact that he wore glasses and in one of their recent actions 'had cracked one of the lenses', which was 'now held together with bits of sticky tape'. As Arnold observed, while he and Swill Sutton did drive, they were both 'cavalry men' and so were 'better at riding horses'.

The Carabinieri barracks was located on a tree-lined square. Having dumped the truck with McQueen at the wheel, the rest flitted through the dark streets towards their target. A carabiniere stood guard at the gate. McGregor split his force into two.

Moving with immense caution around the fringes of the square, half took up a position on one side of the gate and half on the other. When all were ready, Sutton threw an old tin can into the square, to the front of the sentry's position. Predictably, the man took a few steps forward to investigate the source of the mystery noise. Moments later, 'he felt the Boss's gun in his ribs on one side and Pat's knife on the other'.

With Sergeant Pat Mitchell's blade tickling his ribs, the sentry was 'walked a few yards from the gate', to where Nicolich was hiding. The carabiniere's dilemma was then explained to him. McGregor and his band of merry men were British raiders. If he wanted to live, they needed access to the barracks, no noise and no fuss. The guard appeared most biddable. 'Without any trouble he led us in.' Slipping into the barracks building, they discovered four more carabinieri fast asleep on mattresses laid out on the floor. McGregor slammed shut the door to wake them up – 'the look on their faces when they saw us was very funny.'

Again, Nicolich explained who the mystery raiders were and why they were here. By way of response, the captives roused themselves, shaking hands enthusiastically with their captors. One, a sergeant, pulled some keys from his pocket and handed them to McGregor. He told the SAS lieutenant that he and his men could take 'whatever they wanted' from the arms store, but that when they were ready to depart would they please 'tie them up and fire a couple of shots into the ceiling', just for good measure. While McGregor and his cohorts were raiding the weapons store, the carabinieri would be making them some coffee.

McGregor and his men proceeded to take around a hundred weapons, including shotguns, rifles and pistols, plus ammo.

Arnold slipped out of the barracks to fetch McQueen with the grocer's truck. The pilfered arsenal was loaded aboard. Then they 'tied and gagged' the carabinieri, and proceeded to lock them in their own cell. The raiders drove away with their 'loot', feeling 'rather pleased with the night's work'. After a few minutes on the road, McGregor pulled his hand from his pocket to reveal the Carabinieri sergeant's bunch of keys. 'Oh, look, I forgot to give them back their keys.'

They drove directly to what they reckoned was the ideal place to hide their arsenal. In a tiny village some way up the nearest mountain there lay an ancient church. They'd already made contact with the priest, a diehard anti-Fascist. Towards the far end of the village there was a German military vehicle repair depot, but it would be closed and deserted at this time of night. In the church grounds lay an iron grating, which led in turn to a disused sewer. The priest had explained that in times past it had been used to hide those who were being sought by 'some cruel overlord'. It was dry and secure and the priest had given them the key. Having backed the truck into position, 'we got all our loot into the sewer,' Arnold recalled, 'and got out of the grounds and the village.'

Keeping the best for themselves, they 'distributed the guns to various farmers who seemed anxious to turn into guerrillas', McGregor reported. Once he and his men had trained them properly, the plan was for 'all to go up north and do some work against the Germans'. Unfortunately, as McGregor was to learn, a gang of 'British POWs' stole some of the weapons, proceeding to sell them to the highest bidder. McGregor was furious. He launched a secondary hunt now – for the pack of POW-escapees hiding in their midst, who were acting as common bandits or almost as agents of the enemy. In the process, he was to learn of an even deeper level of treachery.

Repeatedly, McGregor and his men had heard rumours of an escaped POW named Bailey, thought to be from the Lancashire Regiment, who was ferried around the hills by a tall, blond German. Accompanied by a small white terrier, Bailey was linking up with other escapees and then informing on them. Presumably he was also cashing in on the 10,000-lire-a-scalp reward for doing so. From one POW-escapee they learned at first hand of the duo's real identity. That escapee was an RAF gunner who'd been shot down over Italy. As with so many, he'd escaped from his POW camp when the Armistice was announced. Making his way across country, he'd fallen in with what seemed like two fellow escapees.

One was the northern lad, Bailey, who 'never stopped talking'. The other was the tall blond individual who 'very rarely spoke at all'. Whenever he did it was in a foreign accent. The RAF man had asked Bailey what was the score with his friend. He was a deserter from the French Foreign Legion, Bailey had explained. But a while later the two of them had turned on the RAF man, taking him captive. Bailey had crowed about how he was an Englishman by birth, but had changed his nationality to German, having been captured. His tall blond pal was a German officer whose 'job was to catch escaped POWs'. Under threat of being shot, the RAF man was placed in a local prison, but he had managed to escape. He described Bailey as having two front teeth missing, a Union Jack tattoo on his left forearm, and a head 'indoctrinated with Nazism'.

While McGregor and his men were well armed once more, after their Carabinieri brigandage, he was starting to learn the same lesson as had OSS Lieutenant Sauro: here in Italy, it was impossible to know who you could trust.

By now, just shy of a thousand POWs had been sent to the coastal rendezvous point by Sauro and McGregor's teams. All of those escapees were relying upon Simonds's rescue fleet, and those SAS manning it, to pluck them to safety.

But sadly, they had sailed into a whole world of trouble.

Chapter 15

THE PIRATE FLEET

The day after the A Force schooner *San Vito* had been sunk at Termoli, Simonds had led a fleet of six caiques north, into the coming storm. His aim was to land SAS 'beach parties' at strategic points between Termoli and Ravenna, 420 kilometres further up the coast. He'd given his teams 'strict instructions to undertake no offensive action; to see, and not to be seen, and to collect, hide, and feed any POWs . . . and to tell us when to fetch the POWs by boat'.

Driven to fight the enemy, it was doubtful whether 'Killer' Couraud, the commander of the French Squadron, particularly gave a damn about such orders. Recognising his pugnacious nature, Simonds had given him and his 'wild' French Squadron the toughest assignment of all. Couraud, de Sablet and their men were to take the first point of landfall, that which lay closest to Termoli and the German positions. It was viewed by Simonds as being 'more dangerous than the others, being very close to the frontlines'.

In fact, even as the A Force fleet had set sail, the battle for Termoli was raging. Roy Farran and his 2 SAS contingent were holding vital terrain, where the coastal rail line ran into the northern outskirts of the town. Deployed beside the rail tracks, with a massive – and highly combustible – oil tank directly behind them, they'd proceeded to hose down any enemy who tried to rush their positions. With the men of 1 SAS and the commandos also holding the line, the fighting proved intense and often at close quarters. In desperation, the SAS had discovered a locomotive and tender packed full of explosives, parked up at the station just to the rear of Farran's position. If all seemed lost, they planned to steam it up the tracks and detonate it in the face of the enemy. Operation Loco II.

Operation Loco III was arguably the caique fleet's present mission. Slipping through the minefields that had supposedly been mapped by the former Polish ambassador, Couraud's vessel turned north, its blunt wooden prow sawing into the midnight dark. Simonds himself was riding in the craft. As he urged the skipper to coax more power from the ancient diesel engine, it sent up 'showers of sparks' from its rusty exhaust high into the night. It seemed impossible that they wouldn't be spotted from the land, especially since every turn of the screw took them closer to the German positions. But somehow, unbelievably, they slipped past unmolested. In fact, their worst adversary wouldn't prove to be the enemy. It would be mother nature herself.

After a day at sea, Simonds signalled to a second ship of the A Force fleet. In mid-ocean, the two caiques converged. Sailing in broad daylight like this seemed to be tempting fate; the open ships felt horribly exposed. Frustratingly, Simonds had been provided with intelligence that lots of small craft were out fishing in these seas. But there was no sign of any at all. The hope that they might 'hide' their fleet among those genuine fishing vessels would prove entirely unfounded. In fact, the Germans had issued warnings that any unidentified craft found at sea would be assumed to be those of the enemy. Few Italian fishermen were about to brave such threats.

Simonds leapt across to the other caique, for he intended to steer it further north on A Force business. Crammed full of 2 SAS men, it was bound for a more distant rendezvous. Another figure leapt aboard the French Squadron's boat, taking Simonds's place. It was one of the OSS men, and he was there to serve as the French Squadron's interpreter. But shortly after the transfer had been made the weather took a turn for the worse. As a report from the time noted, 'It was very tough going with the storm and the rough waters.'

Inching ahead, the French Squadron's caique neared the area where it was supposed to make landfall – Acquabella Point, not far from the town of Ortona. At nightfall the skipper turned towards the darkened coastline, but a powerful storm broke from out of the heavens. The sea was whipped into giant waves, the howling wind driving the underpowered craft further and further away from the shoreline. For a moment Couraud wondered whether they should turn back. But all his men voted to disembark, rather than to attempt to remain on board amid such terrible seas.

Three small dinghies were launched, crammed full of Couraud's men. Gradually, they were 'lost in the night'. Their oars seemed useless, the small boats 'like corks on the stormy sea, sometimes in the depths of the waves, sometimes riding the foaming crest of a liquid mountain'. An extra powerful wave crashed into the dinghy commanded by Corporal Pinchon, one of Couraud's deputies. It flipped it over like a scrap of driftwood. With typical Legion discipline, each man had his lifejacket on and was clipped to the rope that ran around the gunwale of the boat. But they'd lost their packs and some of their weaponry, and their boat was wallowing, turtle-like and useless.

Having tried repeatedly to right it, the exhausted men resigned themselves to their fate. Clinging to the upturned craft, they prayed that the current would prove favourable and drive them towards the shore. After what seemed like an age, the numb and weakened men felt their boots touch the bottom. Ahead, waves crashed into a steep, rocky shoreline. Moments later Corporal Pinchon and his team were able to haul themselves onto dry land. Pinchon himself had lost his boots. Two of his men had lost their weapons. All of their packs were gone. 'No matter!' Reunited with Couraud and the rest of the squadron, all of whom were soaked to the skin, the first priority was to set up a bivouac – a rough camp – to get themselves and what kit they had dry.

Even as they were busying themselves, everyone 'froze in their tracks'. A road and a railway line ran along the coastline. Suddenly, a locomotive had come snorting out of the night. The carriages proved to be crammed full of German troops. All were 'greatly relieved' when it steamed past, with the enemy apparently oblivious to their presence. Couraud tried to establish just where they'd made landfall. It seemed that they'd come ashore seven miles to the south of their intended point of arrival, putting them that much closer to the enemy's lines. As he and his men were starting to realise, such seaborne operations launched from small, cumbersome craft, onto a night-dark coastline heavily populated by the enemy, were going to prove tough enough. How would they fare when trying to evacuate hundreds of POW-escapees?

Bearing in mind their proximity to the enemy, Couraud had

been allocated the greatest number of A Force operators. In addition to his French Squadron, he'd been given Captain Simon Baillie and six of his men. Baillie was the thirty-three-year-old Scot who'd executed the daredevil foray by train to Potenza, returning with the two wounded American pilots plus much useful intelligence. He and his team had been allocated the unenviable task of serving as the 'Beach Party' – those charged to form the coastal rendezvous point, where all escapees were to gather. Couraud and his French Squadron were to act as a 'Protection Party', throwing out a cordon around Baillie's position, with the aim of deterring the enemy. That at least was the plan.

Having dried themselves as best as they could, the two parties set out. Baillie led his team north up the coast, heading for their intended place of landfall, which lay to the south of the city of Pescara. At the place where the Foro river disgorged into the sea he was to establish his base. That was the rendezvous point towards which McGregor and Sauro would steer their hundreds of escapees, and where Simonds would direct his pick-up fleet, should he secure suitable vessels. Thankfully, bearing in mind the task before him, Baillie had some highly motivated men under his command. One, as Baillie noted, was 'a Polish soldier rescued from an internment camp . . . hereafter called Joseph'. This was Josef Lyczak, the former legionnaire who been rescued from Pisticci.

As Baillie's party flitted north along the coast, so Couraud and the main force headed inland. In his strikingly brief official report on the mission, Couraud noted how they were 'to get in touch with Escaped POWs . . . to organise and guide them to Francavilla Beach', the stretch of open coastline adjacent to the mouth of the Foro. Typically, there is no mention in that report of what actually transpired, which was Couraud's first episode of blatantly disobeying orders. But frankly, a leopard rarely changes it spots. As the citation for the high-valour medal that he would be awarded noted, Couraud tended to deliver: 'This officer, in all previous missions as well, has been an inspiration to the men under his command.'

Couraud's citation would be written up by none other than Bill Stirling. It takes up the story. Moving inland, Couraud's patrol ran into an enemy convoy. Unable to resist the temptation, he set a snap ambush. In the ensuing melee, he and his French Squadron shot up one of the trucks, 'killing 5 Germans and wounding another'. With their area being thick with enemy troops, the blowback was swift in coming. For days on end, Couraud and his men were hounded through the hills, being 'hunted by German patrols', while at every juncture they were also collecting scattered POW-escapees. Remembering his A Force mission, Couraud began to filter them east, towards Baillie's beachside location, leaving two relay stations manned by his men to guide the escapees on their way.

But Couraud didn't much appreciate being the mouse in the trap. His instinct was to strike back. Before long he was to alight upon what seemed like the ideal means to do so. As they climbed higher into the mountainous terrain, more escapees rallied to their cause. Collecting fifty in one fell swoop, all were dispatched eastwards, joining the French Squadron's escape line. Yet Couraud hungered for more; for a mission more 'worthy of his ambitions'. Just like McGregor and Sauro had discovered, he was finding POW rescue work to be a costly business. Funds could last for only so long. As one A Force operator would note, 'I was forced to sell my watch, ring, pen and pencil to obtain money for POWs . . . This was in addition to the original money given me.'

Reaching the village of Cugnoli, some 30 kilometres to the south of McGregor's base of operations, Couraud began to question the locals as to the German positions and strengths in the area. Interestingly, he learned that at a nearby enemy headquarters they held the payroll for bankrolling all of their troops. It clearly required significant funds to pay their garrisons. To Couraud's way of thinking, there would be something very fitting about robbing the German military's treasury, to fund the escape of the very people so many of their troops were there to hunt down. But having left Baillie at the beach, and having positioned several relay teams in between, his patrol was spread out, his own forces 'extremely thin' on the ground.

Couraud had recently received a boost, in that two further patrol members had caught up with him. One was Lucien Cieslak, the Polish legionnaire who had been on the Pisticci concentration camp raid. During the long months that Cieslak had spent in North Africa he'd contracted malaria, which was rife in the 2 SAS training camp. He'd suffered a relapse of this debilitating and potentially fatal disease and been left behind, knowing from experience that it would spell 'at least four days of alternate shivering and sweats'. Once Cieslak had recovered, he'd teamed up with a Corporal Felix, another French Squadron stalwart, to sally forth and rejoin their unit.

The chief problem was that the caique allocated to them proved to be 'leaking like mad'. With all the bilge pumps 'operating overtime', they crept up the coast 'in a night that had no moon'. Spying what they figured had to be Captain Baillie's signal light, 'set in the bay that his unit had marked as the rendezvous point', they put ashore. Only, that point of illumination turned out to be no signal light. As Cieslak and Felix crept closer, it resolved itself to be the window of a 'mansion house' surrounded by sweeping lawns. Peering inside, they could barely believe their eyes: the room was full of 'German officers, laughing and talking around a table loaded with food and drink'.

Giving the place a wide berth, the two men decided to head inland, to try to link up with their main force. It was so dark they were forced to use a road. A while later they heard the grinding of gears, as what sounded like a truck convoy approached. Diving into a ditch, they took cover. The lead trucks streamed past, but then there came the squealing of brakes. One stopped. Boots thumped down onto the tarmac. There was the chatter of voices in German, and the distinctive smell of cigarette smoke. Two of the soldiers came to stand on the lip of the ditch where the SAS men were hiding. The seconds dragged by. A glowing cigarette butt was flicked away. It landed on Cieslak's hand. Biting back a cry of pain, he felt as if he had been 'bitten by some kind of snake'.

Eventually, the truck moved on. After days dodging enemy patrols, Cieslak and Felix finally made it to Couraud's position. But even with their arrival, Couraud and de Sablet boasted no more than a dozen fighters to hand. Attacking the German treasury called for a far more substantial force. Learning that McGregor's party was not far away, Couraud reached out. For his part, the combative McGregor was surprised to discover that Couraud was operating in an area that he had believed to 'be his own'. Brushing aside McGregor's discomfiture, and seemingly unaware of how sparks might fly, Couraud immediately launched into a hard sell for his bank raid mission. While McGregor conceded that it was a tempting target, he pointed out that this really wasn't an A Force task.

Couraud tried to argue otherwise. They needed funds to bankroll their A Force activities. They had no way to call any in. The German treasury was the answer. McGregor, unswayed, refused to get involved. Couraud's fiery temper sparked. He began to question McGregor's willingness to fight. His martial prowess. His courage even. McGregor countered icily that his record spoke for itself. Quickly, the scene turned ugly, McGregor's team facing off against the French Squadron, as a fight threatened to break out. The two SAS officers went their separate ways with little love lost between them. Once again, they were learning how hard it was to trust anyone on such missions here in Italy, even those on their side.

Undeterred, Couraud cast about for an alternative target. If they couldn't rob the German treasury, maybe they could cut the head off the Nazi snake. He tasked Cieslak with his new mission. The cinema in the nearby town was known to be patronised by German officers. Couraud decided that Cieslak was going to the pictures. With his blond tresses treated with a black hair-dye, and his face suitably darkened, he was dispatched to the movie theatre laden down with timed explosives. Dressed as an Italian, Cieslak was to pose as a local. His disguise was aided by the fact that he spoke half-decent Italian.

Thus disguised, Cieslak set forth for his 'explosive night out!' He reached the cinema to find that it was packed. But for every German soldier there was also a local, and most were young Italian women enjoying a night out with their foreign paramours. For half an hour Cieslak sat there, watching a Western. Then he got up quietly and left. Like most of his SAS brethren, he 'revelled in a gunfight', but he baulked at the 'slaughter of defenceless civilians'.

Seeing his early exit from the theatre, the Italian manning the pay booth asked, 'You don't like cowboy pictures?'

Cieslak shook his head. 'Too much gunfire,' he replied, before slipping away.

Despite their falling out, Couraud and McGregor were inextricably linked, of course. Couraud and his relay chain formed the escape line by which McGregor's POWs were being channelled to the coast. They had to work together. There was no other option, if A Force was to deliver on a mission decreed by Churchill himself. In due course McGregor sent Couraud a special parcel of POWs. It consisted of five men, four of whom were 1 SAS fighters, and all of whom had only recently been captured. One, Sergeant John Scott, had taken part in Operation Hawthorn, a daring SAS mission to raid airfields across the Italian island of Sardinia. Having laced their target aircraft with explosives, Scott and his comrades had been betrayed, hunted and taken prisoner by the enemy.

Incarcerated in PG 59, near the village of Servigliano, come the Italian Armistice the bulk of the prisoners had attempted to break out. But the senior British officer, Captain Derek-Miller, had other ideas. Ordering the camp's 400 POWs to standfast, all were threatened with court martial if they tried to escape. Regardless, and despite being 'fired upon by the Italian guards', Scott and many others got away. Altogether, 18 SAS escaped from that camp, the majority of whom had been captured during the intense fighting in and around Termoli. In doing so Scott, who hailed from Aberdeen, teamed up with Troopers McMillan and Johnston, and together the three SAS men had 'kept to the hills as much as possible and away from towns and villages'.

Several days after breaking out they'd linked up with 'Lt. McGregor of the 2nd SAS', and McGregor in turn had passed them on to Couraud. With these new additions to his charges, Couraud was now in the business of saving their own. SAS were rescuing SAS. It was high time to head for the coast, to get the seaborne pick-ups under way. Couraud, de Sablet and their force retraced their route through the hills, making for the rendezvous with Captain Baillie. One of the first of Simonds's A Force vessels was expected imminently, to spirit the POW-escapees to safety.

Upon arrival at Francavilla beach, Couraud discovered there were hundreds of hopefuls awaiting rescue by sea. Captain Baillie had his hands more than full. Thankfully, an A Force ship was expected that very evening. As soon as it was dark Baillie headed for the beach and began signalling out to sea. Repeatedly, he flashed the pre-arranged codeword. Unfortunately, no Allied boat materialised from the darkened seas. The following night he and Couraud did a repeat performance. That was the agreed procedure, should a vessel fail to turn up. Repeat the schedule for several nights, in case it had been delayed.

Two hours before midnight, and as Bailie and Couraud readied themselves to head for the beach, an escapee joined them. On his own initiative he'd gone down to the sea and had spied a boat lying offshore. It was flashing its signal light landwards. Mustering all as quickly as they could, Baillie got the POWs arranged into batches of thirty. They were to wait under cover on the western side of the coastal road and railway. That way, if there was any trouble on the beach, they should be able to 'scatter and escape'. That sorted, Baillie and Couraud, together with most of their men, headed down to the sea.

Sure enough, the throb of a motorboat's engines echoed across the dark waters. It sounded like one of the Italian MAS boats; those fast torpedo-armed vessels that had been loaned to Simonds. Couraud and Baillie could see it now. A squat, angular form lying about 200 yards offshore. It had to be an A Force ship, especially since they'd been briefed that there were 'no German surface vessels on this coast'. But oddly, they also spied an answering flash of light, from the patch of beach that lay directly opposite the mystery vessel. Baillie figured it had to be an A Force party that had risked coming ashore: 'our people were determined to contact us as it was the boat night,' he reasoned, 'and had thrown all caution to the wind.'

Couraud counselled caution. His instinct told him that something was amiss, and he 'decided to investigate'. Taking two of his most trusted men, he slipped along the expanse of open sand. There was zero cover, and the mysterious boat and light lay some 400 yards away. Accustomed to the darkness, and moving like wraiths, the trio flitted towards whatever lay ahead. As they neared the mystery source of light, they could make out a smaller motorboat that had been pulled into shore. German voices floated across to them on the still night air. Wasting no time, Couraud opened fire. There were three figures in the beached boat, all of whom were cut down.

A 'brief but intense firefight broke out'. Further up the beach there were more enemy soldiers. Couraud and his men were heavily outnumbered, but they owned the night and they had their 'fingers on the trigger'. A grenade was thrown by the enemy. It fell short. A searchlight pierced the gloom, as those manning the larger vessel tried to ascertain just what on earth was happening ashore. After ten seconds of the light sweeping this way and that, powerful engines roared into life and the E-boat – for that was what it was; a well-armed German *Schnellboot* – raced away, heading for the open sea.

As Couraud and Baillie now realised, Francavilla beach was 'burned'. Another embarkation point would need to be sought. More to the point, the hundreds of escapees that they'd mustered must have overheard the gunshots and grenade blasts. The two men hurried back to where they'd left them. Some groups had already scattered. Rounding up as many as they could, Couraud and Baillie gave it to them straight. Francavilla was a no-go. No A Force vessel had materialised. They should head into the nearest hills, while the SAS would guard their rear and shield them from the enemy. It was hugely frustrating, but they hoped there was still everything to play for.

While Couraud and Baillie were so occupied, de Sablet returned to the scene of the beachside firefight. It was shortly before midnight by the time he began his follow-up reconnaissance. A challenge in German rang out in the darkness. A second firefight broke out. De Sablet and his party cut down one of the enemy with their Tommy guns, while one of his men suffered a graze to his right arm. 'The wound was slight and soon healed up.' That might be so, but there was no fixing Francavilla beach. It was off-limits from now on.

Couraud and Baillie dispatched teams to the north and south, searching for an alternative evacuation point. They discovered a beach some 20 kilometres beyond Pescara, near the tiny coastal settlement of Silvi. It seemed ideal for their purposes. There was also a large fleet of fishing boats moored near by, each of a similar size and capabilities to their own elusive caique fleet. If A Force would not come to them, they would take the escapees to A Force, Couraud reasoned. But the Italian fishermen appeared to be petrified by the enemy, who had declared that any such boats found at sea would be blasted out of the water.

De Sablet had discovered Silvi beach. It fell to Couraud to try to ensure the Italian seafolk would be spurred to help. Kidnapping the son of one of the local fishermen, Couraud proceeded to use him as a bargaining chip. If he released the boy, Couraud declared, would the father agree to put his boat to sea? It was a callous, gangster-like tactic to resort to, but what else was he supposed to do? He had been ordered to get the POW-escapees home. Hundreds had been collected, more were coming, but without a rescue fleet he had no means of accomplishing his mission.

Which begged the question, what on earth had happened to Simonds's fleet?

Why had it so spectacularly failed them?

Chapter 16

PARTY ON THE BEACH

At Simonds's Termoli headquarters there was utter consternation. Under his own steam a POW-escapee had got through the lines. Received by Simonds, that man, Captain Balfour, originally of the Scots Guards, had a shocking story to tell. A prisoner at the notorious POW camp at Chieti, he'd been a member of the escape committee. Prior to the Armistice being announced, the camp's senior British officer had presented him with orders received from MI9 in London. Sent in code to the hidden wireless set secreted in the camp, they stated that 'upon the Armistice happening, no one was to try to escape, and that arrangements were being made by the 8th Army to collect them'.

As would so often prove the case, at Chieti the standfast order had been obeyed to the letter. By most, but not all. A good number of refuseniks had decided not to comply. Captain Balfour was one. He'd hidden among the rafters of one of the huts, lying there for two days and so evading detection by the enemy. Meanwhile, all those POWs who had obeyed the order had been rounded up and transported to Germany by rail. Upon hearing Balfour's story, Simonds was 'astonished and furious'. On two counts. One that such a 'colossal blunder' as the standfast order could have occurred in the first place. Two, that no one had seen fit to warn *him*, the man charged with rescuing Allied POWs trapped behind the lines.

Simonds could not believe that he had been kept in the dark. He had orders from Churchill, passed on to him by General Eisenhower and his British counterpart, General Alexander, that 'everything possible should be done to rescue the Allied POWs'. His A Force mission was a direct result of that. Yet here he was, immersed in the thick of it all, and no one had seen fit to tell him about the abomination that was the standfast order. As no one knew better than Simonds, in all escape and evasion training, soldiers were briefed that if 'captured by the enemy it is their primary duty to escape and to regain the nearest Allied lines'. How could MI9 itself, the so-called escape specialists, have issued an order that ran contrary to that fundamental principle? In short, as Simonds fully appreciated, this 'most costly' mistake 'complicated my problems beyond belief'.

Deane-Drummond concurred. Echoing Simonds's words, he would describe the standfast order as an 'incredible blunder'. As all in A Force fully appreciated, it had 'sentenced a great number of officers and men . . . to an additional eighteen months of hell'. But if anything, the realisation quickened their collective spirit. Those who had disobeyed such an iniquitous order deserved so much better. Those who had risked being shot by their own side, or facing court martial, warranted the very best rescue mission that the Allies could muster. But right then, both Simonds and Deane-Drummond knew that they were failing.

The problem was boats – not enough of them and not the right sort. Only one course of action lay open to Simonds, as far as he could determine. He would go in person to 8th Army headquarters and put his demands to General Alexander himself. In the wake of the A Force teams having sailed north in their fleet of caiques, Simonds set out south in a lone jeep, with one man riding shotgun. Some of the places along the route were still held by the enemy. That much he knew. But right at this juncture he'd thrown caution to the wind.

Driving into the teeth of a bitter October gale, he headed into the city of Foggia, 90 kilometres south of Termoli. Simonds barrelled right through. At times he was under fire from his own side, for Foggia was being shelled by British forces. At other times he found himself neck and neck with 'a German Staff car full of German Officers'. As both parties were intent of getting out of this alive, they 'paid little attention to each other'. With his SAS driver, Simonds pressed on, leaving war-torn Foggia behind. The rain pelted down. The jeep had neither windscreen nor hood. There was a machine gun mounted in front, and one in the rear. And no means to shelter.

It was dark when they reached Bari, site of Allied Headquarters in Italy. Still the rain kept pouring down. Simonds was 'tired and wet' – a masterful understatement, if ever there was one. They'd just completed a 200-kilometre drive non-stop, dodging the enemy, not to mention fire from their own side, and in atrocious conditions. Not knowing his way, Simonds spied a hunched figure beside the road. He was wandering along dressed in a mackintosh, and seemed almost as soaking-wet as those riding in the jeep. Simonds signalled his vehicle to a halt and leaned out.

'Hey, you!' he cried. 'Where the bloody hell is Alex's headquarters?' 'Alex' was short for Alexander – General Harold Alexander, the highly respected commander-in-chief of 15th Army Group. The man who'd signed off on Simonds's letter of authority, which supposedly meant he would enjoy all possible assistance from the military powers.

'I'm going there myself,' the figure answered, mildly.

'Hop in and show me the bloody way,' Simonds fired back.

Obligingly, the stranger climbed aboard. When they reached the General Headquarters building, he pointed Simonds in the direction of the commander-in-chief's quarters.

'You must be very wet and tired, Colonel Simonds,' the figure then remarked. 'Come in and have dinner – I'm Alex!'

Simonds did as he was told, wasting no time in explaining exactly why he'd come. He badly needed 'high octane fuel, rations, bedding', and a whole list of other kit besides. But above all, he needed 'two LCIs, to evacuate from our beachheads the large number of escaped POWs'. After this personal intervention, he got those ships in short order. General Alexander could not have been more understanding or supportive. But from some of his underlings, Simonds was starting to get a clearer sense of the lie of the land. He was an embarrassment. A Force was deeply inconvenient, because its very existence was a reminder of the colossal blunder that was the standfast order, which had emanated from the highest levels in London. In fact, the entirety of his A Force operations 'were an embarrassment', Simonds realised, 'in view of the MI9 War Office instructions'. By his stubborn persistence, Simonds was preventing them all from brushing it under the carpet. Indeed, Simonds was the very worst kind of embarrassment, the sort that stubbornly refused to go away. So be it. He wasn't going anywhere but back to Termoli . . . once more unto the breach, once more.

Arriving back at his harbourside headquarters, Simonds studied his team. He'd asked Alex for more staff. They were in dire need. So far, those that he had managed to cobble together were a fine bunch. A truly eclectic lot, he asked each what they had been doing before the war. Gradually, he realised that apart from himself, only three others were regular army. His SAS recruits included a leading amateur jockey who had won the Grand National, a fashion artist who had been working for the *Daily Express*, a Twining's tea taster and a soldier of fortune, plus there were the former Polish ambassador, an Eton-educated Italian Prince and a mysterious Harvard don.

It was Captain Robert Champion, one of his SAS officers, who was the talented fashion artist by trade. As Simonds noted, 'Whenever he was not on operations, he had a daily task of drawing pretty girls, clothed or unclothed, with which I decorated my "Office".' Over the past few days they had certainly needed something to boost their spirits. Champion's sketches had fitted the bill. But now Simonds had news to truly lift their morale. They had got their ships. Thanks to Simonds meeting with General Alexander, they were about to sail north in their newly acquired fleet of LCIs, in an effort to bring the first of the POW-escapees home.

It was 6 October when the fleet of LCIs prepared to hit the trail. Termoli was still under siege, though the German stranglehold was shortly to be broken. As shells whined down and dive-bombers swooped out of the skies, gouts of blasted spray were thrown up by the explosions. Though the harbour was the focus of the attack, the three LCIs – Simonds had actually got *three* allocated to his force – weathered the storm. That evening they slipped their moorings and motored north into enemy territory.

The commander of Simonds's new fleet was Captain Charles Henry Duffett. He'd received his orders to join A Force only twenty-four hours earlier, arriving in Termoli just before midnight the same day. Then he'd met with Simonds, been apprised of his new mission, and together they had worked out a plan for how the new ships were to be best used. Due to the pressing urgency, all three of his LCIs would be heading into harm's way, targeting different areas along the coastline. Simonds himself would be at the vanguard, riding in one of the fast Italian MAS boats, making for the beaches around Pescara – Couraud and the French Squadron's territory.

Blessed with the superior speed of the new A Force fleet, the entire run north could be accomplished under cover of darkness. Arriving well in time and wallowing off the coast, Simonds spotted a recognition light flashing from the beach. He guided the MAS boat closer to shore. The last leg was accomplished via an inflatable dinghy, after which Simonds hit the beach 'to be greeted by the six foot figure of Sergeant Mitchell, in bedraggled clothing but with an immaculate salute'. Mitchell – part of McGregor's team – had personally brought a party of POW-escapees down to the coast to make sure they got away. But his mission had been plagued by bad luck and trouble.

'Beach party present and correct,' Mitchell, a former Scots Guardsman, barked. 'Thirty-four prisoners in fair order, sir.'

Simonds was aghast at the paucity of numbers. Thirty-four? Where were the hundreds that he had been expecting? Mitchell explained that he had corralled far more – well over a hundred – but they had faced a 'very hazardous trek, culminating in crossing the main coastal road, which was full of German transport'. A dog had kept barking, and a German sentry had ended up shooting it. That burst of gunfire had spooked his POW-escapees. Scores had bolted. No matter what measures the

SAS sergeant had tried, they could not be persuaded to recross that busy highway and 'hide up on the beach and wait to be evacuated'.

In a sense, the escapees were hardly to blame. That coastal road and railway lay only a couple of hundred metres inland, in some places far closer. The strip of open beach beyond appeared horribly cut-off and exposed, a seeming death trap. Hence the SAS sergeant's trials and tribulations in getting the POW-escapees to muster there. Simonds asked Mitchell what he might have seen and learned, as he'd waited for the pick-up boats to arrive. Any useful intelligence? The SAS sergeant drew himself up and saluted once more.

'Sir, my orders were not to be seen, to take no offensive action, to see nobody. So, I have seen nothing!'

While Simonds conceded that it was a 'wonderful example of peerless Guards discipline', he would have far preferred some usable intelligence, especially regarding that coastal highway. As the LCI was yet to arrive – it was far slower than the MAS boat – Simonds figured he might as well take a look himself. He had always believed a man was far safer 'in uniform, miles behind the enemy lines, than those brave men facing danger and discomfort on the frontline'. Taking that as his maxim, he made his way across the beach to the roadside. Before long a convoy of enemy vehicles emerged from the darkness. It consisted of trucks and armour, and all were heading south towards the frontline.

Making no effort to hide, Simonds took out his notebook and began to 'write down the details of the tanks, armoured cars and other vehicles passing on the road'. Standing there in full view and 'in British battle dress', his only 'disguise' was that he had tucked his hat under his arm. No one challenged him, which was fortunate, for Simonds spoke very little German or Italian. All presumed that Simonds was one of their own, for who else would be standing there openly, noting down their passing? After about an hour he returned to the beach. The LCI was due. He signalled the vessel in. It eased towards the shore, but a crisis ensued. Around fifty yards out it struck a sandbank.

Using an improvised system of ropes and folbots – folding commando-style canoes – they managed to ferry all the waiting escapees onto the ship, under the noses of the enemy. Simonds sent the MAS boat on ahead, while he joined those who had boarded the LCI. Sitting in a cabin, about to start the first of his 'interrogations of the POWs', he told himself with a flood of relief, 'Thank God that's over, safe at last!' At that very instant a burst of rounds came tearing through the ship's side. Simonds had presumed that the LCIs were armoured. In fact, they were not, or if at all only lightly. In the nick of time Captain Duffett gunned the engines and got them out of there. What followed proved 'nerve-racking' – steaming south in strengthening daylight, during all of which time Simonds was 'anxiously scanning the sky for enemy aircraft, as we were sitting targets'.

They reached Termoli unscathed, apart from those bullet holes torn in the LCI's flank. 'Feed the POWs, re-clothe them, interrogate them, commandeer transport,' Simonds noted of his priorities, 'and send them back to 8th Army lines for reception.' At last, some of the first of the POW-escapees had been brought out by sea. It was a paltry number. Undaunted, Simonds urged all to redouble their efforts. From then on, 'escape and rescue work continued every night by sea'. Simonds was also sending A Force parties through the lines overland, and POW-escapees were returning via the same means. With the frontline fluid and shifting, it was proving porous and leaky, at least for now.

With his caique fleet also working overtime, Simonds now had some fourteen ships plying the seas, plus 150 SAS and mixed A Force agents operating deep behind the lines. There were also scores of POW interrogations to carry out daily. In addition, he had the all-important intelligence reports to send to headquarters, for the escapees were returning with the choicest snippets of information. Shortly after his first foray north with the MAS boat, Simonds was at it again. Again he searched the beaches around Pescara. Two nights in a row he was there, lying offshore, but not one signal lantern flashed from shore. When he returned for a third try, he spied 'a series of lights, some in a sort of recognition signal . . . faint but irregular'.

As Simonds well appreciated, any light shining out to sea tended to carry a very long distance. Even a match flame or a glowing cigarette might be visible, especially on a calm night such as this. They nosed closer in the MAS boat. The Italian crew feared a trap, but Simonds and Major Symes, his SAS opposite number, decided to investigate. They crammed themselves and what few men they could into a folbot and paddled silently to shore. The mysterious lights still flickered beguilingly. They rode a small wave the final yards to land. Simonds spied a group of shadowy figures higher up the beach.

'Who are you?' he cried.

'British,' came the faint reply.

'Identify yourself by whistling the British Grenadiers,' he instructed.

A feeble rendition of that classic British Army marching song echoed through the darkness. Simonds and Symes discovered a group of around fifteen POW-escapees, 'bedraggled ... and on the point of exhaustion'. In small groups they were ferried to the MAS boat, while Simonds and Symes 'guarded the beachhead'. Once all were aboard, Simonds got some 'hot cocoa into them'. They consisted of a mixed bunch of officers and men, six of whom were South Africans. Among the hundreds that McGregor and Couraud had rounded up, they'd scattered following the gunfight on Francavilla beach. While the SAS had 'fought hard to cover them', this little party had got separated.

Undeterred, they kept at it. Though going without food or water for several days, they'd 'had the guts to stand on that beach at night for two nights running, making their faint recognition signals with a candle and a box of matches'. As Simonds noted, it proved 'a very emotional rescue'. Moments like these made it all worthwhile. En route back to Termoli, and with the MAS boat cutting through the midnight calm, the ship's commander, an Italian lieutenant, made a telling remark to Simonds. 'You know, it's funny, this war. Three weeks ago I helped sink a British ship near here. Now I am fighting for you!'

In the shifting allegiances of this conflict, it was difficult to know who one could trust. But as Simonds saw it, those MAS crews were doing their best under trying circumstances. Even so, it felt odd giving orders to Italian officers who just weeks earlier had been their sworn enemies. Yet even for Simonds, orders were a somewhat fluid concept. Of course, he'd given strict instructions to his A Force teams: 'no offensive action'. Yet he didn't for one moment expect all to abide by such strictures. For Simonds, it was more about emphasising their POW-rescue remit. To keep that foremost in their minds.

As Simonds himself was to demonstrate, sometimes the

temptation for action and intrigue was just too much to resist. He'd managed to recruit into A Force a very interesting individual. A tall, bespectacled American, and a somewhat scholarly-looking figure, Lieutenant Robert Lewis had wandered unannounced into Simonds's Termoli headquarters. Simonds had asked who he might be. 'I'm a Harvard don with a taste for hot jazz,' Lewis had replied. More importantly, he spoke fluent Italian and German, and was an officer serving with the OSS's MIS-X, their nearest equivalent to A Force. Sensing a kindred spirit, Simonds and Lewis had teamed up on several missions heading for enemy shores.

Some 220 kilometres north of Termoli lay the town of Civitanova. At a tiny bay to the south of there, A Force had established another rescue-rendezvous. Arriving in their MAS boat, Lewis and Simonds had paddled ashore in a folbot, seeking to check out that cove. Finding no POW-escapees, the pair were loath to return empty handed. Instead, they'd snuck into a nearby railway station. From the station master's office, Lewis had placed a call to the local German barracks. Raising the 'Commandant', he'd offered to sell him 'a case of Scotch and several cases of good beer'. Lewis was speaking fluent German, of course, and posing as a black marketeer.

In the course of their conversation – and their spirited bargaining – Lewis had discovered the present strength of the enemy garrison. The German officer had eight soldiers under his command. They agreed a meeting place to do the supposed whisky and beer deal: a hidden spot at the edge of the barracks. 'Both sides kept the rendezvous,' as Simonds noted. But rather than getting the 'delivery of booze' the German commander was hoping for, he was pounced on. Taken prisoner at gunpoint, Simonds and Lewis 'brought him back to Termoli by boat'. Of course, such offensive action ran contrary to his own orders. It was decidedly 'naughty', as Simonds confessed, and far from being correct A Force procedures. 'But great fun.'

Fun it might have been, yet fun didn't bring the prisoners home. Practically every night over the month of October 1943 the A Force fleet ran the gauntlet, nosing into darkened shores seeking escapees. During this time, Simonds's most trusted deputy became the man who was supposedly banned from deploying behind the lines – Anthony Deane-Drummond. Nearly every night he was seabound in 'one or other of our strange assortment of craft'. During one episode he'd been riding in a MAS boat, loitering just offshore, when a German vehicle convoy had appeared 'moving south on the main road'. The Italian skipper baulked. He started his engines and made as if to depart.

Deane-Drummond was having none of it. In his best Italian, he told the MAS boat commander that he would hold his station or die, and he drew his Colt .45 pistol to emphasise the point. 'He quickly changed his mind.' Bang on cue there was the flash of a signal light from shore. Keeping one hand on his gun and one eye on the ship's captain, Deane-Drummond dispatched some of his men to the beach, to extract the POWs. Their folbot could carry only two passengers at a time, but he made sure that 'the Italian Navy did not go into reverse' until every last escapee was loaded aboard.

The greatest focus of their efforts was in and around Couraud's territory – the beaches at Pescara. On one night, Deane-Drummond turned shoreward, riding in one of their LCIs, and 'expecting to take off three hundred prisoners'. They found just twenty-three. Gallingly, half an hour earlier a far greater number had been there. But they had 'panicked when a burst of German Schmeisser fire had been heard'. One of the escapees had cried out, 'It's a trap!' Most had bolted. In spite of the efforts of their SAS guardians, the rout could not be halted.

The desperate escapees were forced to run 'back to the farms and hills from where they had been collected'.

Chapter 17

A KING'S RANSOM

Deep in those hills, alarming news was reaching McGregor and his men. The beach-side rescue points appeared to be plagued by insecurities. Undeterred, he and his small team vowed to redouble their efforts. As October bled into November and the weather turned increasingly grim, the plight of the thousands of POW-escapees was worsening. For that reason alone, McGregor and his men felt driven to endure. If the seaborne route was proving so difficult, they would send more out overland. If their coffers were running dry, they would have to find the means to replenish them. If their guns were lacking ammo, they'd seize whatever they needed off the enemy. No matter what, McGregor and his force would not turn aside.

By now, and unbeknown to them, they had been listed as 'missing', fate unknown. The last contact McGregor or any of his men had had with friendly forces had been in October, when Captain Baillie had paid them a fleeting visit. His aim was to warn them that Francavilla beach was burned and unusable. That done, Baillie had returned to his troubled coastal sojourn. Since then, there had been no contact with either McGregor or any of his patrol. Conflicting reports had reached Simonds's headquarters. The first intimated that an officer called McGregor was operating somewhere in the Gran Sasso region, which was roughly where he was known to be based. But the next news was that 'seven parachutists had been found shot by Germans at the roadside in the Chieti area'. That, it was feared, was McGregor and his patrol.

In truth, the SAS lieutenant and his men were still very much at large. As winter bit deep, so too would their claws. The early November chill meant warm clothes were desperately needed for the hundreds of POW-escapees, many of whom 'had only rags to wear'. If they didn't get them, they would die. It was really that simple. McGregor decided that he and his men would have to provide, for unless clothes, food and shelter could be secured, there would be no one left alive to rescue. Desperate times called for desperate measures. McGregor's tactics would become brutally direct, and merciless in the extreme.

In the harsh winter conditions, frontline fighting had ground to a halt. It was obvious that Allied forces wouldn't get through to their area before the spring. Accordingly, McGregor called a 'Chinese parliament', a round table meeting in which all were free to voice their opinions. 'On all our jobs with him he always let everyone have his say,' Arnold noted. It proved hugely empowering. 'No leader could have had more confidence placed in him ... Each man's individual skill and initiative was essential to the safety and success of the whole stick, but the Boss was the directing personality.'

Once again, they considered making every effort to get back to their own lines. But even if they made it, with the stalemate in the fighting there would be precious little for them to do. Better to stay put and 'make ourselves useful in tormenting the enemy', they decided. What McGregor and his men were envisaging 'would not conform to the Geneva Convention', but 'the Germans and for that matter the Fascists had no respect for it, so why should we?' As McGregor put it, anything they did was 'for the benefit and to help the people of Italy to regain a normal life . . . there were still POWs about and it was our duty to try to get them installed in safe houses for the winter'.

Via the extensive local contacts that they'd built up, they had acquired lists of the most prominent 'rabid Fascists' in the region, those with the kind of deep pockets they were looking for. Those who deserved all that was coming to them. 'We were short of money and equipment and we wanted more clothes for the POWS to keep out the winter cold,' as Arnold noted, 'but money was the most urgent, as money talks, even when you are in enemy country. We needed it to give some to the POWs that we had in hiding in safe houses . . . and who better to get this from than our Fascist enemies.' It was time to start 'robbing the rich to feed the poor', in part 'the poor being our very selves'.

In order to pay those diehard Fascists flying visits, McGregor decided that he and his men really did need some usable wheels. Learning of a fabulous car that was in the vicinity, he reckoned this was to be their means of conveyance. Rumour had it that Italy's King Victor Emmanuel III had secreted one of his prized vehicles in the nearby village of Città Sant'Angelo. Hidden away by the king's chauffeur, it was intended to be kept safe until war's end. McGregor and his men paid a visit to the individual in question, and offered to buy whatever that elusive car might be. The chauffeur's response was to eye McGregor and his men 'as if we were a heap of rubbish', and to declare that 'the King's property was not for sale'. Not a smart move.

Shortly, the chauffeur was persuaded to take McGregor and his men to the secret hiding place. At nightfall they drove to a 'very lonely farm'. In one of the barns were hidden 'two beautiful Lagonda cars'. The pair of luxury vehicles – Lagonda was taken over by Aston Martins in 1947 – looked to be in pristine condition.

Having inspected them, McGregor pointed to the best, announcing, 'We'll have that one.'

The chauffeur practically had a heart attack. 'You cannot—'

'I am afraid that is the one we're going to have,' McGregor cut in.

'But Signor, that is the King's car. You cannot take it away. I have promised to look after it until the Tedeschi leave.'

'Well,' countered McGregor, 'I have a paper from the King of England which I will sign and give to you, and when you next see King Victor you can give it to him, and tell him that his car was put to good use helping to fight the Tedeschi and the Fascisti who were making his people so miserable.'

Taking a scrap of paper from his pocket, McGregor proceeded to write the following: 'I, Colonel J. Brown, do hereby confiscate this car, the property of King Victor, in the name of King George of England.' He handed the paper to Nicolich and asked him to read it out in Italian. Leaving the bemused chauffeur with that slip of paper, shortly McGregor and his men were loaded aboard the Lagonda. 'She was a beauty – there was enough room inside for all of us to be seated comfortably.' As a bonus, '300 gallons of petrol were also requisitioned,' reported McGregor.

They drove the vehicle to their present base, an isolated farm situated on top of a high hill. The road leading up to it was no more than a narrow, rutted cart track. 'No driver in his right senses would ever attempt to take a car up it,' which for the SAS made it the perfect hideaway. From there, 'they did some good work with that car'. At sundown, they'd drive thirty-odd kilometres away, so as to hide their tracks. Any German vehicles they came across were treated to a broadside, as McGregor and his men opened up with their weapons, before making a rapid getaway.

One night they ran into trouble, coming across 'our old friends the cavalry'. Up ahead there was a column of mounted troops some thirty strong, riding in pairs. McGregor was behind the Lagonda's wheel. He put his foot down hard, as Sergeant Mitchell leaned out of the passenger window brandishing their captured Breda light machine gun, 'like Gary Cooper in a Western'. Likewise, Arnold and Sutton had their Tommy guns thrust out of the windows. Once the cavalry commander realised the approaching vehicle was not about to stop, he ordered his men to divide the column in two, to allow the speeding car to pass through.

As the Lagonda thundered onwards all opened fire, and the results were 'terrible'. At the rear of the column some managed to dismount and prepared to return fire, but the onslaught from the Lagonda was just too fearsome. 'I think they thought more about staying alive than heroics,' Arnold observed. 'If they had hit any of our tyres we would have had the most awful crash and would have been sitting ducks, or for that matter if they had hit the Boss, who was driving. At the speed we were going we would not have had a chance in hell.'

Having got through the worst of it, McGregor put some miles behind them before stopping to assess the damage. There were a few dents in the Lagonda's bodywork and one or two bullet holes, 'but mechanically she had come through fine'. It was time to start visiting the Fascist bigwigs, on A Force business. Placing two of his men on the running boards – the horizontal side-steps, fixed below both front and rear doors – each with their Tommy guns to hand, plus four inside, McGregor set off a-hunting.

Mobile and heavily armed, he planned to visit carefully chosen targets in Elice, Picciano, Loretto, Collecorvino, Piccianello and Città Sant'Angelo itself. At night, heading into those villages and towns at speed, 'nearly all of which had Germans billeted there', they struck by surprise and often McGregor took no prisoners.

Among their first targets was one Arturo Giuliani, who lived in a farm near Collecorvino. One of the most reviled of individuals, Giuliani was a diehard Fascist who excelled at hunting down escaped Allied POWs. A 'rich man of the town', he was a de facto bounty hunter. To add insult to injury, Giuliani had even taken to pretending to be allied to McGregor and his men. To any POW-escapees, he claimed to be 'working with some British Paras' to 'get them back through the lines to their own people'. Thus lured in, Giuliani would lead the hopefuls down into a valley, pretending it was the rendezvous spot with the 'British Paras'. Instead, he'd hand them over to 'some SS men whose job it was to round up ex-POWs'. His work done, Giuliani would collect his reward.

McGregor felt that robbing Giuliani of all his valuables and money, as well as any warm clothing and bedding that his house might possess, was far from sufficient. In short, he could not be allowed to live. Late one evening they drove to Giuliani's place. Keeping watch in the fading light, they set upon a plan of attack. Sergeant Mitchell and Nicolich walked up to the building, and finding the door unlocked they stepped inside, posing as

POW-escapees. After a few minutes Mitchell came out again and beckoned for the others to join him. He'd told Giuliani that he had to head outside for a pee.

With weapons concealed, the six SAS filed into Giuliani's presence. The Italian looked surprised. 'In broken English he asked if we were ex-POWs.' By way of response, McGregor and his men revealed their arsenal of weapons. With 'a gasp of horror', Giuliani raised his hands. Nicolich was in a fuming rage. He explained how 'the dirty bastard had told them they could stay the night and that tomorrow he would take them to meet the British Paras'.

McGregor eyed the captive, who had all but collapsed into a faint. 'Well, tell him that he has no need to take you to the British Paras, as we are already here.'

Once Nicolich had translated, Giuliani fell to his knees and began gabbling away, begging for mercy, but McGregor shut him up. He was forced to sit in a chair, as the interrogation began. With his face a 'ghastly white', Giuliani admitted that all they had heard about him was true. As the minutes ticked by on a big Italian wall clock, McGregor kept firing in the questions. How many POWs had he handed over? How much was he paid for each one? But then Giuliani played his last, desperate card. If they agreed not to shoot him, he would lead them to where the SS were 'and he would help us to kill them'. No deal, McGregor countered. He already knew where to find that SS base.

As the hands on the old clock ticked away, Giuliani's 'agony and fear became more noticeable'. But not a man in that room could feel an ounce of pity for the captive – 'a man who lures men – our men – to their capture and in some cases death'. They also felt certain that his real target, far from being the POW-escapees, was actually themselves – McGregor and his team. They commanded the highest bounty from the Germans, and they were the most intensively sought. His time up, McGregor ordered Giuliani into his overcoat and he was marched out of the house.

Bundled into the Lagonda, they drove for about twenty miles to an isolated patch of woodland. 'The Boss stopped the car and we all got out,' noted Arnold. With his weapon at the ready, McGregor marched the captive off into the shadows, raising one arm to signal the others to stay where they were. During the drive, he'd told Giuliani that their base was in this woodland. He went to his doom unwittingly. After a few moments the rest of McGregor's men 'heard the sound of his gun firing'. Shortly, McGregor was back, and without a word to anyone they fired up the King's car and left.

Giuliani had been executed. 'In this way,' McGregor observed, simply, 'life for the few remaining POWs in this area became more secure.' While his logic was implacable, in appointing himself judge, jury and executioner, the SAS lieutenant had perhaps overstepped his A Force orders – 'no offensive action'. Yet McGregor had few qualms. As he noted, 'Fascist element small but powerful, and intensely feared. They are dangerous.' More to the point, the locals had laboured under Fascist rule for an age. Many were overjoyed at McGregor's actions.

One, the Carabinieri commander at Collecorvino, proved a staunch ally. When they executed their next target, the foremost Fascist of a nearby town, they got the Carabinieri chief's resounding stamp of approval. Bundled into the Lagonda, the captive was 'driven to the cemetery one night and shot'. By accident, they'd dropped a couple of empty ammo clips. Their carabiniere friend sought McGregor out to return the British soldiers' belongings to them. That way, they would leave no evidence.

It appeared that 2 SAS's commander, Bill Stirling, shared McGregor's convictions. In writing his official report on Operation Begonia, McGregor would make no bones about those extrajudicial killings. They were plainly and simply recorded for all to see. And in the citation for McGregor's subsequent DSO, awarded in recognition of his extraordinary A Force operations, Stirling would praise McGregor's strength of leadership, his initiative and his spirit, which kept the enemy 'guessing as to his whereabouts and the strength of his force' for so long. All of that was very true and quite uncontroversial.

But Stirling would go on to note in some detail McGregor's Fascist-hunting activities: his 'requisitioning one of the Italian Royal cars ... to drive to the homes of notorious Fascists who were helping the Germans to round up escaped prisoners'. Of particular note, the next three lines of McGregor's citation were blacked out. Censored. They are unreadable. No doubt they recorded his executing those 'rabid Fascists' in the local woodlands and cemeteries. The citation was signed off by General Alexander, but clearly someone had decided that those killings were best left unread. Tellingly, the document is also marked: 'NO PUBLICITY IS TO BE GIVEN TO THIS CITATION.'

Not content with those first two executions, McGregor terminated another such figure: he was shot dead in the village of Picciano. At every juncture they confiscated the victims' valuables, their clothes and cash. Then they heard about a local Fascist who was recruiting a cadre of 'Italian boys, to train them to fight the British when they arrived'.

This man deserved the very next visit.

Chapter 18

MIDNIGHT ASSASSINS

McGregor and his men paid their target a midnight call, forcing entry at the rear of his sumptuous residence. They found him sleeping soundly with his wife beside him. McGregor made his silent way to the bedside, and then, 'with his pistol pointing at the man very carefully put his hand on his shoulder and rocked him very gently'. The man awoke and stared at McGregor 'in amazement'. His wife also stirred, her eyes going 'wild with terror' as she 'opened her mouth to scream, but no sound came out'.

They bundled the captives into the living room. The man of the house readily admitted that he was raising a boys' militia, but he claimed that he was doing so 'under orders of the Tedeschi'. McGregor asked him where his cash was kept. He claimed not to have any in the house. McGregor said there was the easy way to do this, or the hard way. Either he told them, or they'd rip the place apart. As there was still no admission, McGregor ordered his men to get to work.

'Okay, wreck the bloody place,' he announced. 'And Nick, tell him will you.'

Even after Nicolich had explained what was about to happen, still the man of the house feigned ignorance. There was a haughtiness in his manner that rankled with McGregor. Arnold and Sutton discovered a locked attic room. Hearing movement on the far side, Sutton barged open the door. The sight that met their eyes was the last thing they'd been expecting. Inside there was a beautiful young woman in a pink nightdress, with a pistol levelled at the intruders. Something about her poise struck Arnold as all wrong. He indicated for Sutton to disarm her. It turned out that the pistol was a toy.

But when Sutton went to take it, the young woman let it fall to the floor. As Sutton bent to pick it up, she pounced upon him, her 'long dark hair falling over him, as she tried her best to scratch or bite him wherever she could'. Arnold fully appreciated that 'to stop a woman like that from hurting you without hitting her is one hell of a job'. Still, somehow Sutton managed it. Once they'd got the young woman to understand that she was not about to be raped or otherwise molested, and that the two strangers weren't Germans, she seemed to rally magnificently.

Muttering to Arnold that she was the best young woman 'I have ever had a fight with', Sutton smiled and asked if she was okay. Moments later she rushed up to him, flung her arms around his neck and 'planted a big kiss on his cheek'. It turned out that she was a lodger, and that she hated her landlord about as much as she hated the Germans. Shortly, she had whisked off the bra she was wearing under her nightie and had thrust it towards the two SAS men. They 'stood there like a couple of fools not knowing what to do'. Almost laughing at them now, she turned it inside out, ripped out the lining, and showed them where it was stuffed with cash. Her donation to the cause.

Moving on to the master bedroom, they zeroed in on the wardrobe. It was locked, but they made short work of that. There were two compartments, one full of men's clothing, the other, ladies'. Among many fine fur coats was one that seemed remarkably heavy. Upon closer inspection, the lining seemed most peculiar. Tearing it asunder, 'out came a pile of expensive jewellery, gold watches, rings, necklaces, bracelets and quite a lot more'. Hidden inside a 'moth-eaten fur cape' they found bundles of thousands of lire.

They returned to the living room bearing their booty. 'The Signor nearly had a fit when he saw what we had,' remarked Arnold. The young woman who'd fought like a 'hissing tigress' was laughing delightedly at the turn of events. As for the man of the house, he begged McGregor to leave him something. McGregor was nothing if not a fine judge of character. Through Nicolich, he told the Signor that he would get some of it back, if he agreed to the following: any militia he formed would not work against the POW-escapees or the British. Instead, its aim would be twofold: to fool the enemy, and to work for McGregor and his men, so that once the British reached the area the Signor would be well positioned. McGregor even offered to 'speak well of him' if he agreed.

At this, the Signor appeared like a changed man. His wife was ordered to fetch some wine, and once glasses were filled, he declared: '*Viva gli Inglesi! Viva gli Inglesi!*' With a little less gusto or feigned conviction, McGregor and his men returned the toast: '*Viva Italiano.*'

Having 'played Robin Hood' it was now time to 'play Father Christmas'. McGregor had bounty aplenty to disperse. While riding around in their purloined vehicle and acting as modern-day highwaymen – and hangmen – McGregor and his small force had expropriated '300,000 lire and some 50 suits of clothes'. Such riches were given out to the neediest POW-escapees. Christmas 1943 was approaching, and McGregor began to consider their possible return to Allied territory. As far as he could imagine, the only means to get back was to split into pairs, and to make their own way through the lines. They'd need to be disguised, he reasoned, but they had the means to ensure that they would be.

Having retained 15,000 lire each from their Robin Hood activities, McGregor and his men commissioned a local tailor to make them some fine 'tweed suits', at 2,000 lire a piece. While waiting for their civilian disguises, McGregor, restless as ever, set upon a little freelance espionage. Changing into a decent suit – 'the property of a Fascist', as he gleefully reported – he headed into Collecorvino, the nearest large German garrison town. Around a hundred enemy troops were based there. In the company of Toni Giganti, one of his Italian comrades, McGregor proceeded to supposedly befriend 'several German NCOs' who frequented the local bars.

Not content with such DIY espionage, McGregor engaged the services of a 'pretty blonde girl, who we persuaded to spy for us'. She organised a dinner party with three German officers, fishing for juicy snippets of intel. But equally, the enemy suspected that McGregor and his men were operating in their midst, and they began to do 'everything possible to secure our capture', as McGregor observed. Fascist agents did the rounds of the farms, spreading reports that British aircraft had dropped a radio set 'for the use of the Parachutists'. Those rural folk, little suspecting, offered to take McGregor and his men to collect their kit. Upon careful investigation, McGregor discovered those houses supposedly holding their radio sets actually concealed 'well planned German ambushes'.

The game was afoot. The question was who would be the first to make a wrong move. By circuitous means, a group of four 'Canadian intelligence officers' made contact with Giganti, McGregor's Italian intermediary. Fluent in Italian, French and English, and dressed in Allied uniforms, they claimed to have an important message for McGregor. An Italian MAS boat operated by A Force was waiting for them off the coast. All they had to do was undertake the trek to get there, and they could be whisked away to Allied lines. The mystery four tried to arrange a face-to-face meeting with Giganti. McGregor refused to let him go. But all the same the SAS lieutenant could sense that the enemy were circling.

One figure proved of particular interest. A German officer hailing from the Alsace region, he spoke fluent French. Giganti offered to introduce him to McGregor. The German officer had been stationed in Paris, and McGregor had spent some time there before the war. In their fine Parisian French they should be able to talk volubly. The evening of their planned rendezvous, Giganti led the SAS lieutenant to a certain Collecorvino cantina – a vaulted wine bar. They were shown to a curtained-off table in one corner, where the German officer was waiting. He was doubly pleased to see them, he explained, for the menu was all in Italian and he could order nothing.

Over copious courses of food and drink, he asked Giganti and McGregor if they might assist him. He'd been dispatched from Paris to Italy to deal with a most thorny problem. In France, he had worked to counter the French Resistance, otherwise known as the Maquis. Here, there was something far worse – 'a band of British paratroopers who are doing the same as the Maquis were doing in France'. In France, he had recruited brave locals to help with his anti-resistance work, the officer explained. Might Giganti and McGregor be able to provide similar services, here in Italy?

By way of response, McGregor vowed to do his utmost to help the German officer, but that first they would have to find out all they could about the 'British paratroopers'. If the officer would be happy to meet them in the cantina in five days' time, they would see what they could discover. The rest of the evening was spent listening to the officer's drunken reminiscences about his amorous adventures in Paris, where he still kept a mistress. At their next meeting, McGregor promised that he was homing in on the elusive British soldiers, but any further updates would have to be after the Christmas holiday, which was almost upon them.

The officer readily agreed, especially since he was about to go on a Christmas break himself, which he would spend in the company of his mistress. In fact, he explained, all such German anti-partisan and anti-British activities would come to a temporary halt over the festive season. All needed a well-earned rest and a break. 'The knowledge of our enemy's plans was too good to be true,' McGregor and his men reasoned. They wondered if they were somehow being led into a cunning trap. In fact, the reverse was true.

Christmas 1943 was spent billeted with an Italian nobleman, who lived in a large house at the foot of the mountains. The 'main attraction' was Lillian, the Signor's niece, who was training to be an opera singer in Rome. She had come to spend the Christmas holidays with her uncle and aunt, and after dinner she would sing for McGregor and his men, who all vied to 'gain her attention and favour'. Despite the fact that the Germans had set up a camp barely half a mile away, no one seemed particularly concerned, as all were busy preparing their Christmas celebrations.

On Christmas Day, McGregor and his men feasted with Giganti's family. After lunch, they went with four of his female cousins to visit Lillian, the trainee opera singer. Mitchell and Arnold were asked by two of the young ladies to go for an afternoon stroll. Walking through the woods with a 'pretty girl holding your hand', the two men almost forgot there was a war on. They passed by the German camp, seeing a body of troops lining up with their mugs in hand, queuing for 'their Christmas drink'. As Mitchell and Arnold walked past with the ladies, several raised their mugs and cried out *Buona Fortuna* (good luck) and *San Nicolo!* (Saint Nicholas; Santa Claus).

They reached a farm where locals were playing accordions and violins, and couples were dancing. The four joined in. The farmer-host had lived in America and spoke decent English. As the wine flowed, he explained that he had a very fine horse which sadly no one could ride. Arnold was busy trying to chat up the girl he was with, but Mitchell never missed a trick.

'My friend could ride her,' he declared. 'He was a cavalryman.'

The farmer fixed Arnold with a hopeful look. 'Signor, I would like you to ride my horse. She is a real beauty, and it is a shame that nobody yet has been able to ride her.'

Their two lady companions joined in, begging Arnold to try, and shortly all the guests were egging him on. Appreciating that faint heart never won fair lady, and being 'a little high on wine', Arnold agreed to give it a whirl.

He asked the farmer to catch the mare, saddle her and he'd see what he could do. In no time it was done, though the reins were little more than two lengths of rope. As Arnold placed a first foot in the stirrups, the mare began to kick and twist. His response was to adopt 'an old cavalry trick': he pulled her head around until it was almost touching his boot, then swung himself up into the saddle, to a rousing cheer from all. Moments later the horse was away 'at breakneck speed'. She'd covered two field lengths before Arnold managed to wrestle back a modicum of control. Giving the mare her head, he galloped her around the fields until she was out of breath.

After a couple of similar episodes 'we became friends', Arnold observed. He slowed her to a trot and left the field for the nearby lane. He cantered past the German camp, intending to execute a circuit to take him back to the farm. Again the German troops waved and wished him the best. Then he came around a corner to find a German truck stopped by the roadside, with troops gathered beside it on the verge. A figure stepped forward, barring Arnold's way. He held up a hand for Arnold to stop. There was nothing he could do but comply. An officer emerged, with a glass of wine in each hand.

He passed one up to Arnold. '*Buona sera, Signor*.' Good evening, sir.

'*Grazie, Signor*.' Thank you, sir. Arnold's Italian seemed good enough to bluff him. He drained the glass and handed it back, then trotted on.

By the time Arnold got back to the farm, a search party was about to set out. All were convinced that he'd either been caught by the enemy or thrown by the mare. The young horse was now 'docile', and Arnold could tell by the look in her eyes that 'she had enjoyed the ride as much as I had'.

A few days later they enjoyed a fine New Year's Eve party, after which McGregor decided it was time to move. 'Our Christmas holiday was over.' He and his men relocated to a cluster of remote farmsteads. As they were still waiting for their tailormade tweed suits, they'd changed into whatever local clothes they could find, and were now dressed as 'rather disreputable civilians'. Posing as escaped POWs, they hid their weapons thereabouts.

It was mid-afternoon on 5 January 1944 when McGregor first sensed trouble. He was sitting with Giganti, plus Troopers Dellow and McQueen, at one of the farms, when a series of shots rang out. Jumping to his feet, McGregor spied a group of thirty German troops, in extended line, advancing on the farmstead through an olive grove. They were no more than forty yards away. Giving a cry of alarm, he raced downhill, heading for the neighbouring farm in an effort to grab his carbine. But as he approached, he could see that a second line of enemy troops had all but encircled it. 'There was no alternative but to run.'

Taking his comrades with him, McGregor made a dash for a nearby stream, 'pursued and shot at by the Germans' all the way. Behind, they could hear that a full-scale battle had broken out, as the enemy assaulted the farmsteads with machine guns. In truth, Sergeant Mitchell, caught in one of the buildings, was in the battle of his life. Hopelessly outnumbered, he 'shot his way out of the trap, and continued firing until all his ammunition was exhausted', killing and injuring several of the enemy. Miraculously, when he was all out of rounds he executed a daring getaway.

In a nearby farmhouse, Arnold had gone to ground. Caught in the middle of shaving, the first rounds had come thumping through the open window. 'How I was not hit was a bloody miracle.' Scrambling upstairs to the bedroom, he'd climbed the ladder into the loft, and tried to loosen some tiles, to escape through the roof. But putting his head through the opening, bullets pinged all round him, ricocheting off the roof. Tumbling back downstairs, he dashed into the cowshed and stables that were attached to the house.

At the far end was a wooden wall, with a little trapdoor set in the middle of it. Diving through he landed in the pigsty. Ahead lay an even smaller trapdoor, which he was just able to wriggle through. On the far side was a sow, with 'piglets at her teats'. By now the shooting had stopped. Lying there next to the sow, he heard German voices and the thump of footsteps. Lifting the tiny trapdoor just a smidgen, he spied a pair of German jackboots on the far side. Knowing the enemy would eventually learn that there was a pig here and come for her, Arnold made his move.

Lifting the tiny trapdoor again, the boots were nowhere to be seen. Wriggling back through, he made a break for it, bending low and running out of the farmyard. He made it across one field, then another, dashing through a dusting of snow and headed for the river below. A line of enemy troops emerged on the slope above him. He ran even faster, as an order rang out. Bullets began to whack into the snow all around his fleeing form. Moments later he'd made the cover of the trees that lined the river, and turned to follow its course downstream. Rounding a corner he spotted some familiar figures. It was McGregor and several of their comrades.

Just then, Nicolich, their OSS man, appeared, sliding down the snowy incline. 'The Germans are everywhere!' he cried out.

Slipping, ducking and cursing, the helter-skelter getaway resumed as they followed the river downhill. Now and again a machine gun barked fire, as the Germans sprayed bullets into any patch of cover that might be hiding their prey. Finally, the 'creek which so far had saved us now ran out into a swamp'. On the far side lay the Tavo river, while a road barred their onwards progress. There was the roar of powerful engines, signifying that a convoy was in-bound, while from behind they could hear the noise of pursuit echoing from the river valley.

'Split up,' hissed McGregor. He glanced at Arnold. 'You take Nick and the POW, and go that way. I'll take Giganti and the rest and go the other.' As the two groups parted company, McGregor yelled out a final instruction: 'Meet you at Giovanni's, forty-eight hours!' Giovanni's was a farmstead some fifteen kilometres away that had always offered them sanctuary.

Once they'd covered a good distance McGregor and his party called a brief halt. He had Giganti and McQueen with him, but somehow, Trooper Dellow had disappeared in the mad rush to get away. The ground was treacherous with snow. McGregor and his two comrades were clearly visible against its stark whiteness and made an excellent target. They moved fast, despite the conditions, fording freezing rivers that were chest deep. Fortunately, none of them were hit. After five hours on the move, the freezing and exhausted fugitives reached a remote farm. They decided to chance it. The owners had no idea that the hue and cry was up. Believing McGregor and his men to be escaped Allied POWs, they offered them succour and shelter.

The following day Giganti managed to get news of the attack. Apparently, none of McGregor's men had been injured or killed. Sergeant Mitchell had managed to slip away, as had Corporal Laybourne and Trooper Sutton. Some 200 German troops had made up that hunter force. Deprived of their kills, they had burned down the farms as they tried to flush out their quarry.

But seemingly all had slipped the net. McGregor hurried on towards the rendezvous at Giovanni's. They reached it, but there was no sign of any of the rest of his patrol.

McGregor had only one of his original party of eight remaining with him, plus their Italian comrade, Giganti. As for the other six, lord only knew what might have happened to them. McGregor hoped they might have pushed further into the mountains, heading for one of the farms they had used as their base back in October. By now, McGregor and his men had spent more than three months behind enemy lines, engaged on a mission whose shelf life was supposed to have been a matter of weeks.

As far as A Force and 2 SAS were concerned, they were lost without trace.

Chapter 19

ROBIN HOOD AND SANTA CLAUS

At their coastal hideouts, Couraud, de Sablet and Baillie had reached a similar conclusion to McGregor: they needed to rob the rich, to feed the poor. They mounted a raid on a Carabinieri headquarters, known to be a hotbed of Fascists. Woken from their sleep by the surprise attack, those carabinieri present in the barracks were rapidly 'disarmed and told to go home'. Warned to change into civilian clothes, they were ordered to return to their families and to stay there. Unfortunately, the SAS had missed the local commander, who happened to be out at the time. Still, they seized all weaponry and ammo, plus 'military blankets and clothing', which were desperately needed.

Incensed at the raid, and the mysterious way in which his men had vanished, the Carabinieri commander called in a company of German troops, with heavy machine guns in support, to track down the elusive British raiders. But long before the hunt got going the SAS had melted away into the hills. The recently rescued 1 SAS veteran, Sergeant John Scott, had taken part in that raid. By now, Couraud had gathered to him seven such 1 SAS escapees, all of whom were desperate to return to Termoli, from where they could get back into the war. As a result of Couraud's extortion, using the kidnapped son of the fisherman as a bargaining chip, they had been promised a boat. It was one of the few vessels that was large enough to carry a substantial number of POW-escapees.

But as luck would have it, that ship was 'damaged in an air-raid'. That left only smaller vessels available. Having been promised the first boat 'and let down', Couraud, Scott, Baillie and a few score POW-escapees gathered at San Silvestro beach, which lay just to the south of Pescara and was a 'suitable part of the coast for embarking'. Out of the cold autumnal night a ghostly vessel emerged. Sure enough, it was the one they were waiting for. The skipper's son had been held hostage until the very last moment; 'until the boat was brought'. While his father had delivered, the caique was far too small for all those who were there. Finally, Couraud decided to depart, taking with him all seven 1 SAS escapees, plus several more. 'The size of the boat would not permit a larger party.'

Before casting off, Couraud told his men to be back at this very beach in two days' time, with all the escapees they could muster. He would return with a vessel large enough to spirit all to Termoli. Baillie, de Sablet and the rest of the SAS were to bring all to that rendezvous, at thirty minutes prior to midnight. If Couraud failed to show, they were to return to the beach at the same hour for five nights running. That way, the pick-up was sure to happen. Couraud would flash from the ship, in Morse, the V for Victory sign. The beach party was to answer with five short bursts of light from their own signal lamps. Plan set, the reluctant Italian skipper fired up his engine and the caique pulled away into the darkness.

As Scott would remark of the moment, 'Captain Lee [Couraud]

left his own men . . . and took us back with him in the fishing boat to Termoli.' Scott's return to Allied lines was to prove short lived. The very next night, he and another 1 SAS escapee, Trooper Rogers, were set to return. Simonds persuaded them to go right back in, laden with parcels of escape aids, compasses and the all-important cash, to oil the wheels of the escape lines. They were to sail in the company of Lieutenant E. C. Lyte, another of the former POWs who had just been rescued. Their orders were crystal clear. Once they'd delivered their escape kits, they were to await Couraud's return, and then be 'under the orders of Captain Lee [Couraud]'.

Couraud sailed with them on the MAS boat. In fact, it took three such journeys, quartering the coast to the south of Pescara, before they finally managed to locate the rendezvous beach. On the night of 27/28 October, Scott, Rogers and Lyte were at last put ashore. As Couraud returned to Termoli on the MAS boat, he reflected upon how their A Force missions were beset by such travails at every turn. They were plagued by confusion, distrust and delay, not to mention the challenges of timing and navigation. But even so, little by little they were getting there. By now, thousands of POW-escapees had been spirited back into Allied hands, either by the seaborne route, or via the escape lines running overland. Bit by bit, the trickle was becoming a flood.

Even the hardnosed 'Killer' Couraud was growing into something of a believer. A convert to the cause. At first, he'd felt such rescue operations were beneath his mettle. But he had been won over by the plight of the POW-escapees. From the deck of that MAS boat, he repeated his promise to the men in the diminutive folbot as they paddled away into the darkness: the following night he would be back. There was more to do. Hundreds more to rescue. He knew the terrain now and vowed that he would return.

Arriving back at Termoli, Couraud received an unexpected boost. De Sablet had managed to make it through, having got his hands on a fishing schooner and cramming it full of escapees. He'd managed to squeeze sixteen aboard, and he came bearing reports of 500 more who needed evacuating, all of whom were facing double jeopardy. They were in danger of being captured, of being hunted for the bounty placed upon their heads. They were also at risk of freezing to death as the winter conditions turned dire.

De Sablet had reached Termoli early on the morning of 1 November. The following evening Couraud set forth, departing the harbour at just after nightfall. Riding in MAS boat No. 33, the captain for this crucial expedition was a British naval officer, Lieutenant D. Calf, who commanded a dozen Italian crew. Lieutenant Calf set a course for Pescara. After three hours' hard steaming, he reduced the ship's speed to six knots, switched to the 'silent engine' and turned his prow towards land. Reducing his speed still further, the sleek vessel glided through the darkness. It was 10.35 p.m. when MAS 33 drew to a standstill, Lt. Calf having brought her to within 'five cables' of the nearest point of landfall, so half a kilometre offshore.

They were almost an hour early, for Baillie and the French Squadron were set for an 11.30 p.m. rendezvous. With one and a half fathoms of water lying beneath his ship, there was not a great deal closer that Calf could bring her. In any case, there was time to kill, before they would begin displaying their V signal, hoping for an answering sequence of flashes from land. Below decks, Lieutenant Lewis, Simonds's intriguing Harvard don turned OSS agent, was chatting to a lad who looked barely out of his teens. Lewis had been sent below to waken everyone. He'd paused to speak with Prince Augusto Ruffo di Calabria, a young Italian nobleman and the brother of the future Queen of Belgium. Despite his youth, the prince, another of Simonds's A Force recruits, was proving 'one of our most quick-witted agents'.

Lewis and the prince were deep in conversation about the coming mission, when the deafening bark of a 'rapid firing cannon' cut through the night. Glancing up the steps to the open ship's door, Lewis caught sight of fiery streams of tracer rounds tearing across the deck. A series of explosions seemed to shake the length of the boat. There was utter consternation, as orders rang out from above. Moments later Lewis watched aghast as his fellow agent, 'in the midst of a sentence, fell forward from the bunk to lie dead on the floor'. A round had torn through the ship's side, hitting the young prince in the back and killing him outright. The fearsome sound of incoming fire, and of the vessel taking repeated hits, continued.

Lewis tried to take cover. Up on deck, all was chaos and carnage. As Lieutenant Calf fully appreciated, his ship had been engaged by 'two enemy guns firing explosive shells of about 20mm calibre', and before he could get his vessel moving they took repeated hits in the engine room. Much as his Italian Engineer Officer tried to get the engines started, they were out of action and the ship was going nowhere. Immobile as they were, and taking heavy fire, the enemy was using some kind of small searchlight to better illuminate the target. Calf's Italian crew had taken cover on the upper deck, but in truth there was nowhere to hide from those fearsome 20mm rounds. Worse still, no one was returning fire with the MAS boat's own guns.

For seven full minutes the onslaught continued. Eventually, one of the torpedo tubes was hit, and an 'air lead' exploded. Moments later, the vessel began to burn. Still the enemy poured in the fire. In desperation, Calf jumped into the water to the seaward side of his ship, where its bulk should shield him from the worst of the incoming rounds. He cried out to his second in command, Midshipman Draper, to do the same, for the stricken vessel was a death trap. 'There was no reply.' Instead, Couraud leapt in beside him. Together, they decided that since there was 'nothing that could be done to save the ship, our best action was to swim for the shore'.

Couraud and Calf set out at around 11 p.m., shortly before Baillie and all were supposed to have made it to the beach and begun their signalling. At first they struck out north, moving away from the source of the enemy fire. As they rounded the burning MAS boat's hull, they spied a rubber dinghy lying a dozen feet away. It appeared overloaded, and neither of the swimmers fancied its chances of weathering the storm of enemy fire. They came across a body in the water. It turned out to be one of Couraud's men, who was badly wounded. Taking him in tow, the two swimmers set out for land.

Behind them, the enemy fire stuttered to a stop. Below decks a figure moved. It was Lieutenant Lewis, who somehow had survived the onslaught. Climbing up the steps to the deck, he was met by a scene of carnage. Six bodies were strewn across the ship, while 'flames were licking along the railings'. Glancing to sea, 'from out of the blackness' he heard 'the desperate appeals of the Italian sailors' in the water. *'Aiuto! Aiuto!'* With the enemy fire having ceased, Lewis took off his glasses and tucked them into his top pocket, removed his trousers and tied them around his waist, before undoing his boots and slinging them around his neck, so that he could grip them with his teeth.

Like that he slipped into the sea and set out for shore. The distance was no more than a few hundred yards, but the lone swimmer kept losing his bearings. Eventually he made it to the beach, whereupon he sat in the shelter of a sand dune, 'spent and shivering'. As he gazed out to sea, the fire on the ship must have reached one of the torpedo tubes, for it blew up in a series of almighty great explosions. Moments later the flaming hulk of the MAS boat slipped beneath the waves.

Two other men had also made it ashore. Couraud and Calf had had a nightmare journey. At first they'd been pushing their injured comrade before them, while trying to keep his head above water. Steering away from the glare of the burning ship, the wounded man grew heavier and heavier and shortly he ceased showing any signs of life. He'd been hit in both legs, which had been shattered, and Couraud didn't doubt that he had bled to death. Realising it was a corpse that they were endeavouring to save, they let the body drift away. Reaching a false beach – a strip of shallow land, separated from the shoreline by another stretch of water – the two cold and fatigued swimmers rested for a while, as they tried to massage life into their cramped limbs.

Finally, they pushed on, before feeling their feet touch the solid ground of the shore. Rousing themselves, they hurried inland. Having covered some two hundred yards, they were just approaching the railway and road, when they realised they were in trouble. A group of shadowy figures came tearing after them, and the two fugitives started taking fire. While the enemy would be fresh, Couraud and Calf were on the brink of exhaustion, but somehow in the thick darkness they shook off their pursuers.

They edged ahead, coming to the road itself – the most dangerous part of their escape and evasion. As they went to dash across it, heading for the open land beyond, there were cries of alarm. The chase was on again, only this time they were pursued by a larger group of enemy troops.

Diving into a 'thicket of reeds', Calf and Couraud became separated. Shots rang out in the darkness. Lying low, Calf remained hidden until the enemy were gone. He crept back to the reed beds looking for Couraud. There was no sign of him anywhere. Glancing out to sea, Calf saw a series of 'very large explosions'. What had once been his ship had been torn to pieces. Calf forced himself to move. This time he managed to cross the road undetected. He followed the course of a river running inland. Just as dawn was breaking, he reached an isolated farm. With few other options he knocked on the door. The owners welcomed him in, dried his clothes, fed him and provided him with a bed so he could rest.

Calf drifted off. He awoke hours later to discover another fugitive from the shipwreck was there. It was his second in command, Midshipman Draper. He'd made it off the ship unscathed and had been brought to the house by an Italian youth. Together, Calf, Draper and their young Italian guide set off to find the SAS base thereabouts. By mid-morning they had reached it. There, they met Captain Baillie and the men of the French Squadron, and shared with them the dire news. There was no sign of Couraud. It looked as if the seemingly invincible SAS captain had either been taken prisoner or killed.

For their part, Baillie and the men of the French Squadron had suffered a night of terrible psychological torture and pain. They'd arrived at the rendezvous early, only to realise that a strong enemy force had staked out the beach. Feeling helpless and unable to act – their priority was their escapee-charges – the best they could do was flash a danger signal out to sea. It was a silent night, and they could hear the sound of German voices. Then they'd detected the distant hum of a motorboat. They'd heard breechblocks being made ready, as the German troops prepared to strike.

Had their 'DANGER signal given from the shelter of the rocks been seen?' Baillie had wondered. The answer came when all hell broke loose, the spectacle made all the more disturbing as the enemy searchlight bathed the tragic scene of the burning ship in its beam. They'd been forced to watch as the MAS boat was repeatedly raked by fire, before the cataclysmic explosion had followed. As far as anyone knew, all who had been sailing on her were lost. So Calf and Draper's appearance at their headquarters seemed little short of a miracle.

Fearing that Couraud was among the dead, there would be a second miracle that very afternoon. A familiar figure stumbled into their farmstead headquarters, though he did not resemble the indestructible SAS commander they all knew. Couraud's upper torso was soaked with blood. Wounded in the right arm and left shoulder, he'd been hit by an 'explosive bullet' which had peppered him with shrapnel, even as he and Calf had tried to evade the enemy. Thrown to the ground, he'd felt around his shoulder and his hand came away covered in blood. While he could move his fingers and forearm, the rest was frozen.

Levering himself up with his one good arm, Couraud had staggered into the darkness, 'fighting against a growing dizziness'. Though his jacket was 'soaked with blood running down to his belt', somehow Couraud had evaded the enemy. 'Shaken and weak', and in considerable pain, still he had pushed inland, and had managed to make it to his comrades' redoubt. As was clear to all, Couraud was in need of urgent medical attention if he was to survive his injuries. A friendly local doctor was persuaded to attend to him, but 'did not do much good'. What Couraud needed was a hospital.

Baillie and Scott cast about for a vessel with which to evacuate their wounded commander, but, having witnessed the sinking of the MAS boat, 'all the fishermen were too frightened to move'. Locals reported that all the beaches in the area were being heavily patrolled, as the enemy did their best to scupper A Force operations and kill or capture the British raiders who were operating in their midst. The coastal road was thick with transport, as tracked vehicles and horse-drawn convoys, mixed with the heavier trucks, headed south. There was no easy route out of there.

That evening, an effort was made to steal a boat. Twelve men headed to the nearest beach. But a 'falling tide' made their attempt to launch their chosen craft nigh-on impossible. While they were still just a few feet short of the water, the vessel slipped from its wooden guide rails and became stuck fast in the sand. Shortly before dawn the attempt had to be abandoned. Returning to their farmstead headquarters, Couraud gave a set of orders. Baillie and the rest of the men were to set out for Roseto degli Abruzzi, a beachside town lying to the north of their present location. Word was that the search for a boat and a willing skipper might prove more fruitful there.

Couraud was to be left behind, for he could 'only move a short distance at a time, and very slowly'. Sergeant Scott, the 1 SAS escapee that Couraud had rescued, volunteered to stay with their injured commander. Supposedly, Scott and Couraud would follow after the others, moving at their own pace. If a boat could be found at Roseto, they would evacuate Couraud that way. That was the best plan they could come up with in the circumstances.

After the main force had left, and with his injured shoulder heavily bandaged and the arm held in a sling, Couraud attempted to move, with Scott supporting him. But very quickly they realised such a journey was beyond him. In truth, it would be the death of Couraud. They had no option but to lie low, and hope for some means of deliverance to materialise.

At Roseto, Baillie struck lucky. A local fisherman promised to take them off the coast and back to Termoli, as soon as 'the state of the surf allowed him to launch his ship'. The offer of a payment of 1,000 lire per POW-escapee doubtless persuaded him. By the evening of 6 November – three days after the sinking of the MAS boat – the Italian skipper declared that all was ready. Now was the time to sail. As there was still no sign of Couraud, Baillie loaded the caique with all they could carry, and at ten o'clock they set sail, steering a course for Termoli. Sneaking past the costal battery set on high ground above the town, they chugged deeper into the night, leaving Couraud and Scott behind them.

As Bailie fully appreciated, Couraud had *ordered* him to sail south with as many men as he could carry, regardless of the SAS commander's fortunes. As luck would have it, their boat would make it. Twenty-four hours after setting sail, the caique pulled into Termoli harbour. There, Baillie was able to acquaint Simonds with the dire news. Not only was MAS 33 lost, but so too were most of those who had sailed with her. Only the ship's commander, Craft, and his deputy, Draper, had been brought back safe and sound.

In addition to the Italian crew, they had to assume that Simonds's A Force agents, the American, Lieutenant Lewis, and the young Italian prince, had also been killed or captured. Among the POW-escapees that Baillie had managed to bring out was Colonel McDonald of the Green Howards. As for SAS commander Couraud, he was badly injured and marooned behind enemy lines, with only Sergeant Scott to care for him. As Baillie would report, a five-kilometre coastal strip along Italy's eastern seaboard seemed to have been turned into a 'free fire zone' by the enemy. Any vessels spied off land, or ship's crew onshore, were fair game, as were unidentified persons moving on the beaches.

At their farmstead hideout, the wounded Couraud and his faithful comrade, Scott, received more grim news. Further inland, a powerful force of enemy troops had raided their POW-escapee hideouts. Dozens of farmsteads had been burned to the ground and prisoners recaptured. As was hardly surprising, the local rural folk, who previously had been so brave and loyal, 'were terrified, and refused to have any further dealings, or give shelter and food' to the POW-escapees. The area was being intensively patrolled, as the enemy sought to clamp down on all that A Force had achieved.

In light of this, the ailing Couraud issued a desperate set of orders: all remaining POW-escapees were to 'make their way south through the lines'. What other options were open to them? Right then, the SAS commander couldn't even get himself back to

255

Allied territory, let alone hundreds of desperate POW-escapees. The architect of Operation Loco, and of so much more besides, was in desperate straits.

Injured, ailing and largely immobile, he was trapped 150 kilometres behind enemy lines.

With the Allies advancing into Italy, Hitler and Mussolini vowed to fight for every inch of Italian soil. Caught amidst the chaos and confusion were some 80,000 Allied prisoners of war. Upon Italy's surrender, tens-of-thousands had broken out of the POW camps, and were in dire need of sustenance and rescue, even as enemy forces hunted them remorselessly.

Winston Churchill vowed that all had to be done to rescue the Allied POWs. Step forward Lieutenant-Colonel Anthony Simonds (above left, and right, on operations with the Chindits), of the top-secret unit A Force, the deception and POW-rescue specialists. As many of the SAS were commando trained, Simonds recruited the Taranto veterans to rescue the POWs via parachute missions and also by sea.

Harried by the enemy at every turn, the SAS pushed north into hostile territory in their heavily armed jeeps. With escorts of Italian MAS boats – the Italian equivalent to British Motor Torpedo Boats (MTBs) - they also sailed hundreds of kilometres into hostile waters, seeking to rescue Allied POWs from coastal rendezvous.

Riding in traditional Italian wooden-hulled boats – caiques – and posing as fishermen, the SAS put ashore deep behind the lines, seeking out the Allied POW-escapees. They sailed back again with their vessels crammed full of those that they had rescued, but their high-risk missions were menaced by the enemy at every turn.

Simonds recruited teams from the Office of Strategic Services (OSS), the American equivalent of Britain's Special Operations Executive (SOE), to his POW-rescue force. Those OSS agents were Italian-Americans, and they would deploy alongside the SAS, carrying out some of the most audacious missions of the war, including assassinating top Italian Fascists.

Legendary SAS commander Major Roy Farran (front right of photo, with German MP40 sub-machine gun), played a key role in both Operation Loco and the POW-rescue operations. One of those POWs so rescued was Sergeant John Scott (right). Typically, he would volunteer to return immediately behind the lines, helping rescue scores more POWs in turn.

Cary-Elwes (right of photo, above) looks on as Churchill lays a wreath of remembrance. Note: he is holding Churchill's cane. Cary-Elwes (below centre, with glasses) at a post-war reunion, together with SAS founder David Stirling (far right of photo), General George Bergé of the French SAS (second from right) and others.

The Pisticci camp memorial and plaque (above and right), in Pisticci town's central square, is one of the few visible efforts to memorialise this history today. Sadly, the concentration camp itself is falling into ruin, with the washing area and guard tower (below left), and chapel (below right) showing signs of abandonment and decay.

A MEMORIA
DEI CONFINATI POLITICI
ANTIFASCISTI

PISTICCI 25 APRILE 1978

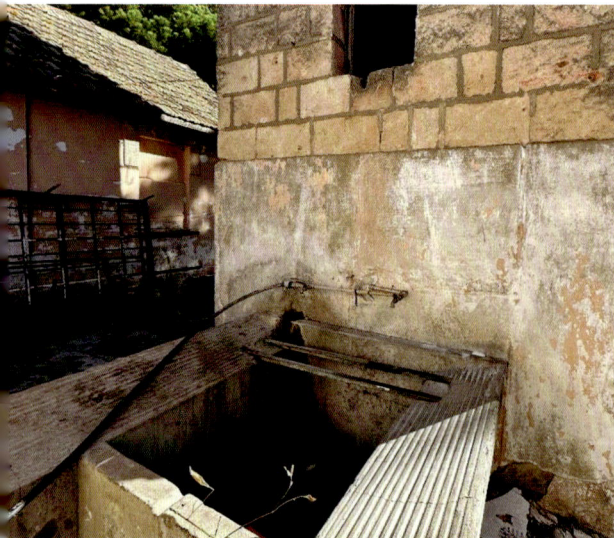

Chapter 20

DODGER SQUADS

A few score kilometres inland of Couraud's hideout, McGregor was also in dire straits. A recent Axis news release had revealed that the enemy knew chapter and verse about the A Force operations. As Guenther Weber, an Axis 'special war correspondent', reported: 'The Allies have been employing, for some time past, chiefly along the Adriatic coast, special squads, which can be best designated as "dodger squads". On dark nights these squads land far inland . . . by means of parachute . . . and are charged with the task of picking up Anglo-American prisoners who escaped from prisoner of war camps . . . Through the vigilance of the German troops and the assistance of the Italian population, many of the commando groups have been caught.'

That last part, 'many of the commando groups have been caught', was open to debate. But as to that phrase 'Dodger squads', right now McGregor felt that pretty much hit the mark. During the time that he had frequented those bars popular with German troops, he'd helped fuel the rumour that there were '4,000 parachutists in the Gran Sasso area', whereas in truth there were only a tiny fraction of that number. He'd also acted as if boasting to the locals, seemingly bragging about how strong were their forces, and knowing that word would get back to the enemy. While the rural folk tended to be welcoming, and loyal to a fault, they didn't seem able to resist the chance of a good gossip. Italy was a nation where news apparently 'spread like wildfire', which meant that 'spreading rumour is easy to do', McGregor had concluded.

But all of that was coming back to haunt him now. The enemy had swallowed the bait and he and his men had become the hunted. As they had fled from the German forces that had pounced on their farm hideouts, they'd had no option but to do so in pretty much what they stood up in, losing all of their weaponry and kit in the process. Apart from the bundles of cash that they carried on their persons, they were as ill-equipped to survive and to fight as were the majority of the POW-escapees. In fact, their own predicament mirrored that of those they had been sent in to rescue. How the tables had turned.

Snow lay thick across the mountains. White-tipped peaks reared on all sides. The cold was intense, and it numbed the bones to the marrow. The area was thick with German troops, necessitating maximum vigilance. While the local farmers had helped scores of POW-escapees in recent months, they warned McGregor, plus his companions, McQueen and Giganti, that it would be foolish for them to move right now in such punishing conditions. The weather, and the deep snowdrifts, would render most of the tried and tested footpaths impassable.

Undeterred, McGregor and McQueen bade farewell to their stalwart Italian companion, Giganti, and set out east, heading for a string of isolated villages where they'd seek word of any boats that might be available. At one, they met an Italian skipper who claimed he knew of a suitable vessel. They made the punishing journey to check, only to discover that the boat lay over a mile away from the sea. Without a vehicle there was no way they could hope to transport it to the coast. In any case, the only things moving on the roads right then were the odd farmer's cart, and German troops. They would stand out a mile.

Then they got word of a seven-metre rowing boat, which lay within easy reach of the water. The question was, could they possibly complete the journey from a beach north of Pescara all the way to Allied lines, riding in such a diminutive vessel and powered only by the strength of the human arm. Much that it seemed like a mission impossible, they went to investigate. The owner of the rowing boat seemed reluctant to let them have it. Bereft of weaponry, McGregor and McQueen were loath to resort to threats. The SAS lieutenant offered the man 100,000 lire for his boat, which amounted to a small fortune in wartime Italy. Still, the owner baulked.

Seemingly a wealthy individual, he also possessed a car. As McGregor made clear, if he wouldn't sell them the rowing boat, they'd have to take his vehicle, for they needed some means to speed them through the bitter winter conditions and back to Allied lines. At last, the man relented. They could take his vessel, but he would have to accompany them, to make sure he got it back again. Shortly before cutting this deal, McGregor and McQueen had come across an American pilot who was also on the run. As they were going to need all possible hands to the oars, that American flier was persuaded to take his chances alongside them. An Italian fighter pilot had also heard of their madcap venture. He volunteered to accompany them, bringing his wife and son along for good measure. As far as McGregor was concerned, the more hands to the pump, the better.

The sun sets at just after 5.00 p.m. in the depths of the Italian winter. It was at that hour that the escapees readied themselves, collecting the four cumbersome oars that they would have to carry, for no sensible boatman stored such things with his rowing boat. Thus heavily laden, they crept towards the coastal road. As bad luck would have it the highway 'happened to be full of passing German trucks'. Waiting for a lull in the traffic, the fugitives staggered across the open space 'with considerable noise and trouble', laden with their loads and relying upon the darkness to hide them from any prying eyes. Then came a repeat performance with the railway line, before they scuttled across the open stretch of sand beyond.

Though they felt horribly exposed, somehow they made it to the water undetected. It was just after 6.00 p.m. as they slid the open wooden craft down the last few feet of the sand and into the surf. With 'only the stars to guide us, and a broken escape compass', they struck out into the forbidding sea. They rowed solidly for thirteen hours, but the weather was worsening, the sea becoming choppy and restive. There was no doubt that they would have to make landfall sometime soon. At first light, McGregor figured they had made it as far south as Ortona, and maybe even beyond.

To the west, they spotted a group of soldiers repairing a bridge. From a distance they had the look about them that suggested they might be Allied troops. 'We hoped fervently that they were British,' observed McGregor, as they turned the prow of their boat towards shore. 'We landed,' he reported. 'They were Canadians. The place was Fossacesia. The time was 0800 hours.' They'd just completed a row through the open sea at night of over 60 kilometres, and all through waters menaced by the enemy.

Shortly, McGregor and McQueen were back at A Force head-quarters. They'd returned from almost four months behind hostile lines, during which time they'd caused untold havoc and chaos for the enemy. Upon reaching Termoli they discovered that they had been listed as 'missing in action', for there had been no news of the patrol's fortunes for an age.

Bill Stirling would recommend McGregor for a DSO, in recognition of his incredible A Force achievements. After praising his 'leadership, coolness and initiative', and having run rings around the enemy for months on end, the citation noted simply: 'On 22 Jan '44 he returned to Allied territory by a stolen rowing boat.' The award of a DSO was a rare honour for one so comparatively junior in rank and so young, and it was wholly deserved.

As the citation also made clear, in the 'space of a fortnight' McGregor's party had 'set over 500 Allied POWs on their way'. In fact, during those long months spent behind enemy lines, their one, eight-man patrol had steered far more POW-escapees 'on their way to freedom'. The true figure would probably never be known, for the means by which those escapees had made it back to Allied lines had been so varied, changeable and fraught. By playing Robin Hood and Santa Claus, and by taking the fight to the enemy, they had delivered on all that Simonds had asked of them and so much more.

Yet right then, in January 1944, their homecoming was something of a bitter-sweet experience, for most of McGregor's patrol were still missing, fate unknown. In truth, those of McGregor's men who remained behind the lines were determined to follow in their commander's footsteps – to make it out alive, while ensuring that the bodies of their enemies piled high in their wake. In doing so, they would make common cause with their

OSS brethren, many of whom were likewise still at large deep behind the lines.

Over the winter months the work of Lieutenant Sauro and his OSS team had echoed that of McGregor and his men, in the sense that they had switched from using the seaborne escape route, to escape lines that cut through or across the mountains. At one stage they had even tried to call in a Douglas C-47 Skytrain ('Dakota' in British service) to land on a makeshift airstrip and pluck hundreds of escapees to safety that way. But the enemy must have learned of their plans. A contingent of SS troops had been dispatched from Rome, seeking to put paid to any such intentions.

As with their British counterparts, the longer the OSS remained at such work, the more the enemy sought them out. Eventually, in late November, Sauro decided that he and his men should try themselves to cross the lines, to prove a route that the POW-escapees might follow. On the way they ran into an enemy patrol. Deciding to ambush the hunters, the OSS team got ready with their 'Marlin' sub-machine guns, the United Defense M42, which was intended to replace the Tommy gun, and was in use already with specialist units. Issued with twenty-five-round magazines, welded face-to-face in pairs to facilitate a rapid magazine change, it could put down a fearsome rate of fire.

Opening up by surprise, they 'killed the officer and six of his men', DeLuca would report. The survivors 'dropped their arms and ran'. Some days later, they came across a jeep-borne force. Studying it closely, in case it was somehow a friendly patrol – after all, the SAS were known to use such vehicles deep behind the lines – it turned out to be nothing of the sort. This was a group of German troops driving a captured Allied vehicle. The enemy had got into the habit of dressing in Allied uniforms, to lure the POW-escapees out of hiding. This looked to be a variation on the theme.

Aiming to shoot them up 'from hidden points', the OSS team ducked behind a series of rocky outcrops and prepared to strike. The lone jeep trundled past very slowly, which enabled the ambushers to lob a grenade into the open-topped vehicle, after which they opened up with their Marlins. As DeLuca reported, they killed 'four of them, an officer, a Sgt. Major, and two lance-corporals'. They then proceeded to seize the jeep, which was still usable.

Such audacious attacks fuelled the German commander's fears that a reputed 4,000 Allied parachutists were menacing these hills. Accordingly, they poured in more and more troops. Eventually, the first of Lieutenant Sauro's men was captured. Corporal Neal Panzarella, Sauro's wireless operator – the man who'd been forced to bury his defunct radio set at the outset of their mission – was run to earth. Panzarella had been sent by Sauro to investigate a mystery target that kept being hit by flights of US warplanes. On a high ridge, he was surprised by German Alpine troops, who were well equipped for such winter conditions and moving fast on skis. While Panzarella tried to shoot it out, he was outnumbered, outmanoeuvred and outgunned.

Taken captive, Panzarella was subjected to numerous interrogations, though he refused to talk. Eventually, he was placed aboard a train and sent north to Nazi Germany. He would not be the last of the A Force warriors to face such a fate. In early January 1944, Sauro and his surviving men linked up with the Italian partisans. By now, they'd mostly switched to their secondary, Operations Group role. Their intention was to cause as much confusion, sabotage and destruction as possible, in order to hurt the enemy where it most mattered – along the routes of their supply lines. But in joining the partisans, they risked facing the same dire fate as those Italian resistance fighters, if they were captured. They could expect little mercy from the enemy.

Based in an isolated hunting lodge on the heights of a mountain, they were operating within what was McGregor and his team's stomping ground. Stirring up a hornet's nest, they were to witness the wrath of the enemy and the price paid for it by the locals. From their vantage point they spied sixty troops leading a mule train, packed with heavy machine guns, explosives and other weaponry. Surrounding a nearby village, they executed a house-to-house search, seeking partisans and their parachutist comrades. Finding none, they looted the houses and rounded up twenty of the male villagers. Before marching them away, they beat up the mayor and his wife, for they had 'received a letter from some spy' claiming that he knew fully well that his village was being used as a base for partisan and OSS operations.

It was true. As with so many ordinary Italians, the mayor hungered to drive out the Nazi occupiers. From their mountaintop bases, the OSS saw the German troops pillaging the local's food – their cattle and their grain – before destroying all of the remainder. Whole villages were burned to the ground. The SS troops were the worst. Fanatics, they had vowed that before they left Italy they would destroy the nation. 'They believe Italy is the country that is causing them to lose the war,' Sergeant DeLuca noted. 'They are even blowing up villages as they leave, just for the sake of destroying.' Being Italian-Americans, Sauro and his men felt such horrors in their hearts, and it drove them to strike back repeatedly.

Bang in their sights, of course, would be the men of the reviled SS.

Chapter 21

COW BOYS

Near by, a second Special Forces team was at work. Over the months that they had spent in these mountains, McGregor had found that one of his most capable deputies was Trooper George Arnold. But when McGregor and Arnold had fled the farmsteads as the enemy had attacked, they'd split into separate groups, after which they'd failed to link up at their planned rendezvous. With 'heavy snow on the ground and snowstorms coming up', Arnold and his fellow escapee, Nicolich, had barely managed to stay one step ahead of the enemy.

Harried and hunted, they'd taken stock of their means of waging war and their supplies. Fortunately, both men had a pistol with them when they'd fled the farmstead, plus a little cash. But that was about all. At one stage, when trying to shake off their pursuers they'd followed a mountain pass leading to the Gran Sasso peak, at night and in the midst of a howling blizzard. When both men had felt as if they'd reached their lowest ebb, and that the storm could take them, Nicolich had made a lifesaving remark and decision.

'Don't go to sleep, you goddamn Limey,' he'd warned Arnold, 'or you will get frostbite.' Up here, lost in this snowbound wilderness, that would spell a death sentence.

'I know,' Arnold muttered, 'but I am so bloody tired.'

'Tell you what,' Nicolich declared, 'let's take one of them Benzedrine tablets out of the escape kit.'

Benzedrine, better known to all as 'bennies', is a euphoric stimulant and the world's first amphetamine. The tablets were included in the escape kits for moments such as these. Though they had no water remaining, there was plenty of snow to melt and to wash the pills down. Shortly after downing two tablets each, Arnold and Nicolich were 'beginning to feel more like our old selves'. Re-energised, they fought on through the blizzard to reach an isolated hut. Inside they found a wizened Italian mountain man, who 'looked like Father Christmas with a long, flowing white beard'. Despite the fact that he could not believe that anyone could have survived crossing the snowbound pass in such conditions, he welcomed them in. Stripping them naked, he got them out of their frozen clothes, thawed them out and then rubbed them down with goose fat.

That done, he prepared them both a meal. He still could not countenance that they had survived the mountains in such conditions. Nicolich produced the Benzedrine tablets, and explained that without those they would never have made it. The old man gazed at the pills in wonder. 'I have lived in these mountains all my life,' he declared, 'but I have never seen a little thing like that that could protect a man from the winds and blizzards and give him strength . . .'

Once recovered, Arnold and Nicolich thanked their host and they got moving again. Their mission now was twofold. One, to find out what had happened to the rest of their patrol, and two, to help any POW-escapees they might come across. As they pressed on, they came to a river which barred their way. Pondering how they might best cross it, an old man arrived on the riverbank leading a cow on a string, followed by her calf. He asked the two men if they might take his cow across the water, while he held on to the calf.

'Go on,' Nicolich urged Arnold, 'you're a bloody donkey man. Get on her goddamn back and ride her across.'

Arnold took up the challenge, climbing onto the homely, placid cow. 'She never moved a whisker.' The old man handed him the rope, and as Arnold patted her head and talked to her, he gave her a couple of kicks and she began to move. Very slowly she stepped into the water, put her head down for a drink, and then off they went, making for the far bank. Having completed the one test journey, Arnold returned to fetch the old man and her calf.

Just as he was loading them up, he heard a voice crying out: '*Halten!*'

A German officer was striding towards them. Without a word he pulled the old man from the cow, mounted up himself, indicated the far bank and cried out '*Schnell! Schnell!*' Quick! Quick! He was clearly after a lift across the river, and pronto. Arnold gave the cow a prompt and before long he'd ferried the German officer to the far side. Upon arrival, Arnold's passenger slid off, took out a cigarette packet and offered it to Arnold. The SAS trooper went to take one, but the German 'closed my hand over the packet, saying "*Danke sehr*," and walked away', Arnold noted, in amazement. After that he went on to complete his ferrying task, which ended with Nicolich in fits of laughter.

'What the hell are you laughing about?' Arnold demanded.

'I've seen it all now. A goddamn Limey riding a cow with a Kraut officer behind him, and then charging him a packet of cigarettes for the journey.'

In due course Arnold and Nicolich managed to link up with two other behind-the-lines raiders – OSS operators Corporal Arthur Roberta and Sergeant Albert Ingegni, two of Sauro's men who had become isolated during recent operations. Together, they formed a gang of four. With their uniforms long hidden, Arnold, Nicolich, Roberta and Ingegni appeared like any group of Italian locals. Dressed in this way they continued with their A Force mission, sending scores more POW-escapees overland to cross the lines, and also working on tracking down 'the worst of the Fascists', as they sought to secure 'money and clothing' for their charges. In this way, they would continue what McGregor had started, for 'a number of Fascists who were actively assisting the Germans were killed', or strongarmed into ceasing the worst of their activities.

The first to be targeted was Alfred Verrocchio, at the town of Elice, north-west of Pescara. Shacked up with a German woman, Verrocchio seemed intent on resuscitating Fascist sentiments across the region. As Elice's mayor, he wielded considerable power. They decided to pay him a midnight visit. While he claimed the German lady was his wife, the visitors knew otherwise. McGregor and his men had paid Verrocchio a previous visit, taking money and clothing from him, during which they'd met his actual spouse. Back then they'd warned the mayor to cease all his Fascist activities. He clearly hadn't listened.

They reached the apartment block where Verrocchio lived with his lover. It was midnight by the time they'd made their way through the main door. The porter saw the intruders, but once they'd explained who they were and their mission he was totally onside. Ushering them into the privacy of his apartment, he pulled out a set of keys and passed them over. Those would give them access to Verrocchio's apartment. He added that no one would try to stop them, for everyone hated the man as much as he did.

Flitting up the stairs, they opened the front door, using the porter's key. Spying a passageway that had to lead to the bedroom, they headed that way. A bedside lamp flickered on even as they stepped inside, and there was Verrocchio sitting up in bed, 'with a pistol in his hand pointing at us', Arnold noted. There was a 'nasty little bang' as Verrocchio fired, but it was only a .22 small calibre weapon and in any case he missed.

Moments later they'd disarmed him and wrestled him to the floor. Meanwhile Verrocchio's 'wife' had sat up in bed and was yelling at him a 'torrent of abuse'. At last she was made to shut up, after which Nicolich began to interrogate her. They knew all about Verrocchio from their last visit. She was a whole different matter. Were she and her 'husband' still Fascists, Nicolich demanded?

'Yes.'

'Are you Italian?'

'Yes.'

'If you don't tell me the truth I will shoot you,' Nicolich warned.

'I am a Yugoslav.'

Niocolich switched to Serbo-Croatian, the main language spoken in Yugoslavia and his native tongue. 'From what part of Yugoslavia do you come?' She failed to reply. 'You are not a Yugoslav. You are a German Nazi.'

'No, I come from Czechoslovakia,' she countered.

Nicolich had lived in that country and he also spoke Czech. When he challenged her again, there was 'nothing but a nervous smile'.

Leaving her in the bedroom under threat of death if she so much as moved, they marched Verrocchio into the living room. Grabbing a suitcase, they made him pile it high with POW-escape kit – 'jackets, socks, underwear, shirts, boots and shoes'. In fact, they took every scrap of clothing they could find. If 'old rat face', as they'd nicknamed him, 'wanted to go out, he would have to go starkers', and they did the same with all of the women's clothing. If nothing else, it should stop the two of them from raising the alarm for a while.

Next they asked Verrocchio for his cash, as a donation to the cause of helping the POW-escapees. He claimed that he had none. They went back into the bedroom and asked the lady of the house the same question.

'If you can find it you can have it,' she answered, with a cold sneer.

Arnold figured it had to be hidden in the bed. He pulled out his fighting knife, and went to remove the sheets, so he could cut open the mattress. Verrocchio's lover tried to grab the bed-sheets, failed and was left uncovered. She was truly a sight to behold – dressed in a see-through pink nightdress decorated all over with silver swastikas. For a moment all in the room froze, as the raiders stared at the Nazi symbols. Once she realised just what they were looking at, she reached up one arm, 'ripped the whole thing off and stood there staring at us stark naked' and with brazen defiance.

Nicolich went to the wardrobe and threw her a dressing gown, telling her to cover up. Verrocchio, meanwhile, disowned her, calling her a 'bloody harlot. This is not my wife, she is a German.'

Her response was to drop the dressing gown, stalk across to Verrocchio, 'with shoulders and buttocks swinging', before delivering 'an awful slap on his face' that all but knocked him off his feet. Perhaps because he had disowned her, she stepped towards the wardrobe, threw all the books off a shelf, then removed a small metal box hidden behind. She passed Nicolich a key, which opened it. Inside, it was stuffed with 100 lire notes.

As they went to leave, Verrocchio even had the cheek to ask if he might come with them, for he was now seemingly scared of his lover. How could he, they countered, for Verrocchio had no clothes. They warned him, plainly, that 'it would be wise not to have anything to do with fascism, or we would pay him another visit, which this time would be fatal'. They left laden with warm clothes, the cash and a bottle of cognac, to warm the cockles of their hearts.

With their bundles of loot, they made their way back into the hills. Using the cash they managed to buy boots for all the POW-escapees that they had gathered together, 'and soon had them all fitted out'. A four-day march followed, pressing south through the mountains. Eventually, they passed that party of escapees on to a trusted guide, who would 'take them through the lines the following night. We left them knowing they were in good hands. All the British lads were in good spirits . . .'

Next they headed inland to Montefino, a small town in the foothills of the mountains. There, the gang of four busted in on a nighttime gathering of the great and the good. They found 'all the officials of the town and they all seemed to be frightened; they said that they were very pleased to see Americans and hoped Allied forces would arrive soon'. It was hardly surprising. Invariably, the four desperadoes struck fear into those they confronted. After months in the hills, they had a strikingly wild appearance, and their civilian guise was augmented by locally acquired 'hunting arms: shotguns, double-barrelled guns, etc. . . . We carried around 200 rounds of ammunition with us at all times.' They appeared more like a band of brigands than any recognisable Allied troops, and as the OSS agents admitted, they were feared like 'American gangsters'.

At Montefino, they warned their audience that they were present 'in great force' in the area. If anyone tried any hostile moves, 'they would be stopped, because we had plenty of support'. The threat wasn't entirely hollow. The gang of four knew where scores of POW-escapees were hiding out. Some of them were armed, and if need be 'we could have counted on the support of our prisoners!' Moving on to other towns, they paid surprise visits to yet more Fascists, to whom they 'gave the third degree', collecting in the process tens of thousands of lire to fund their A Force operations.

Then they learned of a particularly nasty individual who deserved a midnight call. In Sant'Omero lived Aldo Quatsieri, a die-hard Fascist who had tracked down a dozen or more POW-escapees, earning a fortune in bounty. A secretary of the local Fascist party, this was a man who deserved not to live, in their view. Unfortunately, on the night of the gang of four's visit their quarry proved not to be home. Herding his family into the kitchen, they kept them under guard as they awaited Quatsieri's return. Instead, a 'Jerry truck' came roaring up the street towards the house. The four were forced to 'run for it'.

Even as they fled, they vowed to be back. A while later Arnold and Nicolich returned, although this time they staked out the cantina that was their quarry's favourite drinking hole. Having worked out just who he was, they followed him as he left the bar. Reaching the end of the street, Nicolich 'stuck the barrel of his .45 in his back and told him to keep walking and to do as he was told, or else'. Once they were clear of the village, they began to question Quatsieri about selling out POW-escapees to the Germans. For a while he twisted and squirmed, as he tried to avoid admitting the truth.

Then Arnold put a question to him that he never believed would get a straight answer. 'Is it true that the Tedeschi shot two POWs?'

'Yes, Signor, but you see it was their own fault,' Quatsieri answered. 'They were running away and when the Tedeschi called on them to stop they just kept running, so the Tedeschi had no other choice.'

As far as Arnold and Nicolich were concerned, they had heard enough. They knew he was 'telling lies . . . to put himself in the clear. We left him in a ditch,' noted Arnold. 'He would give no more POWs to the Germans or to anyone else for that matter.'

Shortly thereafter, they learned of a partisan group that was based in the mountains to the north, who were in desperate need of some proper training. An RAF warplane had been shot down and they had salvaged its weaponry and ammo. They needed to be shown how to use both, so as to start ambushing German forces in earnest. Arnold and Nicolich agreed to offer their help. Splitting from Roberta and Ingegni, who were busy organising another POW-escapee party, they began the journey north. As both men appreciated, 'It was going to be a very long walk . . .'

On the third night they stopped at 'a lonely little house on a hillside'. The owner turned out to be a kindly spinster. She rustled up a fine meal of minestrone soup, pancakes and fruit, suggesting that her two visitors might sleep the night by the fire. There was only the one bedroom upstairs, she explained, which was hers. In the early hours something woke Arnold. Peering out from the blankets, he saw their host carry a tray of food and drink upstairs. To his surprise he heard voices coming from the bedroom, one of which was that of a male. Arnold woke Nicolich. There were definitely two people upstairs.

Come morning, they tackled the old lady. Who else was in the house, they asked. When she denied that there was anyone, they told her about hearing the voices. If she would not tell them, they would need to go upstairs and investigate. The old lady began to cry. Then she glanced up and said that if they promised not to harm her or her mystery guest, she would tell them all about him. That agreed, she confessed that she was looking after a young German boy who had deserted from the German army.

'A German soldier?' they queried. 'You are telling us you have a German soldier upstairs and an American and British soldier downstairs?'

'Yes.'

'We could have killed each other in the night,' Nicolich objected.

'Oh no, he does not want to kill you or anyone, he is a good boy. He hates the Nazis and the war. When the war is over, he will go to Germany and bring his mother and his girlfriend who he hopes to marry, and live in Italy.'

'That's okay,' said Nicolich, 'but what about us?'

'You too have a mother and perhaps a sweetheart.'

'But we are at war with the Germans,' Arnold objected.

'War, war, war,' the old lady countered, 'are you all mad? It is the mothers that bring you into this world. Do you think we do it so that we can see you go to war and kill each other? Can you not understand that the Tedeschi mother, the American mother and all mothers want to see their sons come safely home?'

Arnold and Nicolich told her to bring the German down, so they could talk to him. She left, and they decided that if her story was true, they would leave the boy be. But if there was any doubt, they would have to kill him. They drew their pistols and stood to either side of the door. The two walked in. Arnold and Nicolich got 'a bit of a shock. The boy was only a lad. He did not look much more than sixteen or seventeen years old.'

Nicolich questioned the boy. He was not yet seventeen. He hated the Nazis for taking away his father, early in the war, after which he had disappeared. He knew there was zero chance of Germany winning the war. He'd even heard their officers talking about it. He also knew that as a deserter he would be shot if discovered, but he was willing to take the chance. All he wanted was to search for his missing father, and then to bring his family to Italy, where 'the people were so peaceful, loving and caring'.

Arnold and Nicolich said they'd have to search the house, but if nothing suspicious turned up then they were happy. They advised the lad to stay with the old lady, keep out of sight, and give himself up to the advancing Allied forces. He would then be held as a POW and at war's end could put his plans into action. The search turned up nothing suspicious. As a final warning they told the lad that if they heard that he had made any kind of a wrong move then they would 'hunt him down and shoot him'.

They shared a meal together and then Arnold and Nicolich went to leave. They tried to pay the old lady for her hospitality, but she would have none of it. She 'did not want money for helping mother's sons to stay alive and to go back to their mothers'. Even so, they managed to hide some cash in a cupboard in the kitchen. Tearfully, their host said she would pray for their fortunes, and that they should visit any time they were passing. The German boy pledged to look after her, for she was 'like a second mother to him'.

A few days later they made their rendezvous with the partisan leader, Alberto. Their base lay in a thickly wooden valley, where they'd constructed huts from tree branches and thatched them with grass. There were several dozen young men in Alberto's group, and Arnold and Nicolich wasted no time getting busy with their training. They concentrated on schooling Alberto's men in the use of the weapons they had to hand, and 'how to plan and execute an ambush'. Once the partisans seemed to have the hang of it, the two instructors said it was time they left. They had other, A Force work to attend to.

In an effort to convince them to stay, Alberto said he had something special he would like to show them. In the thickest patch of the woodland, he scraped away piles of old leaves to reveal some wooden planking. Dragging those aside, he showed where there was a pit. It was full of boxes. He dragged one out and used his knife to prise open the lid. It was packed full of plastic explosives.

'Well,' he beamed, 'what do you think of that?'

'That looks all right,' Arnold admitted, 'but what are you going to do with it?'

'About three miles from here is a German petrol dump. I thought with your help we might be able to blow it up.'

'But you have to have more than just explosives,' Arnold replied.

Alberto ordered more boxes to be dragged out. They were full of timer pencils, pressure switches, gun cotton blocks and more such paraphernalia of demolition work. From what Arnold could see, they had all the accoutrements necessary to cause a tidy few explosions. Alberto asked if they might stay for long enough to teach him and his men how to use it, and then maybe come with them to hit the fuel dump. Arnold and Nicolich said they'd think about it.

When they were alone, Arnold asked Nicolich what he thought they should do.

'Well, I don't know anything about explosives,' Nicolich confessed, but at the same time he made it clear that he didn't want to miss out on any such mission.

Two days later they set out for the fuel dump. The team consisted of Arnold and Nicolich, plus Alberto and three of his men. Six should be more than enough for the job at hand, and 'the fewer the better' was the maxim of the SAS. Since there were three giant fuel tanks, they would work in three teams of two. After trekking through the hills, Alberto announced that they had arrived. Below them lay the fuel plant. Arnold studied it through a pair of binoculars that Alberto had given him. The entire place was surrounded by a barbed wire fence. There was a barracks-like hut, and he could see one sentry at the gate, plus four or five soldiers seated beside the hut who appeared to be playing cards.

As the hut and the gate faced their present position, they'd need to work their way around the ridgeline, in order to strike from the opposite side. That would take some time, so they would attack on the following night, Arnold declared. In the interim they'd note sentry watches, routines and any other key defences.

Once they'd worked their way around to the rear of the plant, Arnold realised they faced a new problem. Between them and their target there lay a river. Around twenty feet wide, there was no way to gauge how deep it might be.

Arnold asked if everyone could swim, and all replied that they could. He then glanced at Nicolich. Earlier, they'd had to cross a wide river during their escape from the enemy. It was only while doing so that Arnold had realised that Nicolich didn't really know how to swim.

'Don't worry about me,' Nicolich growled, 'I'll swim that god-damn river if it's a mile wide and a hundred feet deep.'

That settled, Arnold paired them off. He and one partisan would take the tank nearest to the guard hut, so potentially the riskiest. Nicolich and one other would deal with the one in the middle of the compound, while Alberto and one of his men would hit the one nearest to the fence. Arnold's partner in sabotage, Georgio, was 'a young lad of about twenty, slim, wiry and full of life'. He suggested that when they reached the river he would go first, to gauge its depths. At sundown, Arnold set a watch rota, so the rest could get some sleep. They would be going in at 1.00 a.m. At that point the gate guard would be halfway through his watch and the rest of the enemy should be fast asleep in their barracks hut.

At midnight the raiders got ready. Each carried two-and-a-half pounds of explosives, plus timer pencils and gun cotton. Arnold showed them how to tuck the timer pencils under their hats, but they all seemed to stare at him as if he was mad. He explained that each timer contained a glass tube, filled with acid. If you broke the glass it activated the timer, and if you had them in your pocket or even in your backpack, a fall could set one off accidentally. Tucked under your hat it was all but impossible to break one. The timers Arnold had selected were thirty-minute versions, which left them that time to do their handiwork and get out of there.

They set off for the river, Arnold and Georgio leading, with

Nicolich and his partner coming next, and Alberto and his man bringing up the rear. They were separated by one-minute intervals, so if seen and fired upon they wouldn't make easy targets. The way down was thick with cover – a mixture of bushes and tall grass. Arnold and Georgio reached the river, dropped down onto the bank and proceeded to cover their faces in mud, to camouflage them. As it turned out the water only came up to their knees, so all were able to wade across. They made it to the fence apparently without being detected. Not a sound drifted across from the gate guard or the hut.

One man cut the wire, leaving the upper strands intact, so there was a hole just big enough to crawl through. With the grass being so high, at a glance the fence would appear to still be intact. Having wormed through the gap, the three parties split up. Slipping through the night like ghosts, Arnold and Georgio headed for the tank adjacent to the barracks. The plan was to place a charge on either side of each of the tanks. Upon reaching its vast bulk, Arnold went one way and Georgio the other. Well-practised, it took Arnold just a minute or so to place his explosives, and to trigger the timer. That done, he went to check how Georgio was doing. 'He had almost finished and had made a good job.'

With the second timer crushed and activated, they stole back to the hole in the fence. Having wormed their way through they waited for the others, while 'keeping our eyes on the plant', as Arnold observed. In no time all were reunited. With the seconds ticking by, they forded the river and climbed to a vantage point, from where to observe their handiwork. Arnold glanced at his watch. By his calculations the charge should detonate any moment now. Sure enough, there was 'the first big bang and a huge flame of fire rose to the sky', as the tank nearest the guard block was blasted into fire and ruin. One by one the other charges went up, each tank erupting in a boiling cataclysm of flame and devastation, and belching out a massive plume of black smoke across the sky.

'We had done a good job,' as Arnold noted. 'Alberto and his friends were jumping and hugging each other. They were overjoyed at the success of the mission. Of course, it was their first one.'

Making their way back to Alberto's base, Arnold and Nicolich said they really did have to leave. The partisans did all they could to persuade them to stay, but duty called. On the return journey they stopped off once more with the elderly spinster and her German deserter charge. But their reception there was not as they'd expected. While the old woman invited them in and fed them heartily, she berated Arnold and Nicolich for dishonouring her, for making her a fool, for being 'two very naughty boys', and for making her 'very, very, very unhappy'. Neither had a clue what she was on about. Only when they'd finished eating did she reveal all. Having fetched the German lad, she pulled the wad of lire out of her apron pocket – the money that Arnold and Nicolich had hidden in her kitchen – and plonked it on the table.

'You will take it back,' she instructed. 'You do not know when you might need it.'

All burst out laughing.

A few days later Arnold and Nicolich were back at work, gathering together the next group of POW-escapees to usher towards Allied lines. As SS troops flooded into the region, more and more of their Italian helpers were ending up getting caught, interrogated, tortured and shot. It had reached the stage where they decided that their A Force mission was no longer tenable. By now it was mid-March 1944, and the SAS trooper and OSS agent had been operating behind enemy lines for approaching six months.

Together, they decided to gather a last party of escapees and strike out for Allied lines.

Chapter 22

FIRST IN, LAST OUT

With Arnold and Nicolich poised to make their return across the lines, most of the standout A Force heroes were making their way back to the Allied fold. But OSS Lieutenant Sauro was still missing, as was Lieutenant Lewis, who'd last been seen riding on that doomed MAS boat. As for the inimitable commander of the SAS's French Squadron, somehow the seemingly indestructible Couraud had managed to snatch survival from the jaws of almost certain death or capture.

The wounded Couraud had gone into hiding at a farmstead near the small coastal settlement of Silvi – regular French Squadron territory. Some forty-eight hours after he and Scott had gone to ground, they received unexpected visitors. An Italian officer arrived, bringing with him four POW-escapees. They'd been sent to Couraud by Major Gordon, the mysterious British officer who had done all in his power to frustrate the efforts of the OSS team. In the interim, Couraud had had several dealings with the British major, reaching the conclusion that he was basically all right. It was only with the Italian-Americans that Major Gordon had seemed to have problems. He appeared to be running some kind of freelance escape network, and at times he and the French Squadron had made common cause.

Learning of the parlous state of the wounded Couraud, Major Gordon promised to help. He began 'making arrangements for a boat at Silvi', and a friendly Italian was dispatched to ensure all was in order. Somehow, they would get Couraud out, for he was in desperate need of proper medical care. A boat was procured, but Couraud still needed to get from their place of hiding to the point of embarkation on the seashore. Together with Sergeant Scott and the four POW-escapees, the fugitives set out into a darkening night. With his arm held in its sling, Couraud was assailed by 'long, dull pains' that ran from his 'shoulder and radiated to his fingertips'. At times he felt as if he was 'walking in a fog'. With Scott supporting him, he stumbled on.

Eventually, they made it to the seashore. As Couraud's citation for his Military Cross would relate, 'in spite of his injuries, after a few days he managed to obtain a boat in which he and his party sailed to TERMOLI on 12 November ... He returned ... to our lines with a bullet in one shoulder, which rendered the arm completely useless.' Typically, Couraud had sailed out of enemy territory bringing those last POW-escapees with him, staying loyal to his A Force mission to the very last. As his medal citation concluded, 'During the period October to November, Captain LEE was directly responsible for the ultimate safety of a large number of Allied escapers and showed a fine spirit of endurance and devotion to duty in successfully carrying out his task, even when wounded, under conditions of great difficulty and danger.'

Written up by Bill Stirling and signed off by General Alexander, the citation was also endorsed by Brigadier Dudley Clarke, the commander of A Force. But oddly, as there are no mentions of any extrajudicial executions nor any sections that are redacted, Couraud's MC documentation is also marked: 'NO PUBLICITY TO BE GIVEN TO THIS CITATION'. Even more mysterious is the note that had been stamped across it at a later date: 'CANCELLED SEE LG 21/9/44.' 'LG' stands for *London Gazette*, the official journal of record for HM Government. It appears that Couraud – rarely a stranger to impulsive behaviour or controversy – had been granted an MC for his actions in 1943, but had it taken away again in September 1944, for actions of a questionable nature.

But all of that lay months in the future. For now, Couraud was flown from Italy to Algeria for urgent medical treatment. Again, and typically, one of Couraud's first actions once he was safely ensconced in hospital was to endorse a Military Medal citation for Sergeant Scott, the SAS sergeant who had been his faithful companion to the last. After his own escape from the POW camp at Servigliano, 'Sergeant Scott at once volunteered to assist in the rescue of other POWs ... and was accordingly landed by boat, after two unsuccessful attempts, on the night of 27 October.' As Couraud noted, 'throughout all these operations, Sergeant Scott showed a fine spirit of courage and endurance and ... his conduct in making his own escape and then returning, without rest, to aid the rescue of others, is worthy of the highest praise.'

Even more typically, Couraud's second notable action would prove suitably outrageous: it was to escape from the hospital. With a bullet lodged in his shoulder, the doctors had agonised over how best to treat their patient. Eventually, they'd decided to repatriate Couraud to Britain, for surgery. But the very idea of being removed from the war was anathema to him. And so, with the assistance of some of his SAS comrades, Couraud had 'disappeared from the hospital'. He had two driving reasons to abscond, both of which typified the man. The first, he did not want to 'abandon his unit'. The second, he had 'struck up a romance with a young nurse, Hélène'.

One night, Couraud was out on the town, gallivanting with his arm in a sling, and together with none other than Anthony Greville-Bell, the man who had served as second in command on Operation Speedwell. After an epic escape and evasion, seventy-three days after they had parachuted into northern Italy Greville-Bell had led himself, plus his two companions, Sergeant George 'Bebe' Daniels and Corporal Pete Tomasso, back to Allied lines. He had been awarded the Distinguished Service Order for his incredible achievements. Tonight's Algerian adventures would prove less heroic and somewhat more controversial.

As Greville-Bell drove Couraud and Hélène from one night-spot to another, the shaking of the jeep caused Couraud so much pain that he fell unconscious. Hélène realised at once that this was serious. She and Greville-Bell rushed Couraud to a friend, a surgeon serving with Allied forces. As it was an emergency, he decided to operate immediately and did so using a private, civilian clinic. While the surgery proved a success, the entire venture did not. Alerted to Couraud's illegal absence, and the clandestine medical treatment that he had received, the military authorities were not best pleased. Faced with their wrath, and the threat of a court martial, it took the personal intervention of Bill Stirling to smooth troubled waters. As far as Stirling was concerned, Couraud, and his French Squadron, were far too valuable to lose.

Somehow permitted to share his convalescence with the delightful Hélène, Couraud had further adventures in mind.

Roy Farran had flown out of Italy, as 2 SAS operations there were grinding to a close. After his stalwart defence of Termoli, positioned around the railway line, Farran had remained true to his convictions that A Force work wasn't 'exciting enough and he didn't get to kill anybody'. Instead, he and his squadron had gone on to spearhead a series of coastal raiding operations. But in light of the wild and murderous adventures of McGregor, Couraud and others in the A Force teams, Farran may have regretted his decision to avoid Simonds's call to arms.

Birds of a feather, in Algeria Farran and Couraud made common cause. They set forth on a pilgrimage to the very source of the French Foreign Legion's traditions and its legendary repute – Sidi-bel-Abbès, the site of its training camp and its then headquarters, plus its museum. Of course, Couraud was a deserter from the Legion, which in theory should have attracted serious repercussions. But he had deserted to join SOE, and then the SAS, wherein he and his French Squadron had earned untold renown. In the event, he and Farran were 'shamelessly' toasted by the great and the good of the Legion.

At around this time, Couraud's British wife, Kathleen Davies (now officially Kathleen Lee) wrote to the War Office Casualty Branch, seeking news of her husband. Having heard that he had been injured in Italy, she asked: 'Would it be possible for me to have a report confirming this and telling me how he is getting on? Is there any chance that he will be sent to this country to convalesce?' By way of response, the War Office contacted MO1 (SP), the SOE cover organisation with which Couraud had served. The reply was that they had lost track of Couraud. 'I am afraid I do not know what happened to him,' wrote Lieutenant Colonel J. D. Kennedy, 'although of course we all know that the

2nd SAS Regiment served in a theatre where quite conceivably Lee would have been. I regret very much that I cannot give you any further information.'

Whether by design or not, the mercurial Couraud was proving hard to nail down, even by his own wife. Ensconced for now in Hélène's Algerian home, and enjoying her hospitality, there was little reason for Couraud to break cover. There he would remain for several weeks, convalescing, and entertaining those of his SAS comrades who were then in Algeria, for training, rest and recuperation after the long months at war.

One of the last things that Couraud had done, before being evacuated from Italy, was to report the death of Lieutenant Rob Lewis, the Harvard don turned OSS agent. It was inconceivable to anyone who had escaped from the doomed MAS boat that any of those below decks might have survived. In due course Lewis's family was informed that he was 'missing, believed killed over Italy'. (There was a mix-up in reporting, which suggested Lewis had been shot down 'over' Italy, rather than his vessel sank.) But in truth, the intrepid Lewis was very much alive, and he would make it back to Termoli with one of the greatest tales of escape of any of those involved in A Force operations.

From the point where he had crawled ashore, 'spent and shivering', Lewis was determined that he would get away. Moving south along the coast, he was sheltered and fed by a series of incredibly brave locals – 'kind and unquestioning', as he described them – one family gifting him 'a usefully shabby suit to wear'. While technically this meant that he was 'now in disguise and, if seized by the Germans, could have been treated as a spy', to Lewis it made far better sense than tramping along in full uniform. Thus attired, he was making his way south on the coastal road, when a car drew up beside him, and a question was asked in German.

Without thinking, Lewis answered, being fluent in German himself. Unfortunately, it was a German staff car, and the officer in the rear seemed to have found his quarry. 'Good! An Italian peasant who speaks German – hop in,' he declared, opening a door to usher Lewis into his vehicle. It was an order not an invitation. Thinking fast, Lewis told his captor that he was an Italian who'd spent time living in America and Germany, hence his language skills. Right away he was 'co-opted by the German camp commandant to serve as his interpreter'.

In the days that followed, Lewis worked at the heart of the German military machine, as the camp commandant 'laid out the new German Army Headquarters', which was being set up thereabouts. Having earned the man's 'trust', Lewis had finally managed to slip away. From there, he was sheltered by various locals, as he tried again and again to cross the lines. On each occasion he'd come across heavily fortified enemy positions, offering no way through. At one point he was recaptured and imprisoned in a barn, but managed to squeeze out of a back window and flee.

Finally, in late December 1943, Lewis 'swallowed enough raw red wine' to give himself the 'requisite courage', and he stumbled through the darkness towards the enemy frontline. Passing within feet of the German sentries, the madcap adventure ended as he 'fell into a foxhole'. It happened to be occupied by a Sikh, who served with the British First Indian Division. For a fearful few second the Sikh soldier did his best to cut off Lewis's head, which was hardly surprising since it was dark and he had arrived from the direction of the enemy.

Eventually, Lewis's real identity was established, and he was rushed back to A Force headquarters. Upon arrival, and back from the seeming dead, Lewis greeted Simonds with the following intriguing words: 'Do you think anyone will be interested in the particulars of the German Army Headquarters Camp?' Simonds of course declared himself most interested. Lewis proceeded to sketch out the entire layout of the German commander's position. Simonds sent the intelligence on to Allied headquarters, whereupon a squadron of RAF warplanes duly bombed the target that Lewis had so usefully identified. As Simonds noted, 'I put Lt. Lewis in for a well-earned MBE.'

Of course, having survived the MAS boat's horrendous sinking, and the epic escape and evasion that followed, Lewis went right back to his A Force work. He sent a telegram to his folks alerting them to the fact that he was alive and well. It arrived as they were 'sitting down, not very cheerfully, to Christmas dinner'. But across Britain and America, there were other families still anxiously awaiting news of their loved ones.

First and foremost were Arnold and Nicolich, whose fate remained a mystery.

Chapter 23

HOME RUN

For what was intended to be their last mission in Italy, Arnold and Nicolich assembled a group of five POW-escapees, plus themselves. It was 'just the right number', as Arnold noted. A band small enough to evade from the enemy, yet large enough to maintain morale for whatever lay ahead. The escapees were a mixed bag. There was a Royal Navy sailor, who had been captured by General Rommel's Afrika Korps in North Africa, plus a young infantry lad, and a variety of others, all of whom seemed up for it. The one bugbear was the major who made up their number. Full of pomposity and bluster, Arnold sensed trouble from the start.

The night of their departure, Arnold laid out the ground rules: the order of march, which was to be strictly adhered to, and what each should do if a situation arose wherein the lives of the others 'might depend on the actions of just one of them'. Such tactics and procedures had been tried and tested during countless such A Force operations, but it was now that the major began to show his true colours.

'I don't take orders from anyone here,' he blustered. 'I am the senior ranking person present, therefore I will give the orders, and I most certainly will not take orders from a private soldier and a bloody brigand.'

Arnold's response was to read him the riot act. He could do as he liked, but if he was to come with the rest 'he would have to obey orders to the letter', and if he did not then Arnold 'would shoot him and that goes for everyone. Until we get through the lines your safety is mine and Nick's responsibility. If any of you do not wish to be a member of this party, just say so now and we will leave you. But remember, it is the duty of every soldier to take the chance to get back to his country and to fight again.'

Arnold and Nicolich asked if any had changed their minds. None had. But typically, the major had to have the last word. 'When and if we get back I will report you for threatening an officer of His Majesty's Army.'

Neither Nicolich nor Arnold bothered to answer him. Instead, they arranged the escapees in their line of march. Nicolich would take the lead, and Arnold would bring up the rear. He made sure the major was right in front of him, so he 'could keep an eye on him'. Nicolich had a whistle. If it was blown twice, they would know danger was approaching – very possibly 'Germans in a car or trucks'. Upon hearing those two blasts they were to immediately take cover and to freeze. If there were trees, they were to stand perfectly still beside one. If there was only grass, to dive into it and keep still. On no account were they to run or make any noise. In this way the danger would pass and they would go unnoticed. It was movement that drew the eye.

With the ground rules seemingly agreed, they set off. There were fifteen miles to cover and they'd take a short rest every half an hour, if circumstances allowed. The column of escapees were about halfway to their destination – the frontlines – when they reached a sharp bend in the road that they were following. It was a 'very dark night, no moon', which meant it was 'easy to disappear if circumstances prompted it'. Making their way ahead and spaced well apart, Nicolich and three of the escapees negotiated the corner and were lost to sight. That left only one escapee, the Major and Arnold, the tail end Charlie. Suddenly, they heard two sharp blasts on the whistle – danger was approaching.

With a steep drop on the right, only the left side of the road offered a viable hiding place. It presented a flat expanse of grass, with a clump of trees in the distance. Arnold saw the lead escapee dive into the cover of the grass. Good man. The major followed suit, and Arnold did the same, so all three were well hidden. There was the growl of an engine and headlamps pierced the gloom. A vehicle swung around the bend. Just as the beams were full-on their hiding place, Arnold saw the major spring to his feet and make a run for it, heading for the distant trees.

With both Arnold and the lead escapee down in the grass, the vehicle 'screeched to a halt'. It had come to a stop right opposite where Arnold was lying. Burrowing his face into the grass and with his hands over his head to hide his blond hair, Arnold heard a volley of shots ring out – clearly, whoever was in the car was shooting at the major. Once the firing had stopped footsteps swished through the grass.

A voice yelled out in German. '*Hände hoch! Hände hoch!*'

Arnold rolled onto his back. Standing over him was a German soldier with his machine gun, yelling for Arnold to get to his feet with his hands up. He was frogmarched to the vehicle. It was an open-topped car, which had made it easy for the enemy troops to spot the major breaking cover. 'That bloody stupid major,' Arnold told himself. 'If he had not started to run we would never have been seen.' Beside the vehicle was an officer, who menaced Arnold with his pistol. He was forced into the car, and under close guard driven to a large country house, where he was locked into an upper room.

The following morning some soldiers came in with Arnold's breakfast. To his amazement it consisted of porridge, bacon and eggs, plus three slices of toast and a mug of coffee. Once he had eaten, the questioning began. A young German officer speaking impeccable English asked Arnold to write down his name, rank and regiment. Arnold scribbled down a fictitious name, and gave his unit as the Royal Army Services Corps, a transport and logistics unit. The officer must have checked, for a while later he was marched downstairs for further questioning.

'What you have written on this paper is a lot of lies,' he was told. 'Will you please tell me your right name and number?'

Arnold figured if he was to be held as a POW, he might as well give a fairly accurate account. He wrote down his real name, his rank as trooper and his unit as the 16th Lancers, and not of course the SAS. Glancing at the paper the officer declared that was much better. Then he fired a series of questions at Arnold to check his bona fides, most of which concerned his service in North Africa. When it came to asking what gun the German Tiger tank had, Arnold answered, with a rueful smile, 'A bloody eighty-eight.' The German 88mm gun was hated by Allied troops for its lethality.

The German officer laughed. 'Did you not like the eighty-eight?'

'No, I did not!'

A lot of questions followed, most of which concerned Arnold's supposed time in an Italian POW camp – his cover story – and what he had been up to since escaping. The following morning the inquisition began once more, but this time the atmosphere seemed to be markedly strained. Arnold's interrogator asked him for specific details concerning the POW camp that he claimed to have been held in, before producing a German sergeant who had actually worked there. Very quickly it became evident that Arnold had never set foot in the camp.

'Now, tell me who you are and what you are doing in an enemy country?' the German officer demanded.

'I can only tell you my name, rank and number,' Arnold countered.

'The British agents caught in some farmhouses not long ago – what do you know about them?'

'Nothing, sir.'

'Have you ever taken part in an ambush of German vehicles?'

'No, sir.'

'What about the petrol dump a few nights ago?'

'I don't know what you are talking about.'

Arnold was ordered back to his room.

The next morning he was again marched downstairs. This time the German officer did not ask him to sit. Instead, he continued studying the papers he had before him as the silence lengthened.

Finally, he raised his head. 'I would like to have believed that you are an escaped POW. But I have here information that you are one of a gang of ruthless murderers and as such you will be taken to Germany and tried by a court. If it was left to me, I would shoot you here and now,' he added. 'What do you have to say to that?'

'Nothing, sir.'

The officer began to fire questions at Arnold, to all of which he gave only his name, rank and number. Finaly, the German unholstered his pistol.

He levelled it at Arnold. 'I think I will shoot you now. Have you got anything to say before I do?'

'Yes, sir. If you shoot me, when the British get here they will try you as a war criminal.'

For several seconds the officer stared at Arnold in icy silence. Then, jabbing his pistol into his chest and bringing his face close to his, he cried: 'Me! Me a war criminal? I am an officer of the German Army. I am carrying out my duties in a country that is occupied by my army. You? You are in enemy country dressed as a civilian, you have been murdering German soldiers and Italian civilians. Who is the war criminal? You or me?' He paused. 'I will send you back to your room so you can think about it. Meanwhile, I will be deciding where and how you will be executed.'

Back in his room Arnold pondered his predicament. He'd already checked the place out for any means of escape. There were none. If he admitted any of the charges levelled at him, he was bound to be executed. It was best to stay schtum, and to await an opportunity to break free. That afternoon he was taken downstairs to see the German officer once more.

'I have been ordered to send you to Chieti,' he began. How ironic – that was the point at which he and McGregor had parachuted into Italy in the first place. At Chieti, Arnold would face further interrogations before being sent to Germany. A Feldwebel – sergeant – appeared who was to serve as his escort. He spoke good English, and had orders to shoot to kill if Arnold tried anything. 'Is that clear?'

'Yes, sir.'

'Put your hands on your head and walk to the door.'

Arnold did as instructed. Then the Feldwebel took up position behind him and cried out: 'Quick march!'

With his machine gun sticking in Arnold's back, the Feldwebel propelled Arnold down the track leading to the nearby village. There, a car would be waiting to take him to Chieti. After thirty minutes of fast marching, the Feldwebel called a rest halt. He asked Arnold where he came from in England. London, Arnold answered. The Feldwebel explained that he had been at college in Oxford, 'a beautiful place. I took a degree in law there.'

'What the hell are you doing in the army then?' Arnold demanded.

'Well, we all have to serve the Fatherland.'

The Feldwebel asked if Arnold smoked. He did. He'd love a cigarette. Slinging his weapon on his shoulder, the Feldwebel reached inside his tunic to bring out his smokes. In a flash Arnold brought his knee up into the man's groin, while simultaneously bringing both of his hands down onto the rear of his neck, in a savage strike. It was a move they had been taught and rehearsed time and time again during SAS training, and it proved brutally effective. The Feldwebel's knees buckled and he collapsed onto the ground.

At the same instant Arnold broke away. At first he raced downhill, which was the natural way to flee. But then he decided to do the least expected and to climb. As he switched direction, he heard a burst of fire which had to come from the Feldwebel's machine gun, but this sounded more like shots of alarm than any kind of aimed fire. There were certainly no bullets coming anywhere near Arnold. Climbing hard, he skirted the large house where he had been held captive and made for the mountains beyond.

Over the ensuing days Arnold began a desperate escape and evasion, as the entire countryside seemed awash with German search parties. Living off the land, he ended up 'in a hell of a mess'. At several junctures he fell upon the kindness of the locals, all of whom knew that he was 'the one who had escaped from the Germans'. After many days on the run, he heard news of Nicolich. Apparently the American had also been captured. Remembering what they had promised each other, Arnold decided to make for the Nova Strada, a stretch of newly constructed highway that had never been finished due to the war. As it went nowhere, it was little used. More to the point, there was a cave at one point along its length. Nicolich and Arnold had promised each other that if they were ever separated, they would rendezvous there.

Arnold made it to the shelter of the cave unmolested. He'd been there for forty-eight hours, and hadn't seen a soul, when he heard someone walking along the road and whistling. It was Nicolich, and he was striding ahead 'as if he had not a care in the world'. Breaking from the cave, Arnold yelled out, 'Nick! Nick! Over here!' The American came dashing over and the two 'hugged each other like long lost brothers'.

Back in the cave they swopped stories. After Arnold's capture, Nicolich had led those escapees who remained to the final safe house, after which a local guide took them over the lines. He'd seen not a sign of the major, so he was either dead or on the run. Nicolich had returned to try to find out what had happened to Arnold. But stopped by German guards on a bridge, he'd been taken to their headquarters for questioning. Nicolich claimed to be a Yugoslav who was on his way to enlist in the Black

Brigades, the fascist paramilitary battalions. He gave his interrogators details of his Yugoslav hometown, claiming to be a former soldier who was demobbed when Italy surrendered.

Held prisoner, the Germans had produced a Yugoslav who came from the same area as Nicolich. He asked a raft of questions about Nicolich's hometown. Of course, Nicolich 'had all the answers'. The Yugoslav asked about the cinema, the bars he frequented, the name of his local church. Not only did Nicolich regale him with details, but he fired back some questions of his own. The Yugoslav had no option but to vouch for Nicolich's bona fides. That established, the German officer issued him a pass to travel to Chieti, where he was to volunteer for the local Black Brigade. But he warned Nicolich that if he 'ever caught him wandering about he would shoot him'.

What was clear to the two men was that the enemy knew chapter and verse about their past activities. If they were recaptured, it would amount to a death sentence. They had to make it back across the lines. They resolved to head south, treading the same route as had scores of POW-escapees before them, only now they were seeking to save their own skins. They reached the final safe house, to discover that their trusted guide, 'who had taken so many POWs through', had been arrested. Another young man had taken his place. He went by the name of Ricky, and he worked side by side with his brother, Tino.

Ricky led them to the last stopover before crossing the lines – an ancient 'refugio', a morgue of sorts. It was where the bodies of the dead were kept over winter, when the mountain ground was frozen and too hard to dig any graves. Sure enough, Arnold and Nicolich spent their last night in that cold morgue. 'It was a hell of a place,' Arnold observed. 'It was cold and damp, there were shelves all around where the bodies were put, but now they were taken up with makeshift beds.' As Arnold clambered onto his allotted shelf, he wondered, 'how many corpses had been here before me?'

Strict instructions were issued by Ricky as to how they were to cross the lines. At night, they would descend into a valley, sticking to the cover of a forest. Eventually, they would reach a wire fence. They would skirt along the fence until they reached a hillock, atop of which was a German machine-gun post. It was manned by three Austrians, but they were 'friends of Ricky and Tino and they were on our side'. Five hundred metres below that gun post was a section of the wire that had an opening, about a foot wide. Once through the fence, the danger would be from roving German and British patrols. If they met any, they were to go to ground and freeze, no matter what happened.

Following those instructions to the letter and in complete silence, they snaked their way into the darkness. The onwards journey went like clockwork, including slipping past that machine-gun nest, marked by 'two steel helmets silhouetted against the night sky'. Sliding down a slope they reached the hole in the wire and wormed through. But beyond it they heard the unmistakeable thumps of footfalls. All four men dropped motionless to the ground. Figures emerged in the distance. Arnold and Nicolich prayed they had not been seen. They were in luck, as whoever made up that patrol 'turned and started to walk away in the opposite direction'.

Ricky grabbed Arnold's arm. The two of them would creep forward and try to contact any Allied troops, he explained. 'We will crawl a few yards,' he whispered, 'then when I raise my hand, you just call out softly, "British soldier".'

When the signal came, Arnold did as instructed, but there was no reply. He tried again. Still no answer. But upon a third such cry there was an answer of sorts. A figure rose up ahead with his rifle levelled. 'Stand up and put your hands on your head,' he ordered. Arnold did as instructed and he was ushered into a slit trench. Shortly, the rest of the party – Ricky included – were brought in.

They were taken to a nearby area where there was a squadron of light tanks. An officer asked Arnold who he was. Once he had explained, he was offered a cup of tea. It was sheer bliss, leaning on that tank, 'enjoying a lovely cup of tea and a smoke. It was a good feeling to be free,' reflected Arnold, 'not having to worry about who you might meet next, or where the next food and drink was going to come from.' They were taken from there to the nearest headquarters, whereupon they bade farewell to Ricky and Tino. 'We could not thank them enough for what they had done.'

After a final round of questioning, Arnold and Nicolich were driven to the main Allied HQ at the city of Caserta, which lay a good 100 kilometres to the south of the frontline. After a bath, both men were kitted out in fresh uniforms and shown to a room where they could sleep. 'At last I had a good pair of boots,' remarked Arnold. The next day Nicolich and Arnold saw each other for what would be 'the last time. It was a very sad meeting,' observed Arnold. 'We had become close friends.' Nicolich's parting words were that if ever Arnold was in New York, he should head for the port and ask any docker to be put in touch with him.

Arnold and Nicolich had reached Allied lines in late March 1944, at almost exactly the same time as the two OSS comrades with whom they'd made up the gang of four. As an OSS signal from the time recorded, 'The following personnel reported in person to this HQ on March 23rd, after escaping from enemy territory . . . S/Sgt Albert A. Ingengi, 31214487; T/5 John H. Nicolich, 32655601; Corporal Arthur P. Roberta, 3266445 . . . The men used a secret escape channel . . . Please notify the next of kin.' There were anxious families who had heard nothing of their loved ones for almost half a year. Understandably perhaps, most had presumed that Arnold, Nicolich, Roberta and Ingengi were long dead. It was as if they had risen from the grave.

As Trooper Arnold's Military Medal (MM) citation would state, during many months spent behind the lines he was 'largely responsible for the successful return of a considerable number of British ex-POWs, and continually showed a fine offensive spirit. His devotion to duty during this period is worthy of high praise.' Of course, what men like Arnold and McGregor and the French Squadron – plus their OSS comrades – had also achieved, unwittingly, was to prove Bill Stirling's intent in action. By the law of unintended consequences, their missions deep behind the lines, and their Robin Hood brigandage, had drawn thousands of enemy troops into the region in an effort to hunt them down. Those were troops that, self-evidently, couldn't man the enemy's frontlines.

More importantly, the impact upon the morale of the German troops, and especially on that of their Fascist Italian cohorts, would have been immeasurable. Getting ambushed, harassed, robbed and shot up seemingly at every turn, and across regions that were supposedly hundreds of miles from any fighting and thus assumed to be safe and secure, proved hugely dispiriting, not to mention unsettling. That was especially so, when the attackers came and went like ghosts in the night, and proved so elusive, and so hard to capture or to kill.

As Arnold and his comrades noted, while the physical ability of the German troops was excellent, their 'morale, however, is cracking'. They'd met more than one German soldier who was 'disgusted with Hitler and the war'. Kill the enemy's spirit and you would win the wider war. Right now, there was one team still at large doing just that.

But would the last of the A Force warriors make it home?

Chapter 24

IS IT REALLY YOU?

With Simonds's operations long disbanded, there was no Termoli headquarters for anyone to return to. Instead, Arnold was put on a flight bound for Algiers. In North Africa, there was likewise no SAS base to report to, for all had been recalled to Britain in preparation for the missions to come. Accordingly, Arnold was slated to take an RAF flight back to Britain, but he was bumped by a 'VIP' and for several days running the same thing kept happening.

Arnold had come out of Italy with a fistful of lire. He changed some of that into local currency, and one night he ran into an American pilot in an Algiers bar. The guy offered him a lift in his C47. It was heading out the next morning for Gibraltar, a perfect stepping stone to the UK. True to his word, the American pilot loaded Arnold into his hold, which was crammed with cargo, and off they set. After various adventures they landed in Gibraltar, only for Arnold to get himself arrested. The military police (MPs) couldn't seem to comprehend how he had hitched a lift over from Algiers, still less how he could be carrying no official ID papers (unsurprisingly, he had lost them in Italy).

The MP officer asked Arnold where he had been and what he

had been doing. Arnold answered that he wasn't at liberty to say, but that he'd been serving with 'the SAS Regiment'. His inquisitor looked totally nonplussed. He'd never heard of such a unit. What the hell did the letters 'SAS' stand for anyway? No matter how Arnold might try to explain, he got nowhere. At gunpoint he was locked in the cells for the night. The following morning there was an apology of sorts, before Arnold was bundled aboard a plane bound for London. He touched down in England on 24 April 1944, to be met by two more MPs. Finally, he was issued with a rail warrant and directed to Glasgow, where an officer would guide him to the new base of 2 SAS.

Upon arrival, predictably no one had heard of the SAS. But there were rumours of a secret unit headquartered at the village of Monkton, on the Scottish west coast. Arnold made his way there, and headed to a local café for a cuppa. Inside, he spied a distinctive-looking individual who sported a beret adorned with the 'winged dagger' cap badge. Arnold approached and he turned out to be a member of the French SAS. He explained his story and asked where the 2 SAS base was located. The Frenchman had a jeep outside and offered him a lift: 'I will take you home.'

When the jeep pulled up at the SAS camp, one of the first people Arnold laid eyes upon was Alistair McGregor. The SAS lieutenant 'could not believe that it was me', Arnold recalled, especially since Arnold had been listed as missing for so long. McGregor was able to acquaint Arnold with the news of their patrol. With Arnold's return, every man had made it safely back to Allied lines, barring Trooper Dellow. He'd been caught in the aftermath of the enemy ambush at the farmsteads and was being held as a POW in Germany. Until this moment, all anyone had known regarding Arnold and Nicolich was that they were missing. All had presumed they were either POWS, or dead.

After their emotional reunion, Arnold was taken to Bill Stirling's office to provide a full account of his exploits. After that he was 'very graciously granted ten days leave'. En route to his home, he passed by the Edinburgh army records office, to sort out his back pay. At first he was told that he couldn't have any, for he was still officially listed as missing. Eventually, he managed to convince the bureaucrats of who he was, and finally got some of the money he was owed. In his official army records, the 'Missing' report of 12 December 1943 was eventually crossed out, and replaced with the words 'Cancel Missing Report (Away on Special Duty)'.

From Edinburgh, Arnold travelled home to his grandmother's house in Norwich. Peeping through the window he saw 'my old grandmother sitting in her chair'. Arnold went in. When Granny Webster saw him, she got up and threw her arms around him, crying out, 'Is it really you?' Finally, she stood back with tears streaming down her face, and sobbed, 'I thought you were dead. I was told you were missing. But that was a long time ago. This damn war. Why? Why?'

It was then that Arnold remembered that old lady in Italy who had fed and sheltered him and Nicolich, while she also harboured that young German deserter. He remembered her words: 'What would your mother say if you were reported dead?'

Well, he didn't have a mother. His granny was as good as. And she had been mortified; devastated.

With Arnold's return, that left only Lieutenant Sauro and several of his OSS men unaccounted for. Those OSS agents who had made it through the lines had reported on the fortunes of their comrades. As far as all were concerned, Lieutenant Sauro, their commander, and Sergeant DeLuca, his stalwart deputy, were still at work behind the lines. Only Panzarella, their wireless operator, was known to have been captured. The rest were recorded at OSS headquarters thus: 'latest reports show they are still in that area to first assist British prisoners of war to escape and secondly to cut enemy communications . . .' It was business as usual, as far as Operation Simcol was concerned.

In truth, things were not as sanguine as that report intimated. By March 1944 Sergeant DeLuca had found himself on the summit of a high mountain, hiding out from numerous enemy patrols. He was in the company of two other OSS agents – Sergeants Salvaggio and Gulie – along with several Yugoslavs, who had themselves escaped from camps in Italy. They were desperate for food, especially since few Italian villagers could risk bringing them any. One day DeLuca set out to find some, together with a Yugoslav named Miadrage. They would trek to the nearby village of Castel del Monte, where they had always been able to count upon help.

Halfway down the mountainside a fierce blizzard struck. The snowstorm proved so intense that DeLuca and Miadrage were forced to continue on foot, for they had intended to make the entire journey using skis, having procured several sets from the locals. In an intense whiteout such as this, only by inching forward on foot could you possibly find a safe route. Reaching the village, they made for the house of their local contact, Frank Germain. There they were fed, their clothes were put to dry, and they managed to thaw out frozen limbs. But as the villagers went about collecting food for them, so a group of Fascist Blackshirts entered the village. With the blizzard still raging, DeLuca and Miadrage dreaded having to leave, even though the enemy was right there in their midst.

Eventually they set out, each laden with 40 kilos of flour, cheese and beans gathered from across the village. Still the storm raged and howled. From the bottom of the pass which led to Castel del Monte they heard single gunshots and machine gunfire. The blizzard seemed worse than ever and their route was all uphill. The dark sky became thick with freezing sleet. The fugitives paused to light a fire in the shelter of some trees. But they were shot at and forced to hurry on. Frozen to the core, they eventually made it back to their hideout – that hut set high on the mountain. Dumping their loads, they collapsed into their makeshift beds and fell into an exhausted sleep.

They awoke the following afternoon to hear voices in the hut's kitchen. Crawling to the door of the room, for he could barely walk, DeLuca asked who was there. His eyes were still half-frozen and he could barely see. One of his OSS comrades, Sergeant Salvaggio replied that it was 'Germans'. DeLuca tried to argue that he was an Italian soldier, but he was asked for his ID documents. Shortly, all were taken prisoner. Marched down the mountain, at various junctures the German troops stopped at huts or farmsteads to seize the POW-escapees who were hiding there. Clearly, someone had reported on them all. Later, one of the German troops revealed to DeLuca that 'Fascist spies' were responsible for giving them away.

Loaded onto trucks, the captives were driven to Gestapo headquarters. There, they received a 'thorough interrogation'. Sergeant Gulie was beaten and tortured, and in the process he 'cracked and let slip the name of the OSS'. It was a short stop from there to

Laterina POW camp (PG 82), which was crammed full of 2,500 British and American POWs, most of whom had either abided by the standfast order, or been recaptured since. The conditions at Laterina were terrible, as DeLuca noted: 'very bad, with little food given to us and sometimes none at all.' But in due course, matters were to take a turn for the worse.

On 17 June 1944, the enemy heard that Allied troops had broken through the lines. A column of tanks was headed for Laterina, which meant that the camp was under orders to evacuate. At 8.00 p.m. that evening, the 2,500 POWs were ordered to move. But as the column of men became strung out and the evening darkened, here and there figures broke away in an effort to escape. Shots rang out as escapees were gunned down. Other POWs were caught in the line of fire. Amid all the confusion, DeLuca decided to seize his chance.

Diving off a bridge into the semi-darkness, by luck DeLuca's fall was broken by a patch of thick bush. He crawled away until he reached a seemingly impassable barrier. On either side of the column of prisoners there were patrols of German troops, providing an outer cordon. DeLuca's only hope was to shadow the column's progress and await his chance. For hours he did just that, seeing POWs who tried to break away getting gunned down and finished off with pistol shots to the head. One injured man was run over by a German armoured vehicle. Others were hunted down by the enemy's dog patrols and summarily shot. Eventually, with the night thick all around him, DeLuca managed to slip away.

A while later he heard a voice call out in English: 'Who's that?'

Deluca answered, and he was able to link up with a British escapee. They pressed on, but finally reached a chokepoint. Ahead lay the wall of a sheer mountain. At its base there were two anti-aircraft guns, with a German soldier standing guard. There was no way to turn back. DeLuca and his English partner would have to deal with the sentry. They crawled across to him and attacked. The guard was well fed and rested. They were not. In the resulting struggle, DeLuca was struck in the stomach by the guard's sub-machine gun and floored, whereupon the German jumped on him.

The English escapee grabbed the sentry by the hair and dragged him off, at which point DeLuca got him by the throat and together they managed to strangle him. The noise of the struggle must have been heard, for a German Spandau – an MG 42 – opened fire. DeLuca's comrade was hit in the stomach. The OSS sergeant tried to drag him away, but the Englishman knew that he was finished, and he urged DeLuca to abandon him. As the OSS agent dashed away, he heard German troops finishing off the wounded man, that was 'if he wasn't already dead'. Linking up with several other escapees from that POW column, DeLuca made his way into the mountains, swimming rivers, scaling ravines, and being sheltered by the locals, until he was able to join up with a band of partisans.

Their leader, a man named Raol, welcomed DeLuca and the others. Over the past few weeks he and his resistance fighters had turned the Valdarno, a rugged stretch of terrain carrying the Arno river from Florence to Arezzo, into a no-go zone for the enemy. With a hundred fighters under his command, and equipped with weaponry parachuted into the area by the British, Raol was 'the first to shoot at any vehicle or German column passing'. But the enemy response had been brutal in the extreme. They'd resorted to attacking any village that had had any kind of contact with the partisans and killing indiscriminately – men, women and children were put to the sword.

By now, DeLuca had been behind enemy lines, or in enemy captivity, for over ten months. He figured it was high time he returned to his own side. Together with eight other escaped POWs – a mixture of Americans, British and South Africans – he set out to try to cross the lines on foot. Braving enemy shellfire, and more, the group moved along the highest mountain terrain in an effort to bypass heavy German patrols. Eventually, DeLuca and his comrades made it through, ironically arriving back at Laterina POW camp, which had been taken by the Allies.

Fed, cared for, and in a fresh uniform, DeLuca decided to hitchhike his way to Rome, in an effort to rejoin his unit. His first contact with US troops was when he ran into an American Air Force Headquarters outfit. There he was hospitalised with 'some stomach trouble', but recovered well. Having made it back to Allied territory on 28 July 1944, Sergeant DeLuca was the last of the OSS/A Force teams to do so. Upon his return to OSS headquarters, he asked that his future assignment should be: 'To continue with his unit in Italy, or wherever they go.' Unsurprisingly, he would be assessed by his OSS commanders as showing: 'Superior Motivation, Leadership. Excellent Practical Intelligence, Stability, Ability to Work with Others, Physical Ability. Very favourable.'

Regarding his A Force operations, they would conclude: 'Very independent and self-sufficient, he functioned extraordinarily well when his OG group had to break into small units to escape. He is quick minded, cool, resourceful, daring and courageous . . . Seems a perfect type for special Ops . . . Twice captured by the Germans he escaped and showed the greatest courage, endurance and resourcefulness ... is highly motivated for further work behind the lines, preferably in Italy.'

Sadly, Lieutenant Sauro – DeLuca's commander – would not be returning to Allied lines any time soon. He'd spent the months of January, February and March 1944 'staying in mountain hideouts and farmhouses, and living off the land in the performance of a most difficult mission'. Captured on 26 April 1944, Sauro was shipped north to Germany. Despite numerous escape attempts he would spend the rest of the war in a POW camp, which would not be liberated until June 1945. Recommended for a Silver Star, the United States's third highest decoration for valour, the citation concluded: 'Hundreds of escaped Allied prisoners were contacted by Lieutenant Sauro. They were given food, clothing, money, and they were directed along escape routes that Captain Sauro had mapped out.'

Following his release from captivity, Lieutenant Sauro was promoted to captain. Of the eighteen OSS men that he had taken into the field, only three, including himself, had been captured. All the rest had made it through the lines. Upon his return to OSS headquarters, in Washington, in August 1945, Sauro was selected for 'Hazardous duty with small combat groups in CHINA. This officer will participate in raids against the Japanese and advance sections in enemy held territory.' Of course, the dropping of the atom bombs and the premature ending of the war in the Far East would make no such deployment necessary.

Long before Captain Sauro's release from captivity in Germany, Simonds had wound up A Force operations in Italy. As he noted, by the turn of the year (1943–44) the 'volume and pressure of escapees had by then died down. The majority of the POWs still in camps had been taken over and evacuated to Germany by the German Army. The flow of escapees was dwindling and the German lines were becoming more tightly held.' It was time to disband his 'hasty and improvised Escape Operation ...' Accordingly, by early 1944 the men of 2 SAS were released from his care.

They had returned to North Africa for rest, recuperation and training, before being dispatched to Britain, in preparation for the second great amphibious invasion that was coming: Operation Overlord and the Normandy landings. There too, they would have a crucial role to play. But for now, they could rest on their laurels. In Operation Loco – the Pisticci concentration camp raid – they had pulled off a mission that would be unrivalled in terms of sheer audacity and daring in the entirety of the war.

The Pisticci mission is one of the few examples of an Allied force going far into hostile territory to rescue mostly civilian internees, and the only one to liberate a concentration camp deep behind the lines. It is a powerful example of how the SAS were a law unto themselves. Thankfully, they didn't have to get such borderline-insane missions signed off at a high level. If they had, it is highly likely that the raid would never have happened. It vindicated Churchill's passionate belief in Special Forces doing the utterly audacious and unthinkable, and the dividends such high-risk high-reward operations would yield. Churchill's frustration at the hidebound nature of military strategy and the inherent caution of many commanders was well known.

In the A Force missions that followed, the SAS had done all that Simonds – and Churchill – had asked of them, and much more. The overall achievements of those operations remains hard to assess. As Simonds had realised early in their work, he and his men were an embarrassment. Every success they achieved was an embarrassment, for it reminded those on high of the catastrophic blunder of the standfast order, and of all those that it had condemned to months of horrific suffering and further incarceration at the hands of the enemy. Typically, Simonds himself would play down the numbers of POW-escapees pulled out by sea, estimating it as being 'about 900 . . . A small number compared to the potential 78,000 POWs in POW camps at the time of the Armistice!' Of course, that took little account of all those who had made it through the lines, moving overland.

As Simonds was fully aware, 'a great deal of courage, endurance and effort by all concerned with these escape operations' had been evidenced by 'all ranks, largely unrecognised and unsung'. As he was at pains to point out, 'the gallantry and privations endured by the men of the SAS, 1st Airborne Division, OSS and the A Force personnel should be recognised and admitted in future official accounts of the Italian Campaign.' But in truth there was a 'marked tendency to play down these operations by the powers that be, *because of the magnitude of the errors resulting from the MI9 War Office orders* [Simonds's emphasis]. But this blunder should not be allowed to diminish or decry the work by all ranks concerned.'

The raft of medals given to the British participants in the A Force operations speaks for itself: 'At least 3 Military Crosses, 2 Distinguished Conduct Medals and 3 Military Medals were awarded', not to mention McGregor's DSO. There were also the decorations given to the OSS teams. Of course, several of the British awards were stamped 'NO PUBLICITY IS TO BE GIVEN TO THIS CITATION', due to the unorthodox nature of their behind-the-lines operations. Thankfully, with the passage of time those awards have been released to the public, though some remain partially redacted.

Bill Stirling, 2 SAS's founder, railed against the misuse of the SAS in Italy. His exasperation centred around the inability of 15th Army Group commanders to 'open their minds to the potential of guerrilla warfare' as perfected by the SAS. In the summer of 1943, he had outlined his plans for hundreds of two-to-four-man patrols to be dropped deep into hostile territory, to paralyse the enemy's supply lines and communications. All he had been allowed was to send in the Speedwell saboteurs, who had of course done a magnificent job.

In December 1943, he had submitted a tersely worded memo to high command, questioning why, with 'aircraft and personnel being available, an effective force was not sent against German Lines of Communication in northern Italy', and demanding that 'in the future, advantage may be taken' of such opportunities. Sadly, such an attitude did not win him many friends in high places. Of course, by default – and at Churchill's personal behest – the A Force teams had been sent in. In Lieutenant McGregor's case – and Lieutenant Sauro's – they had proven just how successful Stirling's mass insertion plan for the SAS might have been. With no radio links, no back-up and no means of resupply, those SAS and OSS teams had spent *months* behind the lines spreading havoc and mayhem.

Of course, Simonds shared Stirling's frustrations. He was aware of the unexpected windfall that the Allies had reaped from his A Force operations. Across a vast swathe of territory, the enemy were left 'Qui vive' – permanently on the alert, or on the lookout – as a few dozen Allied troops tied down thousands of enemy soldiers tasked with 'countering our behind the lines operations'. MI9 itself had stated that one of the key aims of escaping from captivity was to 'tie up as many enemy troops as possible'. As Simonds concluded of his A Force operations: 'We certainly did that.' And the price paid by the Allies was infinitesimal. 'The cost in lives was small,' Simonds concluded, especially since 'the great majority of personnel that I dropped behind the lines made their way back to Allied lines.'

EPILOGUE

Outside of the A Force teams featured in this book, there were several other SAS, A Force and 1st Airborne Division units that served under Simonds. Many of them carried out similarly heroic and audacious POW-rescue missions behind the lines, and related actions. Not all could be featured in these pages, yet all contributed materially to the large number of POW escapees that were, against all odds, brought safely back to Allied lines.

As just one example, Deane-Drummond had dispatched two signallers by parachute, to try to link up with Lieutenants McGregor and Sauro's patrols in the field. Those men, Sergeant P. Phillips and Signalman D. Stewart, failed to find either party. Instead, they set up their own escape line and brought out over 400 POWs overland. Not only that, they remained in regular daily contact with A Force headquarters, and managed to charge their radio batteries by an ingenious means. They'd installed their wireless set in an attic above a German Brigade HQ. They recharged their batteries using a German engine that ran all night, without supervision. Fittingly, Phillips and Stewart were both awarded the Distinguished Conduct Medal (DCM) at mission's end.

Of those teams deployed into Italy on Operation Speedwell, both Lieutenant Greville-Bell's, and Sergeants Stokes and Robinson's sticks made it back to Allied lines. Stokes's escape following his Rome adventures would be a truly epic undertaking; he wouldn't return to the Allied fold until towards war's end, having broken out of a POW camp in Germany. Of course, the fortunes of the Speedwell raiders had proven Bill Stirling right in his assessment that many such small SAS teams could have made a war-winning contribution in Italy, if used in a similar way. The SAS's A Force operations had furthered that argument, of course.

Post-Italy, the SAS won itself a reprieve. In the summer 1944 D-Day missions teams were dropped all across France, deep behind the lines, charged with classic SAS tasks. Often linking up with the French Resistance, they carried out highly successful sabotage and guerrilla-style operations. Sadly, Bill Stirling, who had given so much to the SAS, had by then been sidelined. A victim of the fight to get the SAS properly used, he was sacked in May 1944 – his comeuppance for fighting to win suitable missions for the SAS. He'd refused to remain silent in the face of a high command seemingly determined to saddle the unit with borderline-suicidal operations. His place as commander of 2 SAS was taken by Lieutenant Colonel Brian Franks, who would prove himself to be a talented, determined and inspirational leader.

In preparation for the D-Day operations, two French SAS regiments were formed, 3 and 4 SAS. But Couraud and several of his comrades in the French Foreign Legion Squadron opted to remain serving within the ranks of their beloved 2 SAS. Of course, Couraud had taken British citizenship by then, so it was a simple matter for him to do so. In 2 SAS, Couraud would soldier alongside his old comrades, Cary-Elwes, Greville-Bell and Farran, so would find himself in fine company.

Following the liberation of Paris in August 1944, Couraud became involved in an unfortunate episode in which he saved one Freddy Kraus, an Austrian, from a shadowy fate, by spiriting him to Britain. It may well have been an affair of the heart – a favour to one of his many female admirers. Kraus was a beguiling individual – supposedly a director of Siemens, the major German arms manufacturer that had used 80,000 forced labourers at its various facilities. Kraus – whose real name was Alfred Ignatz Maria Kraus – frequented high society circles in Paris, and was married to the aristocratic and wealthy Anglo-French socialite Jacqueline Marguerite, Princess de Broglie, the stepdaughter of Winston Churchill's first cousin once removed. Jacqueline's mother, Daisy Fellowes de Broglie Ducasez, was especially close to her cousin Winston. Her daughter, Jacqueline, had met Kraus in Paris during the war and they had wed. Unbeknown to Couraud, or indeed Kraus's wife, Kraus was long-suspected by the British secret service of being an agent of the Abwehr, the German counter-intelligence service. In due course, this would lead to Kraus being accused of being 'the spy in Churchill's family'.

In what remains a complex and mysterious affair, Jacqueline chose to remain in Paris for the duration of the war, apparently orchestrating her high-society soirées, at which the new masters of Europe, the officers of Nazi Germany, appeared to be wholly welcome. In truth, Jacqueline was playing a dangerous game. Or so she believed. Her apparent hospitality to the forces of Nazi Germany was a mask. Beneath the carefully cultivated pretence, she was serving as a member of the French Resistance, and in due course an agent of the Special Operations Executive (SOE).

Seemingly aided by Kraus, who was avowedly staunchly anti-Nazi, she became a conduit for a secret mail service, letters being spirited from her Paris apartment under Kraus's care to Marseilles, to be passed on to the SOE's couriers and from there to London. Both she and Kraus also hosted British airmen who had been shot down over France, and who were smuggled onto the escape lines and back to the UK.

Shortly after the liberation of Paris, Kraus attended a dinner party hosted by Jacqueline, at which Couraud, and Captain Lord John Manners, a relatively recent recruit to 2 SAS and a comrade of Couraud's, were guests. During their dinner conversations, Manners, the son of the Marquess of Granby, observed that Kraus made clear how desperate he was to get to Britain. He sought 'to do his bit' for the Allied cause, but also to 'get hold of the girl who had caused him and his friends in France a great deal of trouble'. That 'girl' was none other than Mathilde Carré, better known as 'La Chatte', a French Resistance agent turned traitor, who had turned over the Interallié resistance network to the Gestapo, leading to dozens of agents being arrested and the network being destroyed. Under Gestapo control she had been codenamed 'Victoire'.

In claiming to be after La Chatte – who by then was being held in Britain as a suspected double agent – Kraus painted himself as a lynchpin of the French and Allied resistance. Couraud and Manners evidently bought the story. Kraus was helped in this by two factors. First, he and Couraud knew each other from French social circles before the war. Second, Couraud had reached out to Kraus, prior to Manners and their SAS party making it into Paris. With Paris under Nazi occupation, Couraud and his men had based themselves at a farm on the outskirts of the city. At

Couraud's urging, the farmer had made his way into Paris and sought out Kraus. To aid the liberation of Paris, Couraud and his men planned to sneak into the city, he explained, and for that they sought the help of Kraus and his wife Jacqueline.

Kraus sent a message back with the farmer, along with gifts of 'cigarettes for their friends'. What Couraud and his men planned to do was far too risky, he counselled. His 'firm instructions' were to 'dissuade them from attempting to enter Paris', at least while it was still under Nazi control. To all appearances Kraus was a long-standing and stalwart friend of the Allies. Over their Paris dinner, Couraud offered to recruit Kraus into the ranks of the SAS, as the easiest way to get him to Britain. The Austrian queried if such a thing 'was really possible', to which Couraud responded that Kraus shouldn't worry, for he had other Austrians serving in his unit, 'one of them straight from Berlin'.

With Couraud and Manner's backing, things began to move swiftly. Kraus was issued with British Army uniform, so he could pass as a member of the SAS. In early September, he was taken to Bayeux, on the Normandy coast, and on 9 September was dispatched to Britain on a landing craft packed full of German POWs. Ironically, Kraus was posing as one of their SAS escorts. From Southampton, he travelled to London and was accommodated at the Chelsea flat of Couraud and his long-suffering English wife, Katherine. There they proceeded to hide the 'refugee and stowaway' in their London home.

Kraus believed he had been 'genuinely' enlisted into the British Army and as a member of the SAS. Accustomed to recruiting select individuals on the fly – just as they had done with the three Poles rescued from Pisticci concentration camp – Couraud doubtless saw nothing irregular in the proceedings. To him, it appeared as all in a day's work: he had numerous Germans and Austrians serving in his French Foreign Legion Squadron, after all. Indeed, of his second in command on recent SAS operations, a German, Sergeant Mark, he'd declared, 'What a fighter!' But the powers-that-be clearly deemed otherwise, and especially since Kraus was a most irregular recruit.

Shortly after his arrival in Britain, Jacqueline wrote to Kraus from Paris, alarmed at his silence. 'Freddy Darling, I am given to be a little worried about you, as no one seems to have seen or heard of you. This may be all right, but I hear from all sides that Raymond is far more than irresponsible . . .' Whether Couraud's actions were 'irresponsible' or not, his below-the-radar insertion of Kraus into Britain reached the eyes and ears of the intelligence services. On 19 September, ten days after their arrival in the UK, a report from MI5 raised concerns that 'a Freddy KRAUS, son-in-law of Mrs. Reginald FELLOWES, may shortly arrive here from France. He is reported to have been captured by the GESTAPO in 1941 and then become a German agent. He may be coming to join a parachute regiment.'

As the authorities closed in on Kraus and Couraud, the two fugitives were persuaded by another of Couraud's high society contacts, Mary Westley, Lady Swinfen, to come clean. The two men duly handed themselves in to the 'proper authorities', to 'make a full confession'. In the process of doing so, Kraus readily admitted to being arrested by the Gestapo in 1941, and only being released upon his agreement to work for German intelligence 'in the penetration of the Allied Services'. But Kraus argued that this was simply a bluff, and that he had only and ever worked for the Allies. Despite such claims, Kraus was ordered to be detained for interrogation, and Couraud was arrested – 'disciplinary action will be taken against him'.

By late September 1944, the case of Freddy Kraus and Raymond Couraud was being investigated by Colonel William Hinchley-Cooke, otherwise known as 'Britain's Spy-Catcher'. Serving with MI5, Hinchley-Cooke was aware of Kraus's suspect bona fides; as early as 1939 Kraus had been 'refused leave to land' in the UK, for he was suspected of being 'a Nazi agent'. Reporting on the Kraus-Couraud affair, Hinchley-Cooke concluded that 'at least during the second half of the year 1941 Kraus was employed in Paris by the counter-espionage service of the German Intelligence Services and that he played an important role in the penetration and break up of an extremely valuable Allied intelligence organisation in France'.

Rather than seeking to expose La Chatte, as Kraus had claimed, he was actually suspected of being her partner in the penetration and destruction of the Interallié resistance network. He was further suspected of betraying his wife, and rather than acting as a trusted courier for the SOE's mail, he had secretly been steaming open the missives to be copied by the Gestapo. In fact, Kraus was believed to have used Jacqueline as a proxy for the Abwehr, her every move and act being secretly controlled. He was in turn handled by Oberstleutnant (Lieutenant Colonel) Hermann Giskes, a senior Abwehr officer. Incredibly, the deception of Jacqueline had been so complete that Giskes had even acted as the best man for Kraus at their Paris wedding.

Ominously, Hinchley-Cooke concluded, 'I am unable to say whether or not Captain LEE [Couraud] knew that KRAUS had been connected with the German Intelligence Services.' At Couraud's subsequent court martial, his lawyers sought to have

Kraus appear as a witness. By then, MI5 admitted in private that there was 'no evidence that Captain LEE [Couraud] was aware that KRAUS had been connected with the German Intelligence Services'. Even so, they were keen to ensure that the Austrian did not appear as a witness at Couraud's trial. The case of Kraus was 'one of extreme complication', for he clearly had access to members of Britain's high society, including Churchill's extended family. The court martial of Couraud was set to proceed at 'the earliest opportunity', and certainly before Kraus could be released from interrogations.

Kraus, of course, was being investigated for treachery. As those concerned with his case accepted, 'a great deal of work will have to be done . . . by the way of looking up and briefing before you will be in a position to open the case, which . . . will be one of the heaviest that you have tackled.' The more Kraus's case was examined, the more it appeared that many of La Chatte's supposedly traitorous activities were 'more properly attributable to Kraus'. As to his role in Paris at the time when he was 'picked up by Lee', MI5 strongly suspected that Kraus was a Nazi 'stay-behind agent', his role predicated on his ability to 'exploit the qualifications and connections . . . that enabled him to achieve such successes amongst the English speaking community in that city'.

With no Kraus to champion him at trial, Couraud did have other high-profile backers. At his court martial, a supporting statement was read out from Bill Stirling, in which he stated, 'I do not hesitate to say that his record is amongst the best, within the 2nd SAS and before. He made an invaluable contribution to the Allied cause in this war. There have been few officers so constantly and dangerously engaged against the enemy. And few have done so with such distinction. He proved himself to be an elite soldier in a regiment composed exclusively of selected volunteers.' High praise indeed. Stirling also stated how it was customary in the SAS to dress 'useful defectors to the Allies' in military uniform for their own protection, a supporting comment regarding Couraud's actions with Kraus. Captain Manners also provided a 'voluntary statement' to back up Couraud's defence. In subsequent correspondence he would write that the true story concerning Couraud's court martial would prove that 'reality exceeds fiction'. How very true.

But not even Stirling and Manners's spirited interventions could save Couraud. He was unmasked, accused of smuggling an enemy alien to the UK and found guilty. Couraud was apparently stripped of his Military Cross and cashiered – dismissed from military service. Between his Italian exploits and his court martial, Couraud had commanded a six-man team on a mission codenamed Operation Gaff, in which he was parachuted into France, charged to kill or ideally kidnap and bring to Britain Field Marshal Erwin Rommel. His being given command of such an audacious and vital mission reflects how highly he was viewed by those in command of the SAS. The men he chose for his Operation Gaff team were all bar one former French Foreign Legionnaires. But after his court martial and supposed disgrace, Couraud was finished with the British military.

Expelled from his beloved SAS, by early December 1944 he had applied to be re-admitted to the ranks of the French Foreign Legion, under his British name 'Lee'. 'On 7-12-44, Lee J. W. presented himself to the military attaché with the intention of enlisting in the Foreign Legion,' a handwritten note on Couraud's French military file records. Inquiries were made with the British as to his bona fides. A reply from a Captain C. E. C. Eastman, stamped 'SECRET', and on letterhead stating simply 'Whitehall, London, SW1', referred to the 'Ex-Captain J. W. Lee, MC,' a 'British national who is anxious to join the French Foreign Legion'. But as Eastman pointed out, Couraud (Lee) had been 'court-martialled and cashiered for having committed a breach of Travel Control Regulations in that he introduced a German national, named KRAUS, into the United Kingdom'.

Kraus was of course Austrian. Oddly, in the same breath as damning Couraud, Eastman's letter listed his Military Cross as a valid decoration, whereas the decoration's citation suggested that the MC had been 'CANCELLED ... 21/9/44'. Even more mysterious, it appears that subsequently, in June 1945, the War Office reconsidered Couraud's cashiering, and it was reduced simply to Resignation from the Service of His Majesty's Armed Forces. By then, MI5 was adamant that 'there is no evidence, and it is highly improbable that Captain LEE [Couraud] had any real idea of KRAUS' true character when he sent the man over here.' At worst, Couraud had been duped by the wily Austrian. MI5 also concluded that it was highly unlikely that Kraus had perpetrated any espionage acts while at large in London, before his detention and interrogation.

While they stood accused of very similar crimes, the fate of Kraus and La Chatte – Mathilde Carré – are highly divergent. Deported to France to face treason charges, Carré was sentenced to death on 7 January 1949, although it was later commuted to life imprisonment. By contrast, there is no record of Kraus ever facing any kind of trial or formal disciplinary action. Both he and Lieutenant Colonel Giskes were interrogated at length in London. Alerted to Kraus's alleged treachery, his wife Jacqueline instituted divorce proceedings in April 1945. Kraus decided to fight, and especially over the custody of their daughter, three-year-old Rosamund.

Then, one day in the summer of 1945 Kraus's interrogations appear to have come to an abrupt end. He had been engaged upon a series of 'mysterious errands'. It all ended with Jacqueline getting custody of Rosamund, and Kraus getting his freedom. He returned to his native Austria to live in seclusion, and died in 1978. No doubt, his was a case that was seen as being too hot to handle, especially bearing in mind the publicity that any trial might attract. Of course, with Freddy Kraus's quiet disappearance, the 'Churchills no longer had a spy in the family'.

Shortly after the train raid to liberate Pisticci concentration camp, it was overrun by Allied forces. Then placed under Allied control, it became a refugee camp for those fleeing oppression further north in Italy. Some 18,000 such people would pass through the camp until the end of the war in that country. It is worth bearing in mind what fate those held in Pisticci would have faced, had Operation Loco not taken place. After Italy's formal surrender and the Fascist diehards allying themselves with Nazi Germany, orders went out to hunt down all Jews held in such camps, in preparation for their deportation to Germany. For most, such journeys amounted to a death sentence.

The fate of the Yugoslav, Polish, Greek and other detainees was little better, and most of those held at Pisticci had been slated for deportation, even as the SAS had intervened. In short, the rescue mission at Pisticci doubtless saved hundreds of lives. Across the country, the fate of those held in the concentration camps would be stark. For example, on 24 March 1944, in the Ardeatine Massacre, 335 Jews, resistance figures, anti-Fascists, political prisoners and others were murdered by SS death squads in caves on the outskirts of Rome. The youngest victim was fifteen years old.

No awards were given resulting from the Pisticci mission, barring Sapper Elkin, the train driver's Mention in Dispatches. No publicity was given to the raid at the time, and there was precious little mention of it during the war. It was almost as if Operation Loco, and the discovery of the Axis powers' first concentration camp had been buried. Apart from one or two short paragraphs in wartime newspaper reports, and a brief reference to the operation in the 1968 edition of the *Rover and Wizard* annual, entitled 'Who Dares Wins', that was it.

That *Rover and Wizard* piece reads: 'The SAS did amazing work behind the enemy lines in Italy. One of the most astounding stories concerns a squadron of SAS which had captured a train. They calmly drove the train deep into enemy territory up to a concentration camp. They quickly took control of the camp, released all the prisoners and loaded them and the Italian commandant into the train and steamed back to their base.' Other than that, the mission to liberate Pisticci concentration camp appears to have been written out of history. The question is why.

Pisticci was not the last time that the SAS would play a seminal role in the discovery of the Nazi/Fascist concentration camps. In November 1944, Prince Yuri Galitzine, a Russian nobleman recruited into SOE, would stumble upon Natzweiler-Struthof concentration camp, one of the few to have been built upon French soil. Located in the Vosges Mountains, in east-central France, a 2 SAS unit had been highly active in the area, waging sabotage and guerrilla warfare behind the enemy's lines. Having no idea what a 'concentration camp' might be, Galitzine was appalled and sickened by what he discovered. He interviewed some of the survivors, took copious notes and gathered evidence, and then wrote an excoriating report concerning his discoveries.

As Galitzine served with the Political Warfare Executive (PWE), a subsection of SOE concerned with communications and propaganda, he planned a press conference to reveal the existence of such places of hell to the world's public. At the eleventh hour he was ordered to cease and desist. Not only was there to be no press conference, but he was to remain absolutely silent about all that he had discovered at Natzweiler-Struthof. Incredibly, he was also ordered to *destroy* all copies of his investigation into the concentration camp. To bury the evidence. Thankfully, Galitzine was made of the right stuff. He disobeyed the last part of his orders, smuggling several copies of his report into the hands of the SAS.

Galitzine's reasons for doing so were twofold. One, he knew that the SAS were busy investigating a string of suspected war crimes perpetrated by the forces of Nazi Germany in the Vosges region. Two, he had uncovered evidence that captured SAS personnel had been held at Natzweiler-Struthof, and that some had been tortured and murdered there. His report would prove invaluable. In due course the SAS's own War Crimes Investigation Team (WCIT) – otherwise known as the Secret Hunters – would investigate the war crimes committed at Natzweiler-Struthof and bring many of the perpetrators to justice. Galitzine's report proved vital to their work and the successes so achieved – tracking down the Nazi war criminals who had murdered their SAS comrades.

The reasons Galitzine were given as to why he had been silenced and ordered to destroy all evidence were confounding. At a high political level a decision had apparently been taken not to overly demonise the enemy. If the Germans became known for engineering such horrors as the concentration camps, then they would be less likely to surrender, 'fearing little clemency would be extended to them by the Allies'. Likewise, Allied soldiers would be less likely to take their surrender if they knew of such heinous atrocities.

In the wider scheme of things, the Allied publics also needed to be kept onside, and would be unlikely to view the enemy with a great deal of compassion should the existence of the concentration camps become widely known. Eventually, a peace would need to be engineered out of the ruins of war, and of course what was formerly Nazi Germany was going to prove a key ally to the West, with the rise of the Cold War. So were the arguments made, which effectively gagged all those involved in the Natzweiler discovery, and the same very possibly holds true for the earlier Pisticci rescue mission.

In the spring of 1945, the SAS, operating well in advance of the main Allied forces, were ordered to take their jeeps and investigate the Bergen-Belsen concentration camp. Still, few if any knew what such places represented. The team that arrived at Belsen's gates were sickened and horrified beyond words at what they discovered. They had gone to Belsen chiefly to rescue one of their own: a captured SAS comrade had been incarcerated in that place of hell. On the back of their discoveries, and as more Allied forces took over the camp, a team of news cameramen and reporters were given access to Belsen. Finally, the 'unspeakable horrors of the Third Reich' were broadcast to the world. 'Finally, the true scale of the Holocaust was made public.'

Belsen's discovery and the resulting publicity came fully *nineteen months* after those held at Pisticci had been freed by the SAS – 'the very first concentration camp to be uncovered and liberated by the Allies.' One can only assume that the Pisticci camp's discovery, and all that had gone with it, had been quietly hushed up, as had the discovery of Natzweiler-Struthof some fourteen months later. Of course, with the Pisticci and Natzweiler discoveries, we – the Allies – knew of the existence of such camps, and the SAS who were dispatched to Belsen should have been forewarned. (To my knowledge none of the SAS sent to investigate Belsen had taken part in the Pisticci mission. As a point of note, the level of violence, suffering and deaths in Belsen and Natzweiler were on a different order of scale to those in the Italy.)

Sadly, the Italian response to Pisticci and the wider concentration camp system in Italy was woeful. Following Pisticci's liberation, Colonel Ercole Suppa, the concentration camp commandant captured by the SAS, was appointed to a position as the local chief of police. This was not uncommon. Very few of those responsible for the concentration camps in Italy were ever brought to trial. As Dr Robert Sherwood, an expert on such matters, has noted, 'atrocities in Italy were not investigated to the extent they were in Germany, with the exception of the Ardeatine Massacre of 24 March 1944.' Even as the forces of Nazism and fascism were driven out of Italy, the reality of the concentration camps system was covered up. As the highly respected Primo Levi Centre puts it, Italy 'produced a sugarcoated narration of the past that never ceased to emphasise "Italian goodness" as opposed to "German evil"', with the goal of distancing as much as possible fascism from Nazism.

In truth, as the Primo Levi Centre observed, Italy had been 'allied with Germany and jointly liable for many of its ill-fated endeavours'. Fascist Italy was a 'model for totalitarian states built on racial foundations pursued by Hitler . . . It was also the principal European ally of Germany when Nazism launched genocide against the Jewish populations, often collaborating directly with their deportations.' Post-war, the 'history of the concentration camps employed by fascism . . . was therefore rapidly erased from national memory. Even the geographic sites of the camps . . . were forgotten (becoming the exact opposite of "places of remembrance").'

In recent years, historian Carlo Spartaco Capogreco, a renowned expert on Italy's concentration camps, visited all the known sites. One, at Ferramonti, has been turned into a memorial and museum. It is located in the province of Tarsia, near Cosenza, in Calabria – so just in from the toe of Italy and not so far from Pisticci. One of the largest such camps, it housed some 3,800 Jews and other 'undesirable civilians'. Ferramonti was liberated by the forces of the Allied Eighth Army on 14/15 September 1943, saving those who were incarcerated there. But as Capogreco discovered, Ferramonti is the exception. The majority of the camps across Italy have either been demolished or are the objects of shocking neglect.

Nowhere is this more apparent than at Pisticci. Today, Italy's first concentration camp is largely a deserted ghost camp. For decades it has been left in a 'state of abandonment and decay'. Indeed, there are even groups of illegal squatters living there. The once beautiful chapel is now 'closed and dilapidated due to neglect'. The beautiful murals are decaying, the plaster is falling down and the roof is in danger of total collapse. There is no visitor centre, no memorials and few if any efforts are being made to preserve what remains of the camp or to memorialise its history. Indeed, if a rare visitor does try to see the camp, they may be warned that it is 'dangerous' to do so, due to the 'undesirables' who are squatting there.

In the former Pisticci concentration camp, the phrase 'never again' rings terribly hollow. But as has been pointed out in the local press, 'even today, before it is too late, it can become a place of historical memory with the establishment of a museum open to visitors, students and researchers . . . Only in this way can a historical heritage of notable importance be recovered . . . and returned to historical memory.' From my own dealings with the local authorities, there are reports that the Pisticci Town Council is seeking funds to convert buildings at the camp into a museum. Thankfully, the Mayor's Office and the council have preserved extensive archives concerning the camp's history.

Does the history of neglect mean that the efforts of the SAS at Pisticci were somehow in vain? No. Hundreds of lives were saved. Operation Loco was the SAS's calling card for the A Force missions that followed. But the history of the Pisticci concentration camp – including the dramatic liberation of those who were held there – needs to be properly memorialised, lest we forget.

We can only hope it is not too late.

Appendix

AFTER THE WAR

Note: If date and place of death is unspecified, it is not known to the author.

George Arnold: After the war Arnold continued to serve in the British Army and was given an officer's commission. He listed his credentials for officer training as: 'Trained parachutist, Saboteur, Tank Driver, Tank Gunner, Tank Commander, Driver all Vehicles, knowledge all small arms, Trained machine gunner, light and heavy, Trained horseman.' In 1946, he was assessed during officer training as being: 'Cheerful and well mannered, with lots of determination and guts, a great sense of duty and responsibility.' Post-war he separated from his first wife, Helen Morgan, and married Doreen Robinson. Finding it hard to settle into regimented military life, he left the army in 1959 and became a sawmill worker. He married for a third time, to Dorothy Eccles, with whom he would spend the rest of his life. They had a daughter, Debbie. When asked by his daughter if he hated the Germans, Arnold was adamant that you should never hate an entire race. Those German soldiers were under orders, just as their Allied counterparts were. He died in 2005 aged eighty-eight.

Simon Baillie: Baillie was captured by the enemy during Operation Trueform, an SAS mission in August 1944, in Nazi-occupied France. He survived captivity and returned to the UK at war's end. For his 'gallant and distinguished service in Italy' he received a Mention in Dispatches. He retired from military service in 1953 with the honorary rank of lieutenant colonel.

Oswald Cary-Elwes: After Italy operations, Cary-Elwes became the liaison officer between the British and French SAS, in preparation for their D-Day missions. He deployed into Brittany in the summer of 1944, on Operation Lost, a mission to locate a missing band of French SAS, which morphed into a daring escape back across the Channel carrying vital intelligence. Thereafter he served as part of the 4th French SAS Regiment across France and into Belgium. For his wartime service and 'perilous missions' executed with the French SAS, he was awarded the French Croix de Guerre avec palme and the Légion d'Honneur. He was also Mentioned in Dispatches in 1949. After various military postings, much of which concerned furthering Anglo-French military relations, he retired from the army in 1968 with the rank of lieutenant colonel. In 1984, on the fortieth anniversary of the Normandy landings, he joined his wartime comrades in Paris and was awarded the Medaille de la Ville de Paris by then Mayor of Paris and former French Prime Minister Jacques Chirac, in recognition of his great service to France. Cary-Elwes remained a very active member of post-war SAS associations until his death, playing a special role as the link to French veterans. Among many of the French SAS members with whom he maintained close relations was the mercurial Raymond Couraud. Cary-Elwes had six children with his wife, Pamela Brendon. He rarely spoke with his family about his wartime exploits, and he never breathed a word to them about the Pisticci concentration camp mission. He died in 1994 aged eighty.

Wladislas Lucien Cieslak: After Italy operations, Cieslak parachuted into Brittany in August 1944 as part of a ten-man SAS patrol. In short order Cieslak set off in a two-man sabotage team, both of whom were fluent French speakers. Having blown up a German ammunition dump at night, the two raiders came under fire from a German armoured car. Its 37mm gun wounded Cieslak's comrade, who was captured by the enemy, and caused Cieslak horrific injuries. He was left for dead by the enemy, for he was seemingly mortally wounded. In fact, he survived his injuries, refusing to have his leg amputated in an American field hospital. In 1945 he would personally be praised by de Gaulle for his summer 1944 operations as being 'a most brave and courageous man'. He was awarded the Croix de Guerre avec palme. During SAS training in Scotland in 1944, he met his future wife, a Scottish lass called Agnes. They married in 1946. Settling in Dumfries, Scotland, Cieslak found work as a foreman at a Dunlop rubber factory and in his spare time he indulged his love of trout fishing. In 1966 he became a naturalised British citizen. He died in Dumfries of a heart attack in 1999 aged eighty-one.

Raymond Couraud: After the long years of wartime service in the French Foreign Legion, the SOE and the SAS, Couraud left the British military supposedly in disgrace, following his court martial and cashiering. In 1983, former French paratrooper Colonel R. Flamand would write a biography of Couraud, entitled *L'Inconnu du French Squadron*. In the process of researching his story, Flamand spoke to Couraud's various wives and lovers, and his wartime comrades, including Oswald Cary-Elwes. In the process Flamand would conclude that Couraud's 1944 court martial was sheer idiocy, and his wartime disgrace undeserved. While some in the British establishment would say of him that 'Couraud is not a gentleman', few could criticise his wartime record.

While Colonel Flamand's biography is the definitive account of Couraud's wartime exploits, much of his post-war career remains shrouded in mystery. By 1948 Couraud seems to have been serving as the Deputy Chief of Staff of the Nizam of Hyderabad, one of the last independent states of India. He then very possibly saw service with the Chinese nationalists, in Indochina, and in various other obscure conflicts, including Hong Kong and across Africa. He was rumoured to have been locked up in a secret prison in Rome, and to have had several wives and any number of children.

He married the nurse, Hélène, who had cared for him in North Africa following his injuries on A Force operations, and for a while they settled in a village in Burgundy. Couraud's official first child, also named Raymond, was born in 1954 in France. With Hélène he also had a second son, Yvan. By 1958 Couraud listed his address as 13 Rue Lavigerie, Satif, Algeria, so he had returned to his old stalking ground in North Africa. The last correspondence in his French military file concerns his attempts to have various aspects of his Second World War service recognised by the French government. There are reports of Couraud serving in various capacities for the intelligence services, most notably of France, and not without controversy. One of the final entries in his French records consists of a handwritten note dated 27-6-58:

'An inquiry has been opened into this subject by the SDECE.' The *Service de documentation extérieure et de contre-espionnage* (SDECE) was the French foreign intelligence service, the equivalent of Britain's MI6.

In his later years Couraud rejoined his first wife, Katherine, and they moved into her home in Cornwall. He is believed to have died in Cornwall, in 1977. His headstone bears the following inscription: 'Jack William Raymond Couraud, known as Captain Lee, 1920–1977. Brave Soldier, Loving Heart.'

Captain Pat Dudgeon: The SAS captain and his comrade Trooper Bernard Brunt were captured on Operation Speedwell, after ambushing a German vehicle. Under interrogation Dudgeon refused to divulge the nature of his mission, and he was shot by the German commander under Hitler's Command Order. He had already been awarded an MC for a previous mission. Trooper Blunt was likewise executed.

Roy Farran: After his 1943 Italian operations, Farran served with the SAS across France and then back in Italy, in 1945. He ended the war highly decorated, with a DSO, MC and two bars, plus a Croix de Guerre. Having seen service post-war in various theatres, Farran left the military and took work as a quarryman in Scotland, a position arranged for him by Bill Stirling. In the 1950s he emigrated to Canada and worked for the *Calgary Herald*, before founding his own newspaper, the *North Hill News*. In the 1960s he launched his political career in Canada, and was elected as an MP. He also became a visiting professor at the University of Alberta, and was awarded the Légion d'Honneur in 1994. He died in 2006 aged eighty-five.

John Gunston: The SAS captain was killed in action in early March 1944. The operation, codenamed Maple, involved Gunston leading a three-man team behind the lines in Italy to sabotage railway lines. He and his men were last seen on a 22-foot boat putting to sea, to make their way back to Allied lines. Evidence suggests they may all have been captured and executed under Hitler's Commando Order.

Josef Lyczak: A Polish internee from Picticci who volunteered for the SAS, Lyczak served with the unit throughout Italy in 1943, and the following year on Operation Pistol, a behind-the-lines mission in France commanded by his 2 SAS comrade, Sergeant John Alcock. After the war Lyczak moved to Scotland and raised a family there. He died in Manchester in 2002, aged eighty-one.

James Mackie: By war's end 'Big Jim' Mackie had been awarded a Military Cross and bar, for operations across north-west Europe. He died in 1967.

Alistair McGregor: After Italy operations, McGregor was parachuted into the Vosges, France, in August 1944 as part of Operation Loyton, under the cover name 'Captain Beverley'. Deployed on sabotage operations, he was awarded a Military Cross for his coolness, initiative, leadership and personal courage under fire, plus the French Croix de Guerre. He was also at the forefront of jeeping operations during the SAS push into Nazi Germany in 1945. Post-war he saw service as a special operations instructor to the French Foreign Legion and the Greek Army Commando Brigade, again as an instructor, and he was awarded the Greek War Cross with Silver Crown. He would play a key role in refounding the SAS, deploying to Malaya (now Malaysia) as part of the reconstituted unit in the 1950s, and pioneering the art of parachuting into the jungle canopy, along with fellow Second World War veteran and SAS original, Johnny Cooper. In 1953 he returned to the Foreign Legion on attachment, and took part in parachute insertions into Indochina on operations against the Viet Cong. Married to his Hungarian-born wife Magda Feher in 1942, they had a son and a daughter. He retired from the military in 1954 with the rank of major, and found work in sales management. He died in 2020 aged eighty-four.

Neal Panzarella: In March 1944, OSS agent Corporal Panzarella arrived at Stalag VII-IA, the largest POW camp in Nazi Germany, located near the town of Mossberg in Bavaria. En route to the camp, fifteen of those riding in his cattle car had managed to escape, but by then Panzarella was ill, and he was incapable of breaking free. On 29 April 1945 the camp was liberated by the American Third Army and Panzarella was one of the many thousands who were freed.

Philip Hugh Pinckney: The fate of the SAS captain who had disappeared at the outset of Operation Speedwell remains something of a mystery. He is buried in Florence war cemetery, and a commemorative booklet written by his family, entitled, *Your Uncles*, suggests that Pinckney was captured by the Carabinieri, and though in uniform he was executed. This has never been proven. As Italy had signed the Armistice on the day that Pinckney had landed, it seems unlikely. Possibly he was killed in some kind of shootout. Other accounts state that he was executed while being held as a POW. It is more likely that he suffered a horrendous spinal injury upon landing, on top of the back injuries he was already nursing, and that he died from his wounds. That would explain why he was never found by the rest of his men, and is wholly in keeping with the suspicions of Sergeant Stokes, the only one of his men who knew of the injury.

Prince Filippo Andrea VI Doria Pamphilj: After being freed from Pisticci concentration camp, Prince Filippo went on to become the first mayor of a newly liberated Rome, once Italy's capital city had been taken by the Allies in June 1944. In his speech to the city folk, he appealed for 'a spirit of civic and brotherly love', and for 'mutual understanding and harmony of souls, to which, I am sure, the memory of so many dead commits us'. The full story of his anti-fascist exploits is little known, for he rarely if ever talked about it and certainly never boasted. Prior to Pisticci, the prince had been held at two other internment camps, at Agropoli and Arezzo. There are suggestions that the Prince's being freed from Pisticci was at the 'intervention of the Vatican', although how exactly this keys in with Operation Loco remains unclear. In September 1944, the prince's daughter, Orietta, met a handsome Royal Navy commander, Frank Pogson, who she married some years after the war in London. To ensure the family name would not die out, Pogson added the Doria Pamphilj surname to his own. The family's fabulous private art collection was opened to the public in 1950, and has received great critical acclaim. The Doria Pamphilj family's close relations with the British royal family endured and Princess Orietta was made an OBE in 2000. Prince Filippo died in 1958, aged seventy-one.

Gabriel de Sablet: Captain de Sablet was killed in action in Holland on 8 April 1945, during Operation Amhurst. He was reported as 'drowned on landing, Smilde, Holland'.

John Scott: After Italy operations, Scott deployed with the SAS into north-west Europe. He acted as the rear gunner for Lieutenant Colonel Blair 'Paddy' Mayne, 1 SAS commander, as they rescued several men from certain death from an ambush in Germany in April 1945. He would end the war with a MM and a Mention in Dispatches. A captain, Scott met his future wife in Belgium at war's end and after the war he worked in the family's printing business. They settled at Toadsmoor, near Stroud, in Gloucestershire. He died in 1987 aged sixty-seven.

Anthony Charles Simonds: After his extraordinary endeavours with A Force in Italy in 1943, Simonds was exhausted. By way of respite, he went crocodile hunting on the Nile. Returning to A Force work, he orchestrated the rescue of around three thousand Allied POWs and downed airmen from Eastern Europe. Post-war, Simonds collected evidence concerning war crimes perpetrated against Italian civilians who had helped his A Force teams and POW-escapees in Italy. Few if any of the culprits so identified were prosecuted. He would be Mentioned in Dispatches seven times for his wartime service, but his habit of forcefully speaking his mind did not endear him to many of those on high. Eventually he was appointed OBE, in recognition of his wartime role. In 1944 he had married Eirwen Jones, and they had two daughters. Brigadier Dudley Clarke would be made the godfather of one, testament to their enduring friendship. Simonds's motto was *Malo Mori Quam Foedari* – 'I prefer death to dishonour'.

In 1952 he retired from the military and went to Cyprus, to grow flowers for a living. During the war in Cyprus his house was bombed by the Turks and burned down. He returned to Britain towards the end of his life and died in Stevenage, Hertfordshire, in 1999, aged eighty-nine.

Horace Stokes: Following his lifesaving operation in Rome, Stokes went on to train and operate with the Italian partisans. Eventually, he was captured by the Germans and interrogated by the Gestapo. He refused to admit to his true identity and actions – i.e., that he was SAS and had been soldiering with the Italian partisans – maintaining that he was simply a British POW who had escaped from a camp upon the signing of the Armistice. This undoubtedly saved his life. Dispatched to a POW camp in Germany, Stokes executed a series of breathtaking escapes, during each of which he was eventually recaptured. In the spring of 1945 he finally broke free from his POW camp in Germany and made it to the American lines. Demobilised in 1946, he went back to his old profession of greengrocer, and also as a pub land-lord. He married Joan and they had several children. He died in 1986 aged sixty-five.

Felix Symes: Awarded a Mention in Dispatches for his Italy operations, the SAS captain was killed in July 1944. Commanding a unit of 2 SAS troops, he had flown into France as part of Operation Rupert, a mission to sabotage railway lines in Nazi-occupied France. Most aboard were killed, along with the aircrew of the Short Stirling aircraft they were riding in, when it crashed into a hillside near the village of Graffigny-Chemin.

Acknowledgements

First and foremost, thank you to my esteemed readers. You go out and buy my books, in the hope that each will deliver a rewarding, illuminating read, bringing a story to life in vivid detail. Without you, there could be no author such as myself. You enable individuals like me to make a living from writing. You deserve the very first mention.

A huge thank you to all family members of those depicted in these pages, without whose assistance and support I could not have written this book.

My enormous gratitude to all in the Cary-Elwes family, but in particular to Cate Cary-Elwes, the daughter of Lieutenant-Colonel Oswald Cary-Elwes, for our numerous visits and conversations, and for sharing with me the Cary-Elwes family archives and your extensive research into your father's wartime story. I must also thank Charles Cary-Elwes, the son of Lieutenant-Colonel Oswald Cary-Elwes, and his grandchildren, including Richard, Gerald and Thomas. Thank you for the time we have spent together discussing your grandfather's extraordinary wartime exploits. Thanks also to Sir Henry Elwes KCVO, for our fortuitous meeting and for our discussions and subsequent correspondence over the Cary-Elwes clan and military traditions.

Heartfelt thanks to Jo Hussey, for reaching out to me about her grandfather, Trooper George Arnold, and for showing me his wartime records and the unpublished, untitled account he wrote of his time in Italy. Thank you to Jo's parents, Debbie and Peter Hussey, for inviting me into your home to discuss the wartime exploits of Debbie's father and for sharing with me so many recollections and the family archive. I am so glad that your father and grandfather's amazing story has finally been told.

I must also thank Graham Alcock, the son of Sergeant John Jack Alcock, who was hugely helpful in corresponding with me over his father's wartime service, and in providing me with an early draft of his book, *Operation Pistol: Raindrops in Alsace*, which covers his father's full account of his war.

Thank you, once again, to David Farran, son of SAS commander Roy Farran, for your kind permission to quote from your father's excellent writings, and for our correspondence over the years regarding his outstanding wartime service.

Huge thanks also to David Bruce, the grandson of Trooper Wladislas Lucien Cieslak, for sharing with me his wartime correspondence and personal family archive.

Enormous thanks to Rosey Simonds, for corresponding with me regarding your father, Anthony Simonds OBE, and his wartime experiences. Thank you also to Raymond Simonds, for further correspondence and insight into this remarkable man and his wartime career.

Massive thanks to SAS veteran Bob Lancaster for your sterling efforts researching the history of the SAS operation to liberate Pisticci concentration camp on the ground in Italy, and for the documents, personal testimonies and photographs so secured. Above and beyond.

Huge thanks to Professor Giuseppe Coniglio, author of *La Colonia Confinaria Di Pisticci*, and local historian, for all your help, research and advice in the Pisticci area and thereafter. Greatly appreciated. Thanks to Domenico Albano, the Mayor of Pisticci, for all your help and assistance, and to Vittoria Spada, local Italian translator at Pisticci, for your excellent assistance with translations on the ground and thereafter. Thanks also to Marco Dipierro, an expert on the history of the Pisticci Concentration Camp, for all your research and correspondence. Thanks to Mike Adlem, for your research in Italy on my behalf, and for the translations you carried out; invaluable, as always.

Enormous thanks to Peter Stokes, the son of Horace Stokes, for our correspondence over his father's wartime service, and for allowing me to quote from his excellent book, *No Ordinary Life*, which tells of his father's incredible war record.

I extend my immense gratitude to Prince Jonathan Doria Pamphilj for your generous correspondence regarding your grandfather's wartime record, and helping me piece together those elusive elements of his story.

Thanks to Scott Winthrop for your invaluable insights into all things train driving and operating – absolutely invaluable for a story such as this – and for the kind invitation to ride the locomotive on one of Britain's few surviving steam railways, to experience at first hand how such a machine is operated. Enormous thanks to Peter Yeates for our correspondence over the 261 Field Park Company (Airborne), which proved enormously insightful. Thanks also to Bruce Tocher for all the help and advice on all things related to 261 Field Park Company, Operation Freshman and associated topics.

Enormous thanks to Eric Lecomte for our long correspondence

from France on the wartime story and exploits of Raymond Couraud (AKA Jack Lee). Thanks to Adrian Derry for the correspondence concerning his father's wartime service in the French SAS. Thanks to Peter Sichel for our correspondence concerning the SAS raid on Pisticci concentration camp. Thanks to Robert Ashton McKenny, son of Lieutenant R. A. McKenny, SOE agent W18, for sharing with me the unpublished family memoir of his war years.

Thanks again to Thomas Liaudet, Vice-President General of the AFPSAS – see profile that follows – for the help and guidance in researching all things French SAS, which was invaluable. Thank you also to Professor Robert Gordon, Serena Professor of Italian at Cambridge University, for our illuminating correspondence concerning the Italian concentration camps. Thanks also to John McKay, for the early research into Lieutenant Alistair McGregor, which proved hugely helpful.

Thanks also to Dianna Mara Henry, Tony Mckenny, Jozek Stanko, David Sands, Kieran Troy and Adrian Derry, for your kind help and assistance in various ways.

I have benefited greatly in the research for this book from the resources that the British, Italian, American and German governments, and related institutions, have invested in preserving for posterity the archives from the Second World War era. The preservation and cataloguing of a mountain of papers – official reports, personal correspondence, telegrams, etc. – as well as photographic, film and sound archives is vital to authors such as myself. Devoting resources to the preservation of this historical record, and to making it accessible to the public, is something for which these governments and other institutions should be praised.

I extend a special thank you to the Imperial War Museum (IWM), whose archives are a treasure trove of wonderful oral histories and the collections of private papers, without which I would not have been able to render the actions detailed in this book as I have. The IWM archivists deserve special mention, for reaching out to the families of those whose archives they hold, to secure the kind permission that I sought to quote from their private papers.

Equally, all at The National Archives, Kew, deserve fulsome praise for preserving and presenting to the public a wonderful trove of wartime documents, which are vital to authors such as myself. We could not write the books that we do without the wonderful service that you provide.

The superlative Simon Fowler, my UK archives researcher, deserves special praise once again, as does Sim Smiley, his counterpart in the USA. Also, Laurence Abensur-Hazan deserves special thanks for digging deep into the French National Archives.

Enormous thanks to all at my publishers for their committed, enthusiastic and visionary support of this project from the get-go. In the UK, Richard Milner, my long-standing editor, provided seminal guidance and feedback. The wider Quercus team also deserve the highest praise, especially Elizabeth Masters, Dave Murphy and Jon Butler. Huge thanks to my agent, Andrew Gordon at DHA, for his guidance, support and fine judgement. Special thanks again must be extended to Sophie Ransom, of Ransom PR, for all her fine efforts to help me tell this story.

Finally, my immense gratitude to my wife, Eva, and to David, Damien Jr and Sianna, who once again had to put up with 'Pappa' spending far too long locked in his study trying to do justice to this story. That I have – if I have – I owe to you all; to your love and support and kindness, and for putting up with me through it all.

This is a special story for the Lewis family, if for no other reason than my wife has played a very hands-on role in the research, archiving and transcribing the revisions of this book, not to mention overseeing the administration side of things. You stayed the course over the long months that it has taken to come to fruition, for which I am hugely grateful.

Acknowledgements on Sources

I am indebted to the following authors (and/or estates), who have covered some of the aspects of the story I have dealt with in *SAS The Great Train Raid* in their own writing. I extend my gratitude to all those who kindly granted me permission to quote from their material. For those readers whose interest has been piqued by this book, these authors and their titles in particular would reward further reading:

George Arnold, whose unpublished, untitled manuscript telling of his wartime experiences was kindly shared with me by his daughter, Debbie Hussey, and which chronicles in great detail his incredible wartime experiences in Italy in 1943.

Colonel Roger Flamand, whose biography of Raymond Couraud is entitled *L'Inconnu du French Squadron*, and which is an excellent portrayal of this enigmatic figure. It is sadly long out of print and only available in French (see Bibliography for full details).

Graham Alcock, whose memoir about his father's wartime service, *Operation Pistol: Raindrops in Alsace*, is a detailed chronicle of his life and gripping wartime adventures (see Bibliography for full details).

Charlie Hackney, whose unpublished memoir about his wartime service, *A Soldier's Life For Me*, was kindly shared with me by his grandson, Scott Hackney.

I am grateful to the publishers, authors and estates for granting me permission to quote from the following works (full details in Bibliography):

Graham Alcock, *SAS Operation Pistol: Raindrops in Alsace,* Barnsley: Pen & Sword, 2024 – all rights reserved.

George Arnold, untitled manuscript, unpublished, undated – all rights reserved.

Charlie Hackney, *A Soldier's Life For Me*, unpublished, undated – all rights reserved.

Anthony A. C. Simonds, *Pieces of War,* unpublished, undated – all rights reserved.

Sources

Material quoted from the UK archive files listed below, is by kind courtesy of The National Archives, Kew. This book contains public-sector information licensed under the Open Government Licence v3.0.

Material quoted from the French archive files, and other sources listed herein, is by kind courtesy of the Service Historique de la Défense/Ministère des Armées (France).

The National Archives, UK

WO 208/177 – Op Speedwell After Action report
WO 208/3253 – SIMCOL
WO 218/181 – Op Jonquil
WO 218/174 – Operation Hawthorn
WO 204/8277 – Report on Termoli Operation
WO 208/3253 – Summary of MI9 Activities in the Eastern Mediterranean
WO 218/176 – Taranto Ops
WO 218/178 – Op Begonia + McGregor
WO 373/99 – Citations

WO 376/3 – Couraud Citation
WO 373/186 – French Award British Army
HS 9/1647 – Couraud Raymond Jack William, MI5 debrief
KV-2-1727-02 – KRAUS, ALFRED IGNATZ MARIA

USA Archives

U.S. National Archives and Records Administration, RG 226
  Records of the Office of Strategic Services, including:
RG 226 Entry A1 97 Box 2 Fold 18 – OSS Op Simcol
RG 226 Entry A1 99 Box 45 Fold 6 – OSS Op Simcol
RG 226 Entry A1 143 Box 11 Fold 143 – OSS Op Simcol
RG 226 Entry A1 210 Box 57 WN#001521 DeLuca report on
  Simcol Mission – No date – OSS Op Simcol
RG 226 Entry A1 224 Box 178, DeLuca Frank – OSS Op Simcol
RG 226 Entry A1 224 Box 783, Traficante, Paul – OSS Op Simcol
RG 226 Entry UD 92 A Box 67 Fold 1220 Suro – OSS Op Simcol
RG 226 Entry UD 190 Box 97 Fold 119 – OSS Op Simcol
RG 226 Entry UD 190 Box 276 Fold 1090 – OSS Op Jonquil

French Archives – Service Historique de la Défense

GR 16P 147005 – Raymond Couraud

Imperial War Museum

Document 16238 – Copy of J. Amery's book 'Sons of the Eagle'
  and related items, 2002

Document 16075 – Papers of Lieutenant Colonel A. C. Simonds OBE

Catalogue No. 12022 – Hackett, John Winthrop (Oral history)

Catalogue No. 18034 – Roy Farran audio interview, IWM

Catalogue Number 16000 – Private Papers of Captain Y. Galitzine

Author interviews and personal communications

Interviews and personal communications, author with Graham Alcock, 2023–25

Interviews and personal communications, author with Professor Giuseppe Coniglio, 2024–25

Interviews and personal communications, author with Cate Cary-Elwes, 2022–24

Interviews and personal communications, author with Charles Cary-Elwes, 2024–25

Interviews and personal communications, author with Sir Henry Elwes KCVO, 2024

Interviews and personal communications, author with David Farran, 2023–25

Interviews and personal communications, author with Debbie and Jo Hussey, 2025

Interviews and personal communications, author with Professor Robert Gordon, Serena Professor of Italian at Cambridge University, 2024–25

Interviews and personal communications, author with Bob Lancaster et al, 2023–24

Interviews and personal communications, author with Dr Robert Sherwood, 2023–24

Interviews and personal communications, author with Peter Stokes, 2024–25

Interviews and personal communications, author with Peter Yeates, 2024

Published sources and miscellaneous

London Gazette: 24 August 1944
https://www.thegazette.co.uk/London/issue/36668/supplement/3926/data.pdf

London Gazette: 24 August 1944
https://www.thegazette.co.uk/London/issue/36668/supplement/3931/data.pdf

London Gazette: 21 July 1953
https://www.thegazette.co.uk/London/issue/39921/supplement/4051/data.pdf

'Obituaries, Lt-Col Oswald Cary-Elwes (B 31), 1994', *Old Amplefordian News*: http://www.ampleforthjournal.org/ContentsIndex01-119-red.pdf

Major Alistair McGregor, 'Obituary', *The Telegraph*, 3 October 2002

M. R. D. Foot, 'Obituary: Lt.-Col. Tony Simonds', *Independent*, 26 January 1999

'Anti-fascist emigration and political exile between the two wars', Centro Studi Sea, *Ammentu Historical Bulletin* (ABSAC), No. 1, Gennaio-Dicembre 2011

'The Story of Britain's Most Romantic, Most Daring, and Most Secret Army', *Daily Express*, October 1944, courtesy John Menown private collection

'Call of the Curlew', *Derby Evening Telegraph*, 23 April 1972

Mars & Minerva, Vol. 1, No. 9, June 1963

'The Man Who Has No Fear', *The People's Journal*, November–December editions, 1963

'Who Dares Wins', *Rover and Wizard* Annual, 1968

'Exploits of our Special Air Service', *The War Illustrated*, Vol. 8, No. 191, October 1944

Tom Carver, 'Second World War blunder that doomed 50,000 British POWs', *The Observer*, 1 November 2009

Damien Lewis, 'The Great Train Rescue', *Mars & Minerva*, Spring 2025

David McKay, 'Game of the Foxes', *New York Times*, 30 January 1972

Gavin Mortimer, 'An SAS Rescue Mission Gone Wrong', *H is for History*, 4 February 2024

Tim Robinson, 'Operation Speedwell', *Mars & Minerva*, undated

'Operation Simcol (Italy), 2/10/1943–30/11/1943', Paradata, undated

Today Pisticci, Editorial Staff, 106 Express, *The Ionian Magazine*, 15 April 2018

Unpublished sources

Service Records of George Arnold, courtesy of the Arnold family

Service Records of Oswald Cary-Elwes, courtesy of the Cary-Elwes family

Charlie Hackney, 'A Soldier's Life For Me', unpublished MS, undated, courtesy of the Hackney family

Lt-Col. Robert Ashton McKenny, 'The Story of Agent W18, Special Operation Executive, 1941–1946', unpublished MS, undated, courtesy of the McKenny family

Cpl. Eric Mills, 'Op Lost Diary', unpublished MS, undated, courtesy of the Cary-Elwes family

'Notes on 2 SAS, Origins etc.', undated, Paradata Archive

Olivier Porteau and David Portier, '2nd and 3rd Regiments of Parachute Hunters, a Component of the Allied Special Forces of Liberation: Creation – Training – Employment'

'SAS and SOE and Resistance Operations', 5 November 1944, Paradata Archive

SAS War Diary/Intelligence Summary, June 1944

Parachute Training School, Royal Air Force, Ringway, Reports on Course, 111A Course, undated

République Française, Forces Aeriennes Françaises, Attestation, De Gaulle, 17 May 1945

État Signalétique et des Services, 24th Division Aeropodre, Cieslak, Wladislas, 5 November 1945

Online sources

Graham Alcock, 'The SAS raid on the Italian Concentration Camp at Pisticci in 1943', Special Forces Roll of Honour: https://www.specialforcesroh.com/index.php?threads/the-sas-raid-on-the-italian-concentration-camp-at-pisticci-in-1943.60425/

Tom Carver, 'Second World War blunder that doomed 50,000 British POWs', *The Observer*, 1 November 2009:

https://www.theguardian.com/world/2009/nov/01/second-world-war-british-pows

Gerhard Peters and John T. Woolley, 'Franklin D. Roosevelt, Joint Message with Prime Minister Churchill to the Italian People', The American Presidency Project: https://www.presidency.ucsb.edu/node/210265

Capitaine Corentin Pfortner, 'Qui Ose Gagne: Quand les saint-cyriens s'engageaient dans le SAS': https://www.saint-cyr.org/medias/editor/oneshot-images/878050724627a73f650bf9.pdf

Anna Pizzuti, 'Foreign Jews interned in Italy – last location Piscticci': www.annapizzuti.it

https://www.anpibrindisi.it/archivio-storico/due-eccidi-nazisti-in-basilicata/

https://foreignlegion.info/legionnaires-paratroopers-wwii-second-world-war/

https://www.historytoday.com/archivc/intimatc-bctrayal

https://www.ilmetapontino.it/archivio/index.php/22-prima-pagina/cronaca/8578-pisticci-nuova-identita-per-centro-agricolo

https://josefjakobs.info/2014/08/britains-spy-catcher-lt-col-william.html

https://www.militaryintelligencemuseum.org/captain-chamier

https://www.paradata.org.uk/article/history-261-airborne-field-park-squadron-royal-engineers-formerly-261-field-park-company-re

https://paradata.org.uk/content/4639590-general-sir-john-hackett

https://primolevicenter.org/events/ferramonti-70-years-after-the-liberation/

https://primolevicenter.org/printed-matter/the-fascist-concentration-camps/

https://theojclub.wordpress.com/archive/oj-obituary/pogson-lt-cdr-frank-pogson-doria/

https://www.tracesofwar.com/persons/42850/Couraud-Raymond.htm

https://www.vanityfair.com/style/2014/01/prince-jonathan-doria-pamphilj-family-crisis?srsltid=AfmBOoqLDC1NW54ZUuuiC1iIoqt1G45Z7HjXFU6EU5BRvUveTCSZi_aC

https://en.wikipedia.org/wiki/Yvon_Morandat

Selected Bibliography

Graham Alcock, *SAS Operation Pistol: Raindrops in Alsace*, Barnsley: Pen & Sword, 2024

J. Amery, *Sons of the Eagle*, London: Macmillan, 1948

Anon., *The SAS War Diary*, London: Extraordinary Editions, 2011

Carlo Spartaco Capogreco, *Mussolini's Camps*, London: Routledge, 2019

Marie Chaming's, *I Chose The Storm*, independently published, 2022

Gustavo Comollo, *Il Commissario Pietro*, Edizione ANPI, undated

Guiseppe Coniglio, *La Colonia Confinaria di Pisticci, Il Ventennio Fascista a Pisticci*, Legatoria Lucana Metaponto (MT), 1999

Anthony Deane-Drummond, *Return Ticket*, Glasgow: Collins, 1967

Victor Dover, *The Sky Generals*, London: Cassell, 1981

Ladislas Farago, *The Game of the Foxes*, London: Hodder & Stoughton, 1972

Roy Farran, *Winged Dagger*, London: Weidenfeld Military, 1986

Colonel R. Flamand, *L'Inconnu du French Squadron*, l'Imprimerie F. Rozé, 1983

Charles Foley, *Commando Extraordinary*, London: Cassell, 1999

Raymond Forgeat, *Ils ont Choisi de vivre la France Libre*, Issy-Les-Moulineaux: Atlante Éditions, 1999

Roger & Anne Gresham-Cooke, *Your Uncles*, privately printed, undated

Mark Henniker, *An Image Of War*, Barnsley: Leo Cooper, 1987

Gerald Hough, *Desert Raids with the SAS*, Barnsley: Pen & Sword 2021

Anthony Kemp, *The SAS at War*, Harmondsworth: Penguin, 1991

Major Gordon Lett, *Rossano Valley in Flames*, Barnsley: Frontline Books, 2011

Damien Lewis, *SAS Brothers in Arms*, London: Quercus, 2022

——, *SAS Forged in Hell*, London: Quercus, 2023

——, *SAS Great Escapes Two*, London: Quercus, 2023

R. W. B. Lewis, *The City of Florence*, New York: Farrar, Straus and Giroux, 1995

B. H. Liddell Hart, *The Rommel Papers*, New York: Harcourt Brace & Company, 1953

Gavin Mortimer, *2 SAS Bill Stirling and the Forgotten Special Forces Unit of WWII*, Oxford: Osprey, 2023

——, *The SAS in 1943*, Barnsley: Pen and Sword, 2024

Lt-Colonel T. Otway, *Airborne Forces*, London: Imperial War Museum, 1990

Malcolm Pleydell, *Born of the Desert*, Barnsley: Frontline Books, 2015

Jeffrey Quill, *Spitfire: A Test Pilot's Story*, London: Arrow Books, 1999

Peter Stokes, *No Ordinary Life*, FeedARead Publishing, 2017

John Strawson, *A History of the SAS Regiment*, Swindon: Book Club Associates, 1985

Malcolm Tudor, *SAS In Italy,* Stroud: Fonthill, 2018

John Verney, *A Dinner of Herbs*, Philadelphia: Paul Dry Books, 2019

——, *Going to the Wars*, Philadelphia: Paul Dry Books, 2019

Ex-Lance-Corporal X, QGM, *The SAS & LRDG Roll of Honour 1941–47*, SAS-LRDG-ROH, 2016

Index

Paris, France, 319–21
Parrini, Eugenio, 85, 89
Pellegrino Matteucci, Italian
     gunboat, 37
Penne, Italy, 182, 184
Pescara, Italy, 221
Phillips, Sgt P., 317
Picciano, Italy, 231
Pinchon, Corporal, 198–9
Pinckney, Philip Hugh, 3–17, 19–21,
     27, 341–2
  leadership qualities, 13
  North Africa missions, 8–10
  Operation Speedwell and, 12–17,
     19–21
Pinfari, Don Guiseppe, 87
Pisticci concentration camp, Italy,
     84–95, 115, 130–31, 330–33
  'Operation Loco', 91–9, 101–4,
     108–9, 119–32, 313, 327–9,
     333, 342
  post-liberation, 327, 332–3
Pogiano, Italy, 51
Pogson, Frank, 342
Porretta Terme, Italy, 21
Potenza, Italy, 131
POWs (Prisoners of War), 133–43,
     163–4, 172, 174–7, 180–82,
     193–5, 201–2
  PG 21 POW camp (Chieti),
     163–4
  PG 59 POW camp (Servigliano),
     205
  PG 82 POW camp (Laterina), 309
  'standfast' order, 134–5, 163, 205,
     210–12

see also Operation Begonia;
     Operation Jonquil
Primo Levi Centre, 331
Prince Filippo Andrea VI Doria
     Pamphilj, 87–8, 127, 342
Princess Orietta Doria Pamphilj,
     342

Quatsieri, Aldo, 273–4
Quill, Jeffrey, 7–8

RAF (Royal Air Force)
  112 Squadron, 90
Raol (partisan leader), 310
Roberta, Arthur P., 269, 274, 302
Robinson, Doreen, 335
Robinson, Tim 'Robby', 15–17, 19,
     21–8, 318
Rogers, Trooper, 246
Rome, Italy, 29, 88, 342
Rommel, Erwin, 325
Roosevelt, Franklin D., 133–4
Roseto degli Abruzzi, Italy,
     253–4
Rover and Wizard annual, 328

de Sablet, Louis Gabriel, 67–9, 196,
     203, 206, 208–9, 244–7, 343
Sakri (legionnaire), 70
Salvaggio, Sergeant, 307–8
San Silvestro beach, Italy, 245–6,
     252
San Vito schooner, 155–6
SAS (Special Air Service), 2, 4,
     30–31, 35, 304–5, 315
  1 SAS, 157, 244–5

AFPSAS
WHO DARES WINS

The AFPSAS (Association des familles des parachutistes S.A.S. de la France Libre), includes the Free French SAS from 3rd and 4th SAS (Special Air Service) regiments and their families.

The 'French SAS Squadron' traces its origins to 1940 when the 1ère compagnie de l'Air (1ère CIA) was formed by Capitaine Georges Bergé. Initially operating in North Africa, its men joined David Stirling upon the creation of the Special Air Service (SAS). They would return to the UK in 1943 and form the 3rd and the 4th SAS squadron. They would operate across Nazi-occupied territories and in particular in France. Along with the men of 1st and 2nd SAS, they would be the first forces to land on French soil on D-Day, parachuting during the night of 5/6 June 1944. The Regiment would continue to operate throughout the war, undertaking daring missions in occupied territories, harassing enemy troops by organising sabotage and ambushes as well as training the local resistance. The French SAS squadrons would complete their final missions helping to liberate the Netherlands.

The AFPSAS promotes the social well-being of the veterans from those units, as well as supporting their families. It also aims at commemorating the history and *esprit de corps* of the SAS regiment and passing that on to younger generations. It works with the media, researchers, historians and writers focused on the history of the SAS regiment during the Second World War. It also supports specialised re-enacting teams and relevant museums.

The association operates out of France with a local liaison in the UK and also works in partnership with the Belgian and Dutch associations. It supports commemorative events across those countries. In November 2022, it co-sponsored the unveiling of a commemorative plaque dedicated to the 3rd and 4th SAS regiments, in London. In recent years, the AFPSAS has set-up the first freely accessible, online memorial listing of the men of the 3rd and 4th SAS regiments. It can be viewed here: https://memorial.afpsas.fr

The AFPSAS is affiliated to the Souvenir Français au Royaume-Uni a.k.a. the French War Graves Commission in the UK, a registered Charity in England and Wales, charity number 1185088.

It can be contacted at the following address: getintouch@ afpsas.fr

Who Dares Cares supports our Armed Forces, Emergency Services and Veterans, including their families, who are suffering from Post-Traumatic Stress Disorder (PTSD). They provide weekend retreat facilities for individuals and families, Walk, Talk and Brew Groups where teams of volunteers across the United Kingdom meet with groups of people who maybe just want to clear their head and feel supported through participating in some gentle exercise; attending a PTSD awareness session to gain a better understanding of what the signs and symptoms of PTSD are; learning how to manage symptoms and ways that families can better support in a way that is helpful to the individual. The charity recognises the importance of exercise as part of recovery and they work to encourage this and make it accessible for those who are struggling with PTSD and anxiety-related issues.

The charity was founded in Hamilton, Scotland in 2016 by two former serving soldiers, Calum MacLeod (King's Own Scottish Borderers) and Colin Maclachlan (Royal Scots and Special Air Service). After Calum and Colin met, sharing their own stories and becoming friends, bound by their own experiences, they both realised they could help so many other people, who were left 'alone' to deal with their experiences, thoughts and traumas. They decided to build a platform that would provide help and support to individuals and their families, all in the way of Who Dares Cares.

There are a number of volunteers that support the charity, all with varying skills, from military backgrounds to nurses, who offer help and support to all of their followers in many different ways. The volunteers are just that, volunteers. They are dedicated to the charity and give up their own time and effort to support other people in so many different ways. Without them, Who Dares Cares wouldn't be able to provide the dedicated support that they can.

Anyone with a service record and a history of PTSD should apply for support, even if you're not sure you meet the criteria; each application is assessed on an individual basis. For more details, please email the Who Dares Cares Support Team Mailbox on wdc@who-dares-cares.com and if you wish to learn more about this amazing charity and how you can support its vital work, please visit www.who-dares-cares.com.

It is not about suffering from PTSD, it is about learning to live with PTSD!

Alabaré

Alabaré believes no veteran should call the street home. Since 1991, Alabaré has been helping people who are homeless or vulnerable by providing safe accommodation and a pathway of support to help clients move on to bright futures, homes and minds.

Today Alabaré are a national charity with homes and services across the south of England and Wales supporting 3000 people a year. Their support includes dedicated help for street homeless, young people, those leaving the care system, young parents and their babies, Armed Forces veterans and those struggling with their mental wellbeing. Alongside Alabaré's supported accommodation, the charity offers training and activities to help clients to live the fulfilling life they choose.

Alabaré opened their first dedicated Homes for Veterans in Plymouth in 2009, and have since gone on to open houses across the South and South West of England and Wales. Veterans benefit from the camaraderie and understanding of shared experiences that comes from living with others who have served in the British Armed Forces.

Alongside their supported housing, Alabaré's Boots on the Ground programme uses outdoor activities to build confidence, self-esteem and team endeavour, and the charity's Veterans' Self Build Scheme offers veterans training in the construction industry while building a home that they can live in.

Alabaré have given me a lifeline, I felt like I was stranded at sea and Alabaré were the buoyancy aid. Alabaré have provided me with knowing that there are people there who care and are willing to go the extra mile. I am loving life again and feel every day is a positive day and on point. I no longer go to sleep praying I don't wake. I am again hopeful for the future and look forward to what is to come.

Alabaré veteran client.

For more information or to donate go to www.alabare.co.uk

RAISING READERS
Books Build Bright Futures

Dear Reader,

We'd love your attention for one more page to tell you about the crisis in children's reading, and what we can all do.

Studies have shown that reading for fun is the **single biggest predictor of a child's future life chances** – more than family circumstance, parents' educational background or income. It improves academic results, mental health, wealth, communication skills, ambition and happiness.[1]

The number of children reading for fun is in rapid decline. Young people have a lot of competition for their time. In 2024, 1 in 10 children and young people in the UK aged 5 to 18 did not own a single book at home.[2]

Hachette works extensively with schools, libraries and literacy charities, but here are some ways we can all raise more readers:

- Reading to children for just 10 minutes a day makes a difference
- Don't give up if children aren't regular readers – there will be books for them!
- Visit bookshops and libraries to get recommendations
- Encourage them to listen to audiobooks
- Support school libraries
- Give books as gifts

There's a lot more information about how to encourage children to read on our website: **www.RaisingReaders.co.uk**

Thank you for reading.

hachette
UK

---

[1] OECD, '21st-Century Readers: Developing Literacy Skills in a Digital World', 2021, https://www.oecd.org/en/publications/21st-century-readers_a83d84cb-en.html

[2] National Literacy Trust, 'Book Ownership in 2024', November 2024, https://literacytrust.org.uk/research-services/research-reports/book-ownership-in-2024